CONTENTS

INTRODUCTION

Healthy living has never been as important as it is now. A highly stressful lifestyle coupled with the compromises you make in your food choices can result in poor health and diseases that can severely limit your ability to enjoy life.

Unfortunately, some of the most delicious foods around, such as fried chicken and French fries, are not good for your waistline nor for your overall well-being, since cooking them requires vast amounts of oil. Nevertheless, you can enjoy the flavor and texture of deep-fried foods without the negative effects on your health with the use of an air fryer.

Air fryers were first launched in Australia and Europe in 2010. After becoming a big hit, they were soon released in North America and Japan. Now, you can find air fryers practically in most modern kitchens where they are used to cook everything from chips to samosas.

But while air frying can be considered a healthier way of cooking, it doesn't mean you can eat high-fat foods every day without putting your health at risk. Remember that you still need to exercise self-control and stick to cooking mostly healthy foods if you want to stay fit.

If you've ever wondered about how air frying works and whether it is indeed better for you, this eBook has all the information you need. It also contains healthy recipes so you and your whole family can enjoy all the benefits of air frying.

An Overview

What is an Air Fryer and How Does it Work?

An air fryer is a type of kitchen appliance that fries, grills, or roasts food by making extremely hot air move around it.

Hot air is circulated around the food at a high speed using a mechanical fan – a process which cooks the food and creates a crispy outer layer around it.

Air fryers use what is called Rapid Air Technology, which allows the appliance to cook any kind of food that would otherwise need to be deep fried in oil. This new technology can circulate air that can be as hot as 400 degrees F to produce an effect that is similar to frying so you can enjoy "fried" pastries, chips, fish, chicken and others.

The cooking chamber of an air fryer contains a heating element that radiates heat to cook food more appropriately and efficiently. Above the chamber is an exhaust fan that provides the required air flow, which is what allows the hot air to move around the food constantly.

As a result, every part of the food is exposed to the same heating temperature. The air fryer also contains an exhaust system that keeps the temperature in check. The temperature is increased through internal pressure that produces extra air required to cook the food.

Food cooked in an air fryer is healthier and contains fewer calories because it requires very little oil to produce the fried effect. Imagine being able to make crispy chips with only half a tablespoon of oil. Seems impossible? Not with an air fryer. The best part is that cooking doesn't take long. You can have crispy potatoes in just twelve minutes.

Air fryers are not just better for your health, they are also good for the environment because the extra air that is produced to cook the food is filtered thoroughly before it is released, so you don't have the unpleasant odor that lingers in the kitchen whenever you fry foods the traditional way.

While air fryers were originally created to air fry foods, many of the newer models now have the capability of grilling and roasting, so you can cook a variety of other foods like steaks and hamburgers.

Is Air Frying Healthy?

Compared to traditional frying methods, cooking with an air fryer is the healthier alternative, since it uses up to eighty percent less fat to produce food that is crisp and perfectly golden brown.

If you want to live a healthier lifestyle but you can't give up eating deep-fried foods like French fries, fried chicken, and donuts, an air fryer can make you feel less guilty on your cheat days.

Air frying is also a good way to transition from eating too many fast food meals to having more home-cooked options that are healthier for you.

Of course, if you want to be fit and to develop better lifestyle habits, it's important to include healthier foods in your diet.

Tips for Healthy Cooking with Your Air Fryer

Air frying uses very little oil in order to produce the fried food texture of the meals that you cook in it. That in itself makes using an air fryer a healthier way to cook.

Even so, there are other ways to cook healthy foods with your air fryer.

• Use top quality cooking oil - Because you don't need much, use the best quality cooking oil you can afford. These days, 'best quality' also translates to being better for your health, so use coconut or olive oil, which are low in saturated fats.

• Trim excess fat - As with traditional frying or cooking, trimming excess fat from meat makes for a healthier meal. Remove fat from beef and pork, and skin from chicken.

• Use the white meat part – The breast part of the chicken, for example, is lower in fat and cholesterol compared to other parts. Whenever possible, choose this when making air-fried chicken dishes.

• Try new vegetables – Plenty of vegetables benefit from grilling, so use this function of the air fryer to cook vegetables you haven't tried before. You'll not only be eating healthier, but you'll be treated to new taste sensations.

• Use herbs and spices - Herbs and spices, whether fresh or dried, provide not only great flavor but also numerous benefits for the health.

• Use reduced fat and reduced sodium food products - Whenever possible, opt for versions of ingredients that are low in fat, cholesterol, sodium, sugar and so on.

More Healthy Cooking Tips

• Bring food to room temperature before cooking - A good way to ensure that your food cooks properly in the air fryer is to allow it to come to room temperature first. If you put food straight from the fridge or freezer into the appliance, it will take longer to cook and not be as crispy as you'd like it to be.

- Try other recipes - Air fryers aren't just for cooking fried foods since they basically work as a stove-top oven. As a result, you can use it to grill fish and vegetables. You can also make homemade pizza, as well as pasta dishes. Check the product manual to see how versatile the appliance is.
- Always pre-heat the appliance before putting in food - No matter what type of recipe you're making, pre-heating your air fryer is a must if you want to get the results you are looking for. Pre-heating for two to three minutes will suffice.
- When cooking food with fat, add water to the drawer - To prevent the buildup of grease, add some water to the drawer below the basket when cooking food that contains fat. Grease can cause the temperature to spike, which will lead to the production of smoke.
- Turn foods halfway through the cooking – Flipping the food once or twice during the air frying process ensures even cooking on all sides. Doing so also allows the food to have the same texture and color all over.

BREAKFAST & BRUNCH RECIPES

1. Black's Bangin' Casserole

Servings: 4
Cooking Time: 40 Minutes
Ingredients:
- 5 eggs
- 3 tbsp chunky tomato sauce
- 2 tbsp heavy cream
- 2 tbsp grated parmesan cheese

Directions:
1. Preheat your fryer to 350°F/175°C.
2. Combine the eggs and cream in a bowl.
3. Mix in the tomato sauce and add the cheese.
4. Spread into a glass baking dish and bake for 25-35 minutes.
5. Top with extra cheese.
6. Enjoy!

2. Zucchini Noodles

Servings: 3
Cooking Time: 44 Minutes
Ingredients:
- 1 egg
- 1/2 cup parmesan cheese, grated
- 1/2 cup feta cheese, crumbled
- 1 tbsp thyme
- 1 garlic clove, chopped
- 1 onion, chopped
- 2 medium zucchinis, trimmed and spiralized
- 2 tbsp olive oil
- 1 cup mozzarella cheese, grated
- 1/2 tsp pepper
- 1/2 tsp salt

Directions:
1. Preheat the air fryer to 350 F.
2. Add spiralized zucchini and salt in a colander and set aside for 10 minutes.
3. Wash zucchini noodles and pat dry with a paper towel.
4. Heat oil in a pan over medium heat.
5. Add garlic and onion and sauté for 3-4 minutes.
6. Add zucchini noodles and cook for 4-5 minutes or until softened.
7. Add zucchini mixture into the air fryer baking pan. Add egg, thyme, cheeses. Mix well and season.
8. Place pan in the air fryer and cook for 30-35 minutes.
9. Serve and enjoy.

3. Fried Eggs

Servings: 2
Cooking Time: 7 Minutes
Ingredients:
- 2 eggs
- 3 slices bacon

Directions:
1. Heat some oil in a deep fryer at 375°F/190°C.
2. Fry the bacon.
3. In a small bowl, add the 2 eggs.
4. Quickly add the eggs into the center of the fryer.
5. Using two spatulas, form the egg into a ball while frying.
6. Fry for 2-3 minutes, until it stops bubbling.
7. Place on a paper towel and allow to drain.
8. Enjoy!

4. Cheddar And Ham Quiche

Servings: 4
Cooking Time: 15 Minutes
Ingredients:
- 4 oz ham, chopped
- 1 cup Cheddar cheese, shredded
- 1 tablespoon chives, chopped
- ½ zucchini, grated
- ¼ cup heavy cream
- 1 tablespoon almond flour
- ½ teaspoon salt
- ½ teaspoon ground black pepper
- ½ teaspoon dried oregano
- 5 eggs, beaten
- 1 teaspoon coconut oil, softened

Directions:
1. In the big bowl mix up ham, cheese, chives, zucchini, heavy cream, almond flour, salt, ground black pepper, oregano, and eggs. Stir the ingredients with the help of the fork until you get a homogenous mixture. After this, preheat the air fryer to 365F. Then gently grease the air fryer basket with coconut oil. Pour the ham mixture in the air fryer basket. Cook the quiche for 15 minutes. Then check if the quiche mixture is crusty, cook for extra 5 minutes if needed.

5. Broccoli Stuffed Peppers

Servings: 2
Cooking Time: 40 Minutes
Ingredients:
- 4 eggs
- 1/2 cup cheddar cheese, grated
- 2 bell peppers, cut in half and remove seeds
- 1/2 tsp garlic powder
- 1 tsp dried thyme
- 1/4 cup feta cheese, crumbled
- 1/2 cup broccoli, cooked
- 1/4 tsp pepper
- 1/2 tsp salt

Directions:
1. Preheat the air fryer to 325 F.

2. Stuff feta and broccoli into the bell peppers halved.
3. Beat egg in a bowl with seasoning and pour egg mixture into the pepper halved over feta and broccoli.
4. Place bell pepper halved into the air fryer basket and cook for 35-40 minutes.
5. Top with grated cheddar cheese and cook until cheese melted.
6. Serve and enjoy.

6. Spiced Pumpkin Bread

Servings:4
Cooking Time: 25 Minutes
Ingredients:
- ¼ cup coconut flour
- 2 tablespoons stevia blend
- 1 teaspoon baking powder
- ¾ teaspoon pumpkin pie spice
- ¼ teaspoon ground cinnamon
- 1/8 teaspoon salt
- ¼ cup canned pumpkin
- 2 large eggs
- 2 tablespoons unsweetened almond milk
- 1 teaspoon vanilla extract

Directions:
1. In a bowl, mix together the flour, stevia, baking powder, spices, and salt.
2. In another large bowl, add the pumpkin, eggs, almond milk, and vanilla extract. Beat until well combined.
3. Then, add in the flour mixture and mix until just combined
4. Set the temperature of air fryer to 350 degrees F. Line a cake pan with a greased parchment paper.
5. Place the mixture evenly into the prepared pan.
6. Arrange the pan into an air fryer basket.
7. Air fry for about 25 minutes or until a toothpick inserted in the center comes out clean.
8. Remove the pans from air fryer and place onto a wire rack for about 5 minutes.
9. Carefully, take out the bread from pan and put onto a wire rack to cool for about 5-10 minutes before slicing.
10. Cut the bread into desired size slices and serve.

7. Cinnamon Toasts

Servings: 4
Cooking Time: 15 Minutes
Ingredients:
- 10 bread slices
- 1 pack salted butter
- 4 tbsp. sugar
- 2 tsp. ground cinnamon
- ½ tsp. vanilla extract

Directions:
1. In a bowl, combine the butter, cinnamon, sugar, and vanilla extract. Spread onto the slices of bread.
2. Set your Air Fryer to 380°F. When warmed up, put the bread inside the fryer and cook for 4 – 5 minutes.

8. Mozzarella Rolls

Servings: 6
Cooking Time: 6 Minutes
Ingredients:
- 6 wonton wrappers
- 1 tablespoon keto tomato sauce
- ½ cup Mozzarella, shredded
- 1 oz pepperoni, chopped
- 1 egg, beaten
- Cooking spray

Directions:
1. In the big bowl mix up together shredded Mozzarella, pepperoni, and tomato sauce. When the mixture is homogenous transfer it on the wonton wraps. Wrap the wonton wraps in the shape of sticks. Then brush them with beaten eggs. Preheat the air fryer to 400F. Spray the air fryer basket with cooking spray. Put the pizza sticks in the air fryer and cook them for 3 minutes from each side.

9. Breakfast Creamy Donuts

Servings:8
Cooking Time:18 Minutes
Ingredients:
- 4 tablespoons butter, softened and divided
- 2 large egg yolks
- 2¼ cups plain flour
- 1½ teaspoons baking powder
- 1 pinch baking soda
- 1/3 cup caster sugar
- 1 teaspoon cinnamon
- ½ cup sugar
- 1 teaspoon salt
- ½ cup sour cream

Directions:
1. Preheat the Air fryer to 355 °F.
2. Mix together sugar and butter in a bowl and beat until crumbly mixture is formed.
3. Whisk in the egg yolks and beat until well combined.
4. Sift together flour, baking powder, baking soda and salt in another bowl.
5. Add the flour mixture and sour cream to the sugar mixture.
6. Mix well to form a dough and refrigerate it.
7. Roll the dough into 2-inch thickness and cut the dough in half.
8. Coat both sides of the dough with the melted butter and transfer into the Air fryer.

9. Cook for about 8 minutes until golden brown and remove from the Air fryer.
10. Sprinkle the donuts with the cinnamon and caster sugar to serve.

10. Herbed Omelet

Servings: 4
Cooking Time: 20 Minutes
Ingredients:
- 10 eggs, whisked
- ½ cup cheddar, shredded
- 2 tablespoons parsley, chopped
- 2 tablespoons chives, chopped
- 2 tablespoons basil, chopped
- Cooking spray
- Salt and black pepper to the taste

Directions:
1. In a bowl, mix the eggs with all the ingredients except the cheese and the cooking spray and whisk well. Preheat the air fryer at 350 degrees F, grease it with the cooking spray, and pour the eggs mixture inside. Sprinkle the cheese on top and cook for 20 minutes. Divide everything between plates and serve.

11. Vegetable Toast

Servings: 4
Cooking Time: 25 Minutes
Ingredients:
- 4 slices bread
- 1 red bell pepper, cut into strips
- 1 cup sliced button or cremini mushrooms
- 1 small yellow squash, sliced
- 2 green onions, sliced
- 1 tbsp. olive oil
- 2 tbsp. softened butter
- ½ cup soft goat cheese

Directions:
1. Drizzle the Air Fryer with the olive oil and pre-heat to 350°F.
2. Put the red pepper, green onions, mushrooms, and squash inside the fryer, give them a stir and cook for 7 minutes, shaking the basket once throughout the cooking time. Ensure the vegetables become tender.
3. Remove the vegetables and set them aside.
4. Spread some butter on the slices of bread and transfer to the Air Fryer, butter side-up. Brown for 2 to 4 minutes.
5. Remove the toast from the fryer and top with goat cheese and vegetables. Serve warm.

12. Broccoli Cheese Quiche

Servings: 2
Cooking Time: 50 Minutes
Ingredients:

- 1 cup whole milk
- 2 medium broccoli, cut into florets
- 2 medium tomatoes, diced
- 4 medium carrots, diced
- ¼ cup Feta cheese, crumbled
- 1 cup grated Cheddar cheese
- Salt and pepper to taste
- 1 tsp chopped parsley
- 1 tsp dried thyme

Directions:
1. Put the broccoli and carrots in a food steamer and cook until soft, about 10 minutes. In a jug, crack in the eggs, add the parsley, salt, pepper, and thyme. Using a whisk, beat the eggs while adding the milk gradually until a pale mixture is attained.
2. Once the broccoli and carrots are ready, strain them through a sieve and set aside. In a quiche dish, add the carrots and broccoli. Put the tomatoes on top, then the feta and cheddar cheese following.
3. Leave a little bit of cheddar cheese. Pour the egg mixture over the layering and top with the remaining cheddar cheese. Place the dish in the air fryer and cook at 350 F for 20 minutes.

13. Egg Veggie Frittata

Servings:2
Cooking Time:18 Minutes
Ingredients:
- 4 eggs
- ½ cup milk
- 2 green onions, chopped
- ¼ cup baby Bella mushrooms, chopped
- ¼ cup spinach, chopped
- ½ teaspoon salt
- ½ teaspoon black pepper
- Dash of hot sauce

Directions:
1. Preheat the Air fryer to 365 °F and grease 6x3 inch square pan with butter.
2. Whisk eggs with milk in a large bowl and stir in green onions, mushrooms and spinach.
3. Sprinkle with salt, black pepper and hot sauce and pour this mixture into the prepared pan.
4. Place in the Air fryer and cook for about 18 minutes.
5. Dish out in a platter and serve warm.

14. Sausage Frittata

Servings:2
Cooking Time:11 Minutes
Ingredients:
- ½ of chorizo sausage, sliced
- ½ cup frozen corn
- 1 large potato, boiled, peeled and cubed

- 3 jumbo eggs
- 2 tablespoons feta cheese, crumbled
- 1 tablespoon olive oil
- Salt and black pepper, to taste

Directions:
1. Preheat the Air fryer to 355 °F and grease an Air Fryer pan.
2. Whisk together eggs with salt and black pepper in a bowl.
3. Heat olive oil in the Air Fryer pan and add sausage, corn and potato.
4. Cook for about 6 minutes and stir in the whisked eggs.
5. Top with cheese and cook for about 5 minutes.
6. Dish out and serve hot.

15. Mushroom Bake

Servings: 4
Cooking Time: 20 Minutes
Ingredients:
- 2 garlic cloves, minced
- 1 teaspoon olive oil
- 2 celery stalks, chopped
- ½ cup white mushrooms, chopped
- ½ cup red bell pepper, chopped
- Salt and black pepper to the taste
- 1 teaspoon oregano, dried
- 7 ounces mozzarella, shredded
- 1 tablespoon lemon juice

Directions:
1. Preheat the Air Fryer at 350 degrees F, add the oil and heat it up. Add garlic, celery, mushrooms, bell pepper, salt, pepper, oregano, mozzarella and the lemon juice, toss and cook for 20 minutes. Divide between plates and serve for breakfast.

16. French Toast

Servings: 2
Cooking Time: 25 Minutes
Ingredients:
- 4 slices bread of your choosing
- 2 tbsp. soft butter
- 2 eggs, lightly beaten
- Pinch of salt
- Pinch of cinnamon
- Pinch of ground nutmeg
- Pinch of ground cloves
- Nonstick cooking spray
- Sugar for serving

Directions:
1. In a shallow bowl, mix together the salt, spices and eggs.
2. Butter each side of the slices of bread and slice into strips. You may also use cookie cutters for this step.
3. Set your Air Fryer to 350°F and allow to warm up briefly.

4. Dredge each strip of bread in the egg and transfer to the fryer. Cook for two minutes, ensuring the toast turns golden brown.
5. At this point, spritz the tops of the bread strips with cooking spray, flip, and cook for another 4 minutes on the other side. Top with a light dusting of sugar before serving.

17. Mushroom Cheese Salad

Servings: 3
Cooking Time: 15 Minutes
Ingredients:
- 10 mushrooms, halved
- 1 tbsp fresh parsley, chopped
- 1 tbsp olive oil
- 1 tbsp mozzarella cheese, grated
- 1 tbsp cheddar cheese, grated
- 1 tbsp dried mix herbs
- Pepper
- Salt

Directions:
1. Add all ingredients into the bowl and toss well.
2. Transfer bowl mixture into the air fryer baking dish.
3. Place in the air fryer and cook at 380 F for 15 minutes.
4. Serve and enjoy.

18. French Toast Sticks

Servings:4
Cooking Time:5 Minutes
Ingredients:
- 4 bread, sliced into sticks
- 2 tablespoons soft butter or margarine
- 2 eggs, gently beaten
- Salt, to taste
- 1 pinch cinnamon
- 1 pinch nutmeg
- 1 pinch ground cloves

Directions:
1. Preheat the Air fryer at 365 °F and grease an Air fryer pan with butter.
2. Whisk eggs with salt, cinnamon, nutmeg and ground cloves in a bowl.
3. Dip the bread sticks in the egg mixture and place in the pan.
4. Cook for about 5 minutes, flipping in between and remove from the Air fryer.
5. Dish out and serve warm.

19. Peppers Rings

Servings: 2
Cooking Time: 11 Minutes
Ingredients:
- 1 large green bell pepper
- ½ cup ground beef
- 1 egg, beaten
- ½ teaspoon salt

- ½ teaspoon ground black pepper
- ½ teaspoon Italian seasonings
- 1 teaspoon coconut oil, melted

Directions:
1. Remove the seeds from the pepper and wash it. Then cut the pepper into 2 rings. In the bowl combine together egg, ground beef, salt, ground black pepper, and Italian seasonings. Preheat the air fryer to 385F. Brush the air fryer basket with coconut oil. Place the pepper rings in the air fryer and fill them with ground beef mixture. Cook the meal at 385F for 11 minutes.

20. Egg Porridge

Servings: 1
Cooking Time: 15 Minutes
Ingredients:
- 2 organic free-range eggs
- 1/3 cup organic heavy cream without food additives
- 2 packages of your preferred sweetener
- 2 tbsp grass-fed butter ground organic cinnamon to taste

Directions:
1. In a bowl add the eggs, cream and sweetener, and mix together.
2. Melt the butter in a saucepan over a medium heat. Lower the heat once the butter is melted.
3. Combine together with the egg and cream mixture.
4. While Cooking, mix until it thickens and curdles.
5. When you see the first signs of curdling, remove the saucepan immediately from the heat.
6. Pour the porridge into a bowl. Sprinkle cinnamon on top and serve immediately.

21. Perfect Cheesy Eggs

Servings:2
Cooking Time:12 Minutes
Ingredients:
- 2 teaspoons unsalted butter, softened
- 2-ounce ham, sliced thinly
- 4 large eggs, divided
- 3 tablespoons Parmesan cheese, grated finely
- 2 teaspoons fresh chives, minced
- 2 tablespoons heavy cream
- 1/8 teaspoon smoked paprika
- Salt and black pepper, to taste

Directions:
1. Preheat the Air fryer to 320 °F and grease a pie pan with butter.
2. Whisk together 1 egg with cream, salt and black pepper in a bowl.

3. Place ham slices in the bottom of the pie pan and top with the egg mixture.
4. Crack the remaining eggs on top and season with smoked paprika, salt and black pepper.
5. Top evenly with Parmesan cheese and chives and transfer the pie pan in the Air fryer.
6. Cook for about 12 minutes and serve with toasted bread slices.

22. Sausage & Egg Casserole

Servings:6
Cooking Time: 20 Minutes
Ingredients:
- 6 eggs
- 1 red pepper, diced
- 1 green pepper, diced
- 1 yellow pepper, diced
- 1 sweet onion, diced
- 2 cups Cheddar cheese, shredded
- Salt and pepper to taste
- fresh parsley to garnish

Directions:
1. Place a skillet over medium heat on a stovetop, add the sausage and cook until brown, stirring occasionally. Once done, drain any excess fat derived from cooking and set aside.
2. Grease a casserole dish that fits into the fryer basket with cooking spray, and arrange the sausage on the bottom. Top with onion, red pepper, green pepper, and yellow pepper. Spread the cheese on top.
3. In a bowl, beat the eggs with salt and pepper. Pour the mixture over the casserole. Place the casserole dish in the air basket, and bake at 355 F for 13-15 minutes. Serve warm garnished with fresh parsley.

23. Peanut Butter Banana Bread

Servings:6
Cooking Time:40 Minutes
Ingredients:
- 1 cup plus 1 tablespoon all-purpose flour
- 1¼ teaspoons baking powder
- 1 large egg
- 2 medium ripe bananas, peeled and mashed
- ¾ cup walnuts, roughly chopped
- ¼ teaspoon salt
- 1/3 cup granulated sugar
- ¼ cup canola oil
- 2 tablespoons creamy peanut butter
- 2 tablespoons sour cream
- 1 teaspoon vanilla extract

Directions:
1. Preheat the Air fryer to 330 °F and grease a non-stick baking dish.
2. Mix together the flour, baking powder and salt in a bowl.

3. Whisk together egg with sugar, canola oil, sour cream, peanut butter and vanilla extract in a bowl.
4. Stir in the bananas and beat until well combined.
5. Now, add the flour mixture and fold in the walnuts gently.
6. Mix until combined and transfer the mixture evenly into the prepared baking dish.
7. Arrange the baking dish in an Air fryer basket and cook for about 40 minutes.
8. Remove from the Air fryer and place onto a wire rack to cool.
9. Cut the bread into desired size slices and serve.

24. Buttered Eggs In Hole

Servings:2
Cooking Time: 11 Minutes
Ingredients:
- 2 eggs
- Salt and pepper to taste
- 2 tbsp butter

Directions:
1. Place a heatproof bowl in the fryer's basket and brush with butter. Make a hole in the middle of the bread slices with a bread knife and place in the heatproof bowl in 2 batches. Break an egg into the center of each hole. Season with salt and pepper. Close the air fryer and cook for 4 minutes at 330 F. Turn the bread with a spatula and cook for another 4 minutes. Serve as a breakfast accompaniment.

25. Beef And Cabbage Wrap

Servings: 2
Cooking Time: 15 Minutes
Ingredients:
- ½ cup ground beef
- ½ jalapeno pepper, chopped
- ¼ teaspoon ground black pepper
- ½ teaspoon salt
- 1 teaspoon keto tomato sauce
- 1 teaspoon olive oil
- ¼ teaspoon minced garlic
- ¼ teaspoon onion powder
- 1 teaspoon dried cilantro
- ½ teaspoon ground cumin
- 2 oz avocado, chopped
- 2 big cabbage leaves, steamed
- 2 tablespoons water

Directions:
1. Preheat the air fryer to 360F. In the mixing bowl mix up ground beef, salt, ground black pepper, tomato sauce, olive oil, minced garlic, onion powder, dried cilantro, water, and ground cumin. Then add jalapeno and

stir gently. Transfer the ground beef mixture in the preheated air fryer basket. Cook the meat mixture for 15 minutes. Stir it with the help of the spatula after 8 minutes of cooking. Then place the mixture over the cabbage leaves. Top the ground beef with chopped avocado and roll into the burritos.

26. Easy & Tasty Salsa Chicken

Servings: 4
Cooking Time: 30 Minutes
Ingredients:
- 1 lb chicken thighs, boneless and skinless
- 1 cup salsa
- Pepper
- Salt

Directions:
1. Preheat the air fryer to 350 F.
2. Place chicken thighs into the air fryer baking dish and season with pepper and salt. Top with salsa.
3. Place in the air fryer and cook for 30 minutes.
4. Serve and enjoy.

27. Cheesy Pancake

Servings: 2
Cooking Time: 8 Minutes
Ingredients:
- 5 eggs, beaten
- ¼ cup almond flour
- ½ teaspoon baking powder
- 1 teaspoon apple cider vinegar
- ¼ cup Cheddar cheese, shredded
- 1 teaspoon butter
- 1 tablespoon mascarpone
- ½ teaspoon sesame oil

Directions:
1. Brush the air fryer basket with sesame oil. Then in the mixing bowl mix up all remaining ingredients. Stir the liquid until homogenous. Pour it in the air fryer pan and place it in the air fryer. Cook the pancake for 8 minutes at 360F. Remove the cooked pancake from the air fryer pan and cut it into servings.

28. Cheesy Omelet

Servings:1
Cooking Time: 15 Minutes
Ingredients:
- Black pepper to taste
- 1 cup cheddar cheese, shredded
- 1 whole onion, chopped
- 2 tbsp soy sauce

Directions:
1. Preheat your air fryer to 340 F. Drizzle soy sauce over the chopped onions. Place the

onions in your air fryer's cooking basket and cook for 8 minutes. In a bowl, mix the beaten eggs with salt and pepper.

2. Pour the egg mixture over onions (in the cooking basket) and cook for 3 minutes. Add cheddar cheese over eggs and bake for 2 more minutes. Serve with fresh basil and enjoy!

29. Coriander Sausages Muffins

Servings: 4
Cooking Time: 12 Minutes
Ingredients:
- 4 teaspoons coconut flour
- 1 tablespoon coconut cream
- 1 egg, beaten
- ½ teaspoon baking powder
- 6 oz sausage meat
- 1 teaspoon spring onions, chopped
- ½ teaspoon ground coriander
- 1 teaspoon sesame oil
- ½ teaspoon salt

Directions:
1. In the mixing bowl mix up coconut flour, coconut cream, egg, baking powder, minced onion, and ground coriander. Add salt and whisk the mixture until smooth. After this, add the sausage meat and stir the muffin batter. Preheat the air fryer to 385F. Brush the muffin molds with sesame oil and pour the batter inside. Place the rack in the air fryer basket. Put the muffins on a rack. Cook the meal for 12 minutes.

30. Cheese Omelet

Servings:2
Cooking Time: 8 Minutes
Ingredients:
- 4 eggs
- ¼ cup cream
- Salt and freshly ground black pepper, to taste
- ¼ cup cheddar cheese, grated

Directions:
1. Set the temperature of Air Fryer to 350 degrees F. Lightly, grease a 6"x3" pan.
2. In a bowl, mix together the eggs, cream, salt, and black pepper.
3. Then, pour the egg mixture into the prepared pan and Air Fry for about 4 minutes.
4. Once done, sprinkle the cheese over the top and cook for another 4 minutes at 350º F.
5. When the time is up, take out the pan from air fryer and use a spatula to flip the omelet onto the pan.
6. Serve hot.

31. Cheesy Frittata

Servings: 6
Cooking Time: 20 Minutes
Ingredients:
- 1 cup almond milk
- Cooking spray
- 9 ounces cream cheese, soft
- 1 cup cheddar cheese, shredded
- 6 spring onions, chopped
- Salt and black pepper to the taste
- 6 eggs, whisked

Directions:
1. Heat up your air fryer with the oil at 350 degrees F and grease it with cooking spray. In a bowl, mix the eggs with the rest of the ingredients, whisk well, pour and spread into the air fryer and cook everything for 20 minutes. Divide everything between plates and serve.

32. Bacon Pockets

Servings: 6
Cooking Time: 4 Minutes
Ingredients:
- 6 wontons wrap
- 1 egg yolk, whisked
- 2 oz bacon, chopped, cooked
- ½ cup Edam cheese, shredded
- 1 teaspoon sesame oil
- ½ teaspoon ground black pepper

Directions:
1. Put the chopped bacon in the bowl. Add Edam cheese and ground black pepper. Stir the ingredients gently with the help of the fork. After this, put the mixture on the wonton wrap and fold it in the shape of the pocket. Repeat the steps with remaining filling and wonton wraps. Preheat the air fryer to 400F. Brush every wonton pocket with whisked egg yolk. Then brush the air fryer with sesame oil and arrange the pockets inside. Cook the meal for 2 minutes from each side.

33. Coconut Veggie And Eggs Bake

Servings: 6
Cooking Time: 30 Minutes
Ingredients:
- Cooking spray
- 2 cups green and red bell pepper, chopped
- 2 spring onions, chopped
- 1 teaspoon thyme, chopped
- Salt and black pepper to the taste
- 1 cup coconut cream
- 4 eggs, whisked
- 1 cup cheddar cheese, grated

Directions:
1. In a bowl, mix all the ingredients except the cooking spray and the cheese and whisk

well. Grease a pan that fits the air fryer with the cooking spray, pour the bell peppers and eggs mixture, spread, sprinkle the cheese on top, put the pan in the machine and cook at 350 degrees F for 30 minutes. Divide between plates and serve for breakfast.

34. Air-fried Sourdough Sandwiches

Servings:2
Cooking Time: 25 Minutes
Ingredients:
- 2 tbsp mayonnaise
- 2 slices ham
- 2 lettuce leaves
- 1 tomato, sliced
- 2 slices mozzarella cheese
- Salt and pepper to taste
- Cooking spray

Directions:
1. On a clean board, lay the sourdough slices and spread with mayonnaise. Top 2 of the slices with ham, lettuce, tomato, and mozzarella cheese. Season with salt and pepper.
2. Top with the remaining two slices to form two sandwiches. Spray with oil and transfer to the air fryer. Cook for 14 minutes at 340 F, flipping once halfway through cooking. Serve hot!

35. Ranch Risotto

Servings: 2
Cooking Time: 40 Minutes
Ingredients:
- 1 onion, diced
- 2 cups chicken stock, boiling
- ½ cup parmesan OR cheddar cheese, grated
- 1 clove garlic, minced
- ¾ cup Arborio rice
- 1 tbsp. olive oil
- 1 tbsp. unsalted butter

Directions:
1. Set the Air Fryer at 390°F for 5 minutes to heat up.
2. With oil, grease a round baking tin, small enough to fit inside the fryer, and stir in the garlic, butter, and onion.
3. Transfer the tin to the Air Fryer and allow to cook for 4 minutes. Add in the rice and cook for a further 4 minutes, giving it a stir three times throughout the cooking time.
4. Turn the fryer down to 320°F and add in the chicken stock, before gently mixing it. Leave to cook for 22 minutes with the fryer uncovered. Before serving, throw in the cheese and give it one more stir. Enjoy!

36. Salmon Omelet

Servings: 2
Cooking Time: 15 Minutes
Ingredients:
- 3 eggs
- 1 smoked salmon
- 3 links pork sausage
- ¼ cup onions
- ¼ cup provolone cheese

Directions:
1. Whisk the eggs and pour them into a skillet.
2. Follow the standard method for making an omelette.
3. Add the onions, salmon and cheese before turning the omelet over.
4. Sprinkle the omelet with cheese and serve with the sausages on the side.
5. Serve!

37. Spinach Balls

Servings: 4
Cooking Time: 20 Minutes
Ingredients:
- 1 carrot, peeled and grated
- 1 package fresh spinach, blanched and chopped
- ½ onion, chopped
- 1 egg, beaten
- ½ tsp. garlic powder
- 1 tsp. garlic, minced
- 1 tsp. salt
- ½ tsp. black pepper
- 1 tbsp. nutritional yeast
- 1 tbsp. flour
- 2 slices bread, toasted

Directions:
1. In a food processor, pulse the toasted bread to form breadcrumbs. Transfer into a shallow dish or bowl.
2. In a bowl, mix together all the other ingredients.
3. Use your hands to shape the mixture into small-sized balls. Roll the balls in the breadcrumbs, ensuring to cover them well.
4. Put in the Air Fryer and cook at 390°F for 10 minutes.

38. Green Beans Bowls

Servings: 2
Cooking Time: 20 Minutes
Ingredients:
- 1 cup green beans, halved
- 2 spring onions, chopped
- 4 eggs, whisked
- Salt and black pepper to the taste
- ¼ teaspoon cumin, ground

Directions:
1. Preheat the air fryer at 360 degrees F, add all the ingredients, toss, cover, cook for 20

minutes, divide into bowls and serve for breakfast.

39. French Toast With Vanilla Filling

Servings:3
Cooking Time: 15 Minutes
Ingredients:
- 2 eggs
- ¼ cup heavy cream
- ⅓ cup sugar mixed with 1 tsp ground cinnamon
- 6 tbsp caramel
- 1 tsp vanilla extract
- Cooking spray

Directions:
1. In a bowl, whisk eggs and cream. Dip each piece of bread into the egg and cream. Dip the bread into the sugar and cinnamon mixture until well-coated. On a clean board, lay the coated slices and spread three of the slices with about 2 tbsp of caramel each, around the center.
2. Place the remaining three slices on top to form three sandwiches. Spray the air fryer basket with oil. Arrange the sandwiches into the fryer and cook for 10 minutes at 340 F, turning once.

40. Toasted Cheese

Servings: 2
Cooking Time: 20 Minutes
Ingredients:
- 2 slices bread
- 4 oz cheese, grated
- Small amount of butter

Directions:
1. Grill the bread in the toaster.
2. Butter the toast and top with the grated cheese.
3. Set your Air Fryer to 350°F and allow to warm.
4. Put the toast slices inside the fryer and cook for 4 - 6 minutes.
5. Serve and enjoy!

41. Grilled Apple And Brie Sandwich

Servings:1
Cooking Time: 8-10 Minutes
Ingredients:
- ½ apple, thinly sliced
- 2 tsp butter
- 2 oz brie cheese, thinly sliced

Directions:
1. Spread butter on the outside of the bread slices. Top with apple slices. Place brie slices on top of the apple. Top with the other slice of bread. Cook for 5 minutes at 350 F. Serve cut diagonally.

42. Spinach Eggs And Cheese

Servings: 2
Cooking Time: 40 Minutes
Ingredients:
- 3 whole eggs
- 3 oz cottage cheese
- 3-4 oz chopped spinach
- ¼ cup parmesan cheese
- ¼ cup of milk

Directions:
1. Preheat your fryer to 375°F/190°C.
2. In a large bowl, whisk the eggs, cottage cheese, the parmesan and the milk.
3. Mix in the spinach.
4. Transfer to a small, greased, fryer dish.
5. Sprinkle the cheese on top.
6. Bake for 25-30 minutes.
7. Let cool for 5 minutes and serve.

43. Coconut Eggs Mix

Servings: 4
Cooking Time: 8 Minutes
Ingredients:
- 1 tablespoon olive oil
- 1 and ½ cup coconut cream
- 8 eggs, whisked
- ½ cup mint, chopped
- Salt and black pepper to the taste

Directions:
1. In a bowl, mix the cream with salt, pepper, eggs and mint, whisk, pour into the air fryer greased with the oil, spread, cook at 350 degrees F for 8 minutes, divide between plates and serve.

44. Almond Pesto Salmon

Servings: 2
Cooking Time: 12 Minutes
Ingredients:
- 2 salmon fillets
- 2 tbsp butter, melted
- ¼ cup pesto
- ¼ cup almond, ground

Directions:
1. Mix together pesto and almond.
2. Brush salmon fillets with melted butter and place into the air fryer baking dish.
3. Top salmon fillets with pesto and almond mixture.
4. Place dish in the air fryer and cook at 390 F for 12 minutes.
5. Serve and enjoy.

45. Cheesy Sandwich

Servings: 1
Cooking Time:18 Minutes
Ingredients:
- 2 bread slices
- 2 cheddar cheese slices

- 2 tsp. butter
- A pinch of sweet paprika

Directions:
1. Spread butter on bread slices, add cheddar cheese on one, sprinkle paprika, top with the other bread slices, cut into 2 halves; arrange them in your air fryer and cook at 370 °F, for 8 minutes; flipping them once, arrange on a plate and serve.

46. Pumpkin & Yogurt Bread

Servings:4
Cooking Time: 15 Minutes
Ingredients:
- 2 large eggs
- 8 tablespoons pumpkin puree
- 6 tablespoons banana flour
- 4 tablespoons honey
- 4 tablespoons plain Greek yogurt
- 2 tablespoons vanilla essence
- Pinch of ground nutmeg
- 6 tablespoons oats

Directions:
1. Take a bowl, add in all the ingredients except oats and with a hand mixer, mix until smooth.
2. Add the oats and mix them well using a fork.
3. Set the temperature of Air Fryer to 360 degrees F. Grease and flour a loaf pan.
4. Place the mixture evenly into the prepared pan.
5. Arrange the loaf pan into an Air Fryer basket.
6. Air Fry for about 15 minutes or until a toothpick inserted in the center comes out clean.
7. Remove the pans from Air Fryer and place onto a wire rack for about 5 minutes.
8. Carefully, take out the bread from pan and put onto a wire rack to cool for about 5-10 minutes before slicing.
9. Cut the bread into desired size slices and serve.

47. Espresso Oatmeal

Servings: 4
Cooking Time:27 Minutes
Ingredients:
- 1 cup steel cut oats
- 1 cup milk
- 1 tsp. espresso powder
- 2 tsp. vanilla extract
- 2 ½ cups water
- 2 tbsp. sugar

Directions:
1. In a pan that fits your air fryer, mix oats with water, sugar, milk and espresso powder; stir, introduce in your air fryer and cook at 360 °F, for 17 minutes.

2. Add vanilla extract, stir; leave everything aside for 5 minutes; divide into bowls and serve for breakfast.

48. Egg & Mushroom Scramble

Servings:2
Cooking Time: 10 Minutes
Ingredients:
- 4 eggs
- Salt and freshly ground black pepper, as needed
- 2 tablespoons unsalted butter
- ½ cup fresh mushrooms, finely chopped
- 2 tablespoons Parmesan cheese, shredded

Directions:
1. Set the temperature of Air Fryer to 285 degrees F.
2. In a bowl, mix together the eggs, salt, and black pepper.
3. In a baking pan, melt the butter and tilt the pan to spread the butter in the bottom.
4. Add the beaten eggs and Air Fry for about 4-5 minutes
5. Add in the mushrooms and cheese and cook for 5 minutes, stirring occasionally.
6. Serve hot.

49. Sausage Bacon Fandango

Servings:4
Cooking Time:20 Minutes
Ingredients:
- 8 bacon slices
- 8 chicken sausages
- 4 eggs
- Salt and black pepper, to taste

Directions:
1. Preheat the Air fryer to 320 °F and grease 4 ramekins lightly.
2. Place bacon slices and sausages in the Air fryer basket.
3. Cook for about 10 minutes and crack 1 egg in each prepared ramekin.
4. Season with salt and black pepper and cook for about 10 more minutes.
5. Divide bacon slices and sausages in serving plates.
6. Place 1 egg in each plate and serve warm.

50. Ground Pork Bake

Servings: 2
Cooking Time: 12 Minutes
Ingredients:
- 8 oz ground pork
- 1 tablespoon keto tomato sauce
- ½ teaspoon dried basil
- 1/3 cup Mozzarella, shredded
- ½ teaspoon butter, melted
- ¼ teaspoon dried oregano
- Cooking spray

Directions:

1. Preheat the air fryer to 365F. Then spray the air fryer basket with cooking spray. In the mixing bowl mix up ground pork, marinara sauce, dried basil, oregano, butter, and Mozzarella. Put the mixture in the air fryer basket and spread gently with the help of the spatula. Cook the morning pizza for 12 minutes.

51. Breakfast Omelet

Servings: 2
Cooking Time: 30 Minutes
Ingredients:

- 1 large onion, chopped
- 2 tbsp. cheddar cheese, grated
- 3 eggs
- ½ tsp. soy sauce
- Salt
- Pepper powder
- Cooking spray

Directions:

1. In a bowl, mix the salt, pepper powder, soy sauce and eggs with a whisk.
2. Take a small pan small enough to fit inside the Air Fryer and spritz with cooking spray. Spread the chopped onion across the bottom of the pan, then transfer the pan to the Fryer. Cook at 355°F for 6-7 minutes, ensuring the onions turn translucent.
3. Add the egg mixture on top of the onions, coating everything well. Add the cheese on top, then resume cooking for another 5 or 6 minutes.
4. Take care when taking the pan out of the fryer. Enjoy with some toasted bread.

52. Chicken And Cream Lasagna

Servings: 2
Cooking Time: 25 Minutes
Ingredients:

- 1 egg, beaten
- 1 tablespoon heavy cream
- 1 teaspoon cream cheese
- 2 tablespoons almond flour
- ¼ teaspoon salt
- ¼ cup coconut cream
- 1 teaspoon dried basil
- 1 teaspoon keto tomato sauce
- ¼ cup Mozzarella, shredded
- 1 teaspoon butter, melted
- ½ cup ground chicken

Directions:

1. Make the lasagna batter: in the bowl mix up egg, heavy cream, cream cheese, and almond flour. Add coconut cream. Stir the liquid until smooth. Then preheat the air fryer to 355F. Brush the air fryer basket with butter. Pour ½ part of lasagna batter in the air fryer basket and flatten it in one layer. Then in the separated bowl mix up tomato sauce, basil, salt, and ground chicken. Put the chicken mixture over the batter in the air fryer. Add beaten egg. Then top it with remaining lasagna batter and sprinkle with shredded Mozzarella. Cook the lasagna for 25 minutes.

53. Breakfast Spanish Omelet

Servings: 4
Cooking Time:20 Minutes
Ingredients:

- 3 eggs
- 1/2 chorizo; chopped
- 1 tbsp. parsley; chopped.
- 1 tbsp. feta cheese; crumbled
- 1 potato; peeled and cubed
- 1/2 cup corn
- 1 tbsp. olive oil
- Salt and black pepper to the taste

Directions:

1. Heat up your air fryer at 350 °F and add oil.
2. Add chorizo and potatoes; stir and brown them for a few seconds.
3. In a bowl; mix eggs with corn, parsley, cheese, salt and pepper and whisk.
4. Pour this over chorizo and potatoes; spread and cook for 5 minutes. Divide omelet on plates and serve for breakfast.

54. Cauliflower Rice And Spinach Mix

Servings: 4
Cooking Time: 15 Minutes
Ingredients:

- 12 ounces cauliflower rice
- 3 tablespoons stevia
- 2 tablespoons olive oil
- 2 tablespoons lime juice
- 1 pound fresh spinach, torn
- 1 red bell pepper, chopped

Directions:

1. In your air fryer, mix all the ingredients, toss, cook at 370 degrees F for 15 minutes, shaking halfway, divide between plates and serve for breakfast.

55. Protein-rich Breakfast

Servings:4
Cooking Time:23 Minutes
Ingredients:

- 1 tablespoon unsalted butter, melted
- 1 pound fresh baby spinach
- 4 eggs
- 7-ounces ham, sliced
- 4 teaspoons milk
- 1 tablespoon olive oil
- Salt and black pepper, to taste

Directions:

1. Preheat the Air fryer to 355 °F and grease 4 ramekins with butter.
2. Heat olive oil on medium heat in a skillet and add spinach.
3. Cook for about 3 minutes until wilted and drain the liquid completely from the spinach.
4. Divide the spinach into prepared ramekins and top with ham slices.
5. Crack 1 egg over ham slices into each ramekin and drizzle with milk evenly.
6. Season with salt and black pepper and transfer into the Air fryer.
7. Bake for about 20 minutes and serve hot.

56. Breakfast Banana Bread

Servings:2
Cooking Time: 50 Minutes
Ingredients:
- 1 tbsp flour
- ¼ tsp baking soda
- 1 tsp baking powder
- ⅓ cup sugar
- 2 mashed bananas
- ¼ cup vegetable oil
- 1 egg, beaten
- 1 tsp vanilla extract
- ¾ cup chopped walnuts
- ¼ tsp salt
- 2 tbsp peanut butter
- 2 tbsp sour cream
- Cooking spray

Directions:
1. Preheat the air fryer to 330 F. Spray a small baking dish, that fits inside, with cooking spray or grease with butter. Combine the flour, salt, baking powder, and baking soda, in a bowl.
2. In another bowl, combine bananas, oil, egg, peanut butter, vanilla, sugar, and sour cream. Mix both mixtures. Stir in chopped walnuts. Pour the batter into the dish. Cook for 40 minutes and serve chill.

57. Kale Omelet

Servings: 1
Cooking Time: 10 Minutes
Ingredients:
- 3 eggs, lightly beaten
- 1 tbsp parsley, chopped
- 1 tbsp basil, chopped
- 3 tbsp kale, chopped
- 3 tbsp cottage cheese, crumbled
- Pepper
- Salt

Directions:
1. Spray air fryer baking dish with cooking spray.
2. In a bowl, whisk eggs with pepper and salt.

3. Add remaining ingredients into the egg and stir to combine.
4. Pour egg mixture into the prepared dish and place into the air fryer.
5. Cook at 330 F for 10 minutes.
6. Serve and enjoy.

58. Broccoli Casserole

Servings: 4
Cooking Time: 25 Minutes
Ingredients:
- 1 broccoli head, florets separated and roughly chopped
- 2 ounces cheddar cheese, grated
- 4 eggs, whisked
- 1 cup almond milk
- 2 teaspoons cilantro, chopped
- Salt and black pepper to the taste

Directions:
1. In a bowl, mix the eggs with the milk, cilantro, salt and pepper and whisk. Put the broccoli in your air fryer, add the eggs mix over it, spread, sprinkle the cheese on top, cook at 350 degrees F for 25 minutes, divide between plates and serve for breakfast.

59. Spinach Egg Breakfast

Servings: 4
Cooking Time: 20 Minutes
Ingredients:
- 3 eggs
- 1/4 cup coconut milk
- 1/4 cup parmesan cheese, grated
- 4 oz spinach, chopped
- 3 oz cottage cheese

Directions:
1. Preheat the air fryer to 350 F.
2. Add eggs, milk, half parmesan cheese, and cottage cheese in a bowl and whisk well. Add spinach and stir well.
3. Pour mixture into the air fryer baking dish.
4. Sprinkle remaining half parmesan cheese on top.
5. Place dish in the air fryer and cook for 20 minutes.
6. Serve and enjoy.

60. Cauliflower Hash Brown

Servings:4
Cooking Time:10 Minutes
Ingredients:
- 2 cups cauliflower, finely grated, soaked and drained
- 2 tablespoons xanthan gum
- Salt, to taste
- Pepper powder, to taste
- 2 teaspoons chili flakes
- 1 teaspoon garlic
- 1 teaspoon onion powder

- 2 teaspoons vegetable oil

Directions:
1. Preheat the Air fryer to 300 °F and grease an Air fryer basket with oil.
2. Heat vegetable oil in a nonstick pan and add cauliflower.
3. Sauté for about 4 minutes and dish out the cauliflower in a plate.
4. Mix the cauliflower with xanthum gum, salt, chili flakes, garlic and onion powder.
5. Mix well and refrigerate the hash for about 20 minutes.
6. Place the hash in the Air fryer basket and cook for about 10 minutes.
7. Flip the hash after cooking half way through and dish out to serve warm.

61. Air Fryer Bacon

Servings:6
Cooking Time:9 Minutes
Ingredients:
- 6 bacon strips
- ½ tablespoon olive oil

Directions:
1. Preheat the Air fryer to 350 °F and grease an Air fryer basket with olive oil.
2. Cook for about 9 minutes and flip the bacon.
3. Cook for 3 more minutes until crispy and serve warm.

62. Butternut Squash Stew

Servings: 5
Cooking Time: 15 Minutes
Ingredients:
- 1½ pounds butternut squash, cubed
- ½ cup green onions, chopped
- 3 tablespoons butter, melted
- ½ cup carrots, chopped
- ½ cup celery, chopped
- 1 garlic clove, minced
- ½ teaspoon Italian seasoning
- 15 ounces canned tomatoes, chopped
- Salt and black pepper to taste
- ⅛ teaspoon red pepper flakes, dried
- 1 cup quinoa, cooked
- 1½ cups heavy cream
- 1 cup chicken meat, already cooked and shredded

Directions:
1. Place all the ingredients in a pan that fits your air fryer and toss.
2. Put the pan into the fryer and cook at 400 degrees F for 15 minutes.
3. Divide the stew between bowls, serve, and enjoy.

63. Bacon Mushrooms

Servings: 2
Cooking Time: 11 Minutes
Ingredients:
- 2 Portobello mushroom caps
- 2 eggs, beaten
- ½ cup coconut flakes
- ½ teaspoon chili flakes
- ½ teaspoon salt
- ½ teaspoon ground paprika
- 2 mozzarella slices
- 2 oz bacon, chopped
- 1 garlic clove, chopped
- 1 teaspoon olive oil

Directions:
1. Mix up beaten egg, ground paprika, salt, and chili flakes. Then dip the mushroom caps in the beaten egg mixture and coat in the coconut flakes. After this, preheat the air fryer to 400F. Place the chopped bacon in the air fryer basket and add olive oil and garlic. Cook the ingredients for 6 minutes at 400F. Stir the mixture every 2 minutes. When the bacon is cooked, fill the mushrooms caps with it. Put the mushroom caps in the air fryer basket and cook them for 5 minutes at 400F.

64. 'no Potato' Shepherd's Pie

Servings: 6
Cooking Time: 70 Minutes
Ingredients:
- 1 lb lean ground beef
- 8 oz low-carb mushroom sauce mix
- ¼ cup ketchup
- 1 lb package frozen mixed vegetables
- 1 lb Aitkin's low-carb bake mix or equivalent

Directions:
1. Preheat your fryer to 375°F/190°C.
2. Prepare the bake mix according to package Directions:. Layer into the skillet base.
3. Cut the dough into triangles and roll them from base to tip. Set to the side.
4. Brown the ground beef with the salt. Stir in the mushroom sauce, ketchup and mixed vegetables.
5. Bring the mixture to the boil and reduce the heat to medium, cover and simmer until tender.
6. Put the dough triangles on top of the mixture, tips pointing towards the center.
7. Bake for 60 minutes until piping hot and serve!

65. Sausage Balls

Servings: 6
Cooking Time: 25 Minutes
Ingredients:
- 12 oz Jimmy Dean's Sausage
- 6 oz. shredded cheddar cheese
- 10 cubes cheddar (optional)

Directions:
1. Mix the shredded cheese and sausage.
2. Divide the mixture into 12 equal parts to be stuffed.
3. Add a cube of cheese to the center of the sausage and roll into balls.
4. Fry at 375°F/190°C for 15 minutes until crisp.
5. Serve!

66. Thanksgiving Sprouts

Servings: 6
Cooking Time: 20 Minutes
Ingredients:
- 1 ½ lb. Brussels sprouts, cleaned and trimmed
- 3 tbsp. olive oil
- 1 tsp. salt
- 1 tsp. black pepper

Directions:
1. Pre-heat the Air Fryer to 375°F. Cover the basket with aluminum foil and coat with a light brushing of oil.
2. In a mixing bowl, combine all ingredients, coating the sprouts well.

3. Put in the fryer basket and cook for 10 minutes. Shake the Air Fryer basket throughout the duration to ensure even cooking.

67. Mediterranean Vegetables

Servings: 4
Cooking Time: 30 Minutes
Ingredients:
- 1 cup cherry tomatoes, halved
- 1 large zucchini, sliced
- 1 green pepper, sliced
- 1 parsnip, sliced
- 1 carrot, sliced
- 1 tsp. mixed herbs
- 1 tsp. mustard
- 1 tsp. garlic puree
- 6 tbsp. olive oil
- Salt and pepper to taste

Directions:
1. Pre-heat the Air Fryer at 400°F.
2. Combine all the ingredients in a bowl, making sure to coat the vegetables well.
3. Transfer to the fryer and cook for 6 minutes, ensuring the vegetables are tender and browned.

68. Cabbage Stew

Servings: 4
Cooking Time: 20 Minutes
Ingredients:
- 14 ounces tomatoes, chopped
- 1 green cabbage head, shredded
- Salt and black pepper to the taste
- 1 tablespoon sweet paprika
- 4 ounces chicken stock
- 2 tablespoon dill, chopped

Directions:
1. In a pan that fits your air fryer, mix the cabbage with the tomatoes and all the other ingredients except the dill, toss, introduce the pan in the fryer, and cook at 380 degrees F for 20 minutes. Divide into bowls and serve with dill sprinkled on top.

69. Zucchini Casserole

Servings: 4
Cooking Time: 30 Minutes
Ingredients:
- 1 cup ground chicken
- ½ cup ground pork
- 2 oz celery stalk, chopped
- 1 zucchini, grated
- 1 tablespoon coconut oil, melted
- ½ teaspoon salt
- 1 teaspoon ground black pepper
- ½ teaspoon chili flakes
- 1 teaspoon dried dill
- ½ teaspoon dried parsley

- ½ cup beef broth

Directions:
1. In the mixing bowl mix up ground chicken, ground pork, celery stalk, and salt. Add ground black pepper, chili flakes, dried dill, and dried parsley. Stir the meat mixture until homogenous. Then brush the air fryer pan with coconut oil and put ½ part of all grated zucchini. Then spread it with all ground pork mixture. Sprinkle the meat with remaining grated zucchini and cover with foil. Preheat the air fryer to 375F. Place the pan with casserole in the air fryer and cook it for 25 minutes. When the time is finished, remove the foil and cook the casserole for 5 minutes more.

70. Bacon Chops

Servings: 2
Cooking Time: 20 Minutes
Ingredients:
- 2 pork chops (I prefer bone-in, but boneless chops work great as well)
- 1 bag shredded brussels sprouts
- 4 slices of bacon
- Worcestershire sauce
- Lemon juice (optional)

Directions:
1. Place the pork chops on a baking sheet with the Worcestershire sauce inside a preheated grill for 5 minutes.
2. Turnover and cook for another 5 minutes. Put to the side when done.
3. Cook the chopped bacon in a large pan until browned. Add the shredded brussels sprouts and cook together.
4. Stir the brussels sprouts with the bacon and grease and cook for 5 minutes until the bacon is crisp.

71. Mu Shu Lunch Pork

Servings: 2
Cooking Time: 10 Minutes
Ingredients:
- 4 cups coleslaw mix, with carrots
- 1 small onion, sliced thin
- 1 lb cooked roast pork, cut into ½" cubes
- 2 tbsp hoisin sauce
- 2 tbsp soy sauce

Directions:
1. In a large skillet, heat the oil on a high heat.
2. Stir-fry the cabbage and onion for 4 minutes until tender.
3. Add the pork, hoisin and soy sauce.
4. Cook until browned.
5. Enjoy!

72. Cheeseburger Sliders

Servings: 3

Cooking Time: 20 Minutes
Ingredients:
- 1 lb. ground beef
- 6 slices cheddar cheese
- 6 dinner rolls
- Salt and pepper

Directions:
1. Pre-heat the Air Fryer to 390°F.
2. With your hands, shape the ground beef into 6 x 5-oz. patties. Sprinkle on some salt and pepper to taste.
3. Place the burgers in the cooking basket and cook for 10 minutes. Take care when removing them from the Air Fryer.
4. Top the patties with the cheese. Put them back in the Air Fryer and allow to cook for another minute before serving.

73. Rocket Salad

Servings: 4
Cooking Time: 35 Minutes
Ingredients:
- 8 fresh figs, halved
- 1 ½ cups chickpeas, cooked
- 1 tsp. cumin seeds, roasted then crushed
- 4 tbsp. balsamic vinegar
- 2 tbsp. extra-virgin olive oil
- Salt and pepper to taste
- 3 cups arugula rocket, washed and dried

Directions:
1. Pre-heat the Air Fryer to 375°F.
2. Cover the Air Fryer basket with aluminum foil and grease lightly with oil. Put the figs in the fryer and allow to cook for 10 minutes.
3. In a bowl, combine the chickpeas and cumin seeds.
4. Remove the cooked figs from the fryer and replace with chickpeas. Cook for 10 minutes. Leave to cool.
5. In the meantime, prepare the dressing. Mix together the balsamic vinegar, olive oil, salt and pepper.
6. In a salad bowl combine the arugula rocket with the cooled figs and chickpeas.
7. Toss with the sauce and serve right away.

74. Mozzarella Bruschetta

Servings: 1
Cooking Time: 10 Minutes
Ingredients:
- 6 small loaf slices
- ½ cup tomatoes, finely chopped
- 3 oz. mozzarella cheese, grated
- 1 tbsp. fresh basil, chopped
- 1 tbsp. olive oil

Directions:
1. Pre-heat the Air Fryer to 350°F. Place the bread inside and cook for about 3 minutes.

2. Add the tomato, mozzarella, prosciutto, and a drizzle of olive oil on top.
3. Cook the bruschetta for an additional minute before serving.

75. Mozzarella Burger

Servings: 2
Cooking Time: 12 Minutes
Ingredients:
- 4 sausage patties
- 1 teaspoon butter, softened
- ½ teaspoon ground black pepper
- ¼ teaspoon salt
- 1 oz Mozzarella, chopped
- 4 bacon slices
- Cooking spray

Directions:
1. Sprinkle the sausage patties with ground black pepper and salt. Then put the cheese and butter on the patties. Make the balls from the sausage patties with the help of the fingertips. After this, roll them in the bacon. Preheat the air fryer to 390F. Put the bacon bombs in the air fryer and spray them with the cooking spray. Cook the bombs for 12 minutes – for 6 minutes from each side.

76. Monkey Salad

Servings: 1
Cooking Time: 10 Minutes
Ingredients:
- 2 tbsp butter
- 1 cup unsweetened coconut flakes
- 1 cup raw, unsalted cashews
- 1 cup raw, unsalted s
- 1 cup 90% dark chocolate shavings

Directions:
1. In a skillet, melt the butter on a medium heat.
2. Add the coconut flakes and sauté until lightly browned for 4 minutes.
3. Add the cashews and s and sauté for 3 minutes. Remove from the heat and sprinkle with dark chocolate shavings.
4. Serve!

77. Tuna Bake

Servings: 6
Cooking Time: 15 Minutes
Ingredients:
- 2 spring onions, diced
- 1 pound smoked tuna, boneless
- ¼ cup ricotta cheese
- 3 oz celery stalk, diced
- ½ teaspoon celery seeds
- 1 tablespoon cream cheese
- ¼ teaspoon salt
- ½ teaspoon ground paprika

- 2 tablespoons lemon juice
- 1 tablespoon ghee
- 4 oz Edam cheese, shredded

Directions:
1. Mix up celery seeds, cream cheese, ground paprika, lemon juice, and ricotta cheese. Then shred the tuna until it is smooth and add it in the cream cheese mixture. Add onion and stir the mass with the help of the spoon. Grease the air fryer pan with ghee and put the tuna mixture inside. Flatten its surface gently with the help of the spoon and top with Edam cheese. Preheat the air fryer to 360F. Place the pan with tuna melt in the air fryer and cook it for 15 minutes.

78. Garlic Pork Stew

Servings: 4
Cooking Time: 30 Minutes
Ingredients:
- 1 and ½ pounds pork stew meat, cubed
- 1 red cabbage, shredded
- 1 tablespoon olive oil
- Salt and black pepper to the taste
- 2 chili peppers, chopped
- 4 garlic cloves, minced
- ½ cup veggie stock
- ¼ cup keto tomato sauce

Directions:
1. Heat up a pan that fits the air fryer with the oil over medium heat, add the meat, chili peppers and the garlic, stir and brown for 5 minutes. Add the rest of the ingredients, toss, introduce the pan in the fryer and cook at 380 degrees F for 20 minutes. Divide the into bowls and serve for lunch.

79. Coconut Tomato

Servings: 4
Cooking Time: 5 Minutes
Ingredients:
- 1/3 cup coconut cream
- ½ pound cherry tomatoes, halved
- 2 avocados, pitted, peeled and cubed
- A pinch of salt and black pepper
- Cooking spray

Directions:
1. Grease the air fryer with cooking spray, combine the tomatoes with avocados, and the other ingredients and cook at 350 degrees F for 5 minutes shaking once. Divide into bowls and serve

80. Chicken Rolls

Servings: 4
Cooking Time: 18 Minutes
Ingredients:
- 2 large zucchini
- ½ cup Cheddar cheese, shredded

- 1-pound chicken breast, skinless, boneless
- 1 teaspoon dried oregano
- ½ teaspoon olive oil
- 1 teaspoon salt
- 2 spring onions, chopped
- 1 teaspoon ground paprika
- ½ teaspoon ground turmeric
- ½ cup keto tomato sauce

Directions:
1. Preheat the skillet well and pour the olive oil inside. Put the onions in it and sprinkle with salt, ground paprika, and ground turmeric. Cook the onion for 5 minutes over the medium-high heat. Stir it from time to time. Meanwhile, shred the chicken. Add it in the skillet. Then add oregano. Stir well and cook the mixture for 2 minutes. After this, remove the skillet from the heat. Cut the zucchini into halves (lengthwise). Then make the zucchini slices with the help of the vegetable peeler. Put 3 zucchini slices on the chopping board overlapping each of them. Then spread the surface of them with the shredded chicken mixture. Roll the zucchini carefully in the shape of the roll. Repeat the same steps with remaining zucchini and shredded chicken mixture. Line the air fryer pan with parchment and put the enchilada rolls inside. Sprinkle them with tomato sauce Preheat the air fryer to 350F. Top the zucchini rolls (enchiladas) with Cheddar cheese and put in the air fryer basket. Cook the meal for 10 minutes.

81. Italian Chicken Mix

Servings: 4
Cooking Time: 20 Minutes
Ingredients:
- 1 cup chicken stock
- Salt and black pepper to taste
- 8 chicken drumsticks, bone-in
- 1 teaspoon garlic powder
- 1 yellow onion, chopped
- 28 ounces canned tomatoes, chopped
- 1 teaspoon oregano, dried
- ½ cup black olives, pitted and sliced

Directions:
1. Add all the ingredients to a baking dish that fits your air fryer and toss.
2. Place the dish in your air fryer and cook at 380 degrees F for 20 minutes.
3. Divide the mix into bowls and serve.

82. Beef Pie

Servings: 4
Cooking Time: 6 Minutes
Ingredients:
- 2 cup cauliflower, boiled, mashed
- 2 oz celery stalk, chopped

- 1 cup ground beef
- ½ teaspoon salt
- ½ teaspoon ground turmeric
- 1 tablespoon coconut oil
- ½ teaspoon avocado oil
- 1 teaspoon dried parsley
- 1 tablespoon keto tomato sauce
- 1 garlic clove, diced

Directions:
1. Toss the coconut oil in the skillet and melt it over the medium heat. Then add celery stalk. Cook the vegetables for 5 minutes. Stir them from time to time. Meanwhile, brush the air fryer pan with avocado oil. Transfer the cooked vegetables in the pan and flatten them in the shape of the layer. Then put the ground beef in the pan. Add salt, parsley, and turmeric. Cook the ground meat for 10 minutes over the medium heat. Stir it from time to time. Add tomato sauce and stir well. After this, transfer the ground beef over the vegetables. Then add garlic and top the pie with mashed cauliflower mash. Preheat the air fryer to 360F. Put the pan with shepherd pie in the air fryer and cook for 6 minutes or until you get the crunchy crust.

83. Thyme Green Beans

Servings: 6
Cooking Time: 20 Minutes
Ingredients:
- 1 pound green beans, trimmed and halved
- 2 eggplants, cubed
- 1 cup veggie stock
- 1 tablespoon olive oil
- 1 red chili pepper
- 1 red bell pepper, chopped
- ½ teaspoon thyme, dried
- Salt and black pepper to the taste

Directions:
1. In a pan that fits your air fryer, mix all the ingredients, toss, introduce the pan in the machine and cook at 350 degrees F for 20 minutes. Divide into bowls and serve for lunch.

84. 'i Love Bacon'

Servings: 4
Cooking Time: 90 Minutes
Ingredients:
- 30 slices thick-cut bacon
- 12 oz steak
- 10 oz pork sausage
- 4 oz cheddar cheese, shredded

Directions:
1. Lay out 5 x 6 slices of bacon in a woven pattern and bake at 400°F/200°C for 20 minutes until crisp.

2. Combine the steak, bacon and sausage to form a meaty mixture.
3. Lay out the meat in a rectangle of similar size to the bacon strips. Season with salt/peppe.
4. Place the bacon weave on top of the meat mixture.
5. Place the cheese in the center of the bacon.
6. Roll the meat into a tight roll and refrigerate.
7. Make a 7 x 7 bacon weave and roll the bacon weave over the meat, diagonally.
8. Bake at 400°F/200°C for 60 minutes or 165°F/75°C internally.
9. Let rest for 5 minutes before serving.

85. Chicken & Veggies

Servings: 4
Cooking Time: 30 Minutes
Ingredients:
- 8 chicken thighs
- 5 oz. mushrooms, sliced
- 1 red onion, diced
- Fresh black pepper, to taste
- 10 medium asparagus
- ½ cup carrots, diced
- ¼ cup balsamic vinegar
- 2 red bell peppers, diced
- ½ tsp. sugar
- 2 tbsp. extra-virgin olive oil
- 1 ½ tbsp. fresh rosemary
- 2 cloves garlic, chopped
- ½ tbsp. dried oregano
- 1 tsp. kosher salt
- 2 fresh sage, chopped

Directions:
1. Pre-heat the Air Fryer to 400°F.
2. Grease the inside of a baking tray with the oil.
3. Season the chicken with salt and pepper.
4. Put all of the vegetables in a large bowl and throw in the oregano, garlic, sugar, mushrooms, vinegar, and sage. Combine everything well before transferring to the baking tray.
5. Put the chicken thighs in the baking tray. Cook in the Air Fryer for about 20 minutes.
6. Serve hot.

86. Quinoa And Spinach Pesto Mix

Servings: 4
Cooking Time: 15 Minutes
Ingredients:
- 1 cup quinoa, cooked
- 3 tablespoons chicken stock
- ¾ cup jarred spinach pesto
- 1 green apple, chopped
- ¼ cup celery, chopped
- Salt and black pepper to taste

Directions:

1. Mix all the ingredients in a pan that fits your air fryer; toss.
2. Place the pan in your fryer and cook at 370 degrees F for 15 minutes.
3. Divide into bowls and serve right away.

87. Salmon Salad

Servings: 4
Cooking Time: 8 Minutes
Ingredients:
- 4 salmon fillets, boneless
- 2 tablespoons olive oil
- Salt and black pepper to the taste
- 3 cups kale leaves, shredded
- 2 teaspoons balsamic vinegar

Directions:
1. Put the fish in your air fryer's basket, season with salt and pepper, drizzle half of the oil over them, cook at 400 degrees F for 4 minutes on each side, cool down and cut into medium cubes. In a bowl, mix the kale with salt, pepper, vinegar, the rest of the oil and the salmon, toss gently and serve for lunch.

88. Cast-iron Cheesy Chicken

Servings: 4
Cooking Time: 10 Minutes
Ingredients:
- 4 chicken breasts
- 4 bacon strips
- 4 oz ranch dressing
- 2 green onions
- 4 oz cheddar cheese

Directions:
1. Pour the oil into a skillet and heat on high. Add the chicken breasts and fry both sides until piping hot.
2. Fry the bacon and crumble it into bits.
3. Dice the green onions.
4. Put the chicken in a baking dish and top with soy sauce.
5. Toss in the ranch, bacon, green onions and top with cheese.
6. Cook until the cheese is browned, for around 4 minutes.
7. Serve.

89. Tomato And Eggplant Casserole

Servings: 4
Cooking Time: 20 Minutes
Ingredients:
- 2 eggplants, cubed
- 1 hot chili pepper, chopped
- 4 spring onions, chopped
- ½ pound cherry tomatoes, cubed
- Salt and black pepper to the taste
- 2 teaspoons olive oil
- ½ cup cilantro, chopped

- 4 garlic cloves, minced

Directions:
1. Grease a baking pan that fits the air fryer with the oil, and mix all the ingredients in the pan. Put the pan in the preheated air fryer and cook at 380 degrees F for 20 minutes, divide into bowls and serve for lunch.

90. Nearly Pizza

Servings: 4
Cooking Time: 30 Minutes
Ingredients:
- 4 large portobello mushrooms
- 4 tsp olive oil
- 1 cup marinara sauce
- 1 cup shredded mozzarella cheese
- 10 slices sugar-free pepperoni

Directions:
1. Preheat your fryer to 375°F/190°C.
2. De-steam the 4 mushrooms and brush each cap with the olive oil, one spoon for each cap.
3. Place on a baking sheet and bake stem side down for 8 minutes.
4. Take out of the fryer and fill each cap with 1 cup marinara sauce, 1 cup mozzarella cheese and 3 slices of pepperoni.
5. Cook for another 10 minutes until browned.
6. Serve hot.

91. Tofu Bites

Servings: 3
Cooking Time: 65 Minutes
Ingredients:
- 2 tbsp. sesame oil
- ¼ cup maple syrup
- 3 tbsp. peanut butter
- ¼ cup liquid aminos
- 3tbsp. chili garlic sauce
- 2 tbsp. rice wine vinegar
- 2 cloves of garlic, minced
- 1 inch fresh ginger, peeled and grated
- 1 tsp. red pepper flakes
- 1 block extra firm tofu, pressed to remove excess water and cubed
- Toasted peanuts, chopped
- 1 tsp. sesame seeds
- 1 sprig cilantro, chopped

Directions:
1. Whisk together the first 9 ingredients in a large bowl to well combine.
2. Transfer to an airtight bag along with the cubed tofu. Allow to marinate for a minimum of a half hour.
3. Pre-heat the Air Fryer to 425°F.
4. Put the tofu cubes in the fryer, keep any excess marinade for the sauce. Cook for 15 minutes.

5. In the meantime, heat the marinade over a medium heat to reduce by half.
6. Plate up the cooked tofu with some cooked rice and serve with the sauce. Complete the dish with the sesame seeds, cilantro and peanuts.

92. Italian Sausages

Servings: 4
Cooking Time: 12 Minutes
Ingredients:
- 4 pork Italian sausages
- ½ cup keto tomato sauce
- 4 Mozzarella sticks
- 1 teaspoon butter, softened

Directions:
1. Make the cross-section in every sausage with the help of the knife. Then fill the cut with the Mozzarella stick. Brush the air fryer pan with butter. Put the stuffed sausages in the pan and sprinkle them with tomato sauce. Preheat the air fryer to 375F. Place the pan with sausages in the air fryer and cook them for 12 minutes or until the sausages are golden brown.

93. Sweet Potato Casserole

Servings: 6
Cooking Time: 60 Minutes
Ingredients:
- 3 big sweet potatoes; pricked with a fork
- 1 cup chicken stock
- 1/4 tsp. nutmeg; ground
- 1/3 cup coconut cream
- Salt and black pepper to the taste
- A pinch of cayenne pepper

Directions:
1. Place sweet potatoes in your air fryer; cook them at 350 °F, for 40 minutes; cool them down, peel, roughly chop and transfer to a pan that fits your air fryer.
2. Add stock, salt, pepper, cayenne and coconut cream; toss, introduce in your air fryer and cook at 360 °F, for 10 minutes more. Divide casserole into bowls and serve.

94. Chickpea & Avocado Mash

Servings: 4
Cooking Time: 30 Minutes
Ingredients:
- 1 medium-sized head of cauliflower, cut into florets
- 1 can chickpeas, drained and rinsed
- 1 tbsp. extra-virgin olive oil
- 2 tbsp. lemon juice
- Salt and pepper to taste
- 4 flatbreads, toasted
- 2 ripe avocados, mashed

Directions:

1. Pre-heat the Air Fryer at 425°F.
2. In a bowl, mix together the chickpeas, cauliflower, lemon juice and olive oil. Sprinkle salt and pepper as desired.
3. Put inside the Air Fryer basket and cook for 25 minutes.
4. Spread on top of the flatbread along with the mashed avocado. Sprinkle on more pepper and salt as desired and enjoy with hot sauce.

95. Chicken, Eggs And Lettuce Salad

Servings: 3
Cooking Time: 8 Minutes
Ingredients:
- 3 spring onions, sliced
- 8 oz chicken fillet, roughly chopped
- 1 bacon slice, cooked, crumbled
- 2 cherry tomatoes, halved
- ¼ avocado, chopped
- 2 eggs, hard-boiled, peeled, chopped
- 1 cup lettuce, roughly chopped
- 1 tablespoon sesame oil
- ½ teaspoon lemon juice
- ½ teaspoon avocado oil
- ½ teaspoon ground black pepper
- ½ teaspoon salt
- 1 egg, beaten
- 2 tablespoons coconut flakes

Directions:
1. Sprinkle the chopped chicken fillets with salt and ground black pepper. Then dip the chicken in the egg and after this, coat in the coconut flakes. Preheat the air fryer to 385F. Place the chicken fillets inside and sprinkle them with avocado oil. Cook the chicken pieces for 8 minutes. Shake them after 4 minutes of cooking. After this, in the mixing bowl mix up spring onions, bacon, cherry tomatoes, hard-boiled eggs, lettuce, and lemon juice. Add sesame oil and shake the salad well. When the chicken is cooked, add it in the cobb salad and mix up gently with the help of the wooden spatulas.

96. Herbed Butter Beef Loin

Servings: 4
Cooking Time: 25 Minutes
Ingredients:
- 1 tbsp. butter, melted
- ¼ dried thyme
- 1 tsp. garlic salt
- ¼ tsp. dried parsley
- 1 lb. beef loin

Directions:
1. In a bowl, combine the melted butter, thyme, garlic salt, and parsley.
2. Cut the beef loin into slices and generously apply the seasoned butter using a brush.

3. Pre-heat your fryer at 400°F and place a rack inside.
4. Cook the beef for fifteen minutes.
5. Take care when removing it and serve hot.

97. Pork And Mushrooms Mix

Servings: 4
Cooking Time: 20 Minutes
Ingredients:
- 1 pound pork stew meat, ground
- 1 cup mushrooms, sliced
- 2 spring onions, chopped
- Salt and black pepper to the taste
- 1 teaspoon Italian seasoning
- ½ teaspoon garlic powder
- 1 tablespoon olive oil

Directions:
1. Heat up a pan that fits the air fryer with the oil over medium high heat, add the meat and brown for 3-4 minutes. Add the rest of the ingredients, stir, put the pan in the Air Fryer, cover and cook at 360 degrees F for 15 minutes. Divide between plates and serve for lunch.

98. Smoked Chicken Mix

Servings: 4
Cooking Time: 25 Minutes
Ingredients:
- 1 and ½ pound chicken breasts, skinless, boneless and cubed
- Salt and black pepper to the taste
- ½ cup chicken stock
- 2 teaspoons smoked paprika
- ½ teaspoon basil, dried

Directions:
1. In a pan that fits the air fryer, combine all the ingredients, toss, introduce the pan in the fryer and cook at 390 degrees F for 25 minutes. Divide between plates and serve for lunch with a side salad.

99. Wrapped Zucchini

Servings: 2
Cooking Time: 10 Minutes
Ingredients:
- 2 zucchinis, trimmed
- 8 bacon slices
- 1 teaspoon sesame oil
- ¼ teaspoon chili powder

Directions:
1. Cut every zucchini into 4 sticks and sprinkle with chili powder. Then wrap every zucchini stick in bacon and sprinkle with sesame oil. Preheat the air fryer to 400F. Put the zucchini sticks in the air fryer in one layer and cook for 10 minutes. Flip the zucchini sticks after 5 minutes of cooking.

100.Beef And Sauce

Servings: 4
Cooking Time: 20 Minutes
Ingredients:
- 1 pound lean beef meat, cubed and browned
- 2 garlic cloves, minced
- Salt and black pepper to the taste
- Cooking spray
- 16 ounces keto tomato sauce

Directions:
1. Preheat the Air Fryer at 400 degrees F, add the pan inside, grease it with cooking spray, add the meat and all the other ingredients, toss and cook for 20 minutes. Divide into bowls and serve for lunch.

101.Green Beans Stew

Servings: 4
Cooking Time: 15 Minutes
Ingredients:
- 1 pound green beans, halved
- 1 cup okra
- 1 tablespoon thyme, chopped
- 3 tablespoons keto tomato sauce
- Salt and black pepper to the taste
- 4 garlic cloves, minced

Directions:
1. In a pan that fits your air fryer, mix all the ingredients, toss, introduce the pan in the air fryer and cook at 370 degrees F for 15 minutes. Divide the stew into bowls and serve.

102.Sweet Onions & Potatoes

Servings: 6
Cooking Time: 30 Minutes
Ingredients:
- 2 large sweet potatoes, peeled and cut into chunks
- 2 medium sweet onions, cut into chunks
- 3 tbsp. olive oil
- 1 tsp. dried thyme
- Salt and pepper to taste
- ¼ cup s, sliced and toasted

Directions:
1. Pre-heat the Air Fryer at 425°F.
2. In a bowl, combine all of the ingredients, except for the sliced s.
3. Transfer the vegetables and dressing to a ramekin and cook in the fryer for 20 minutes.
4. When ready to serve, add the s on top.

103.Radish And Tuna Salad

Servings: 2
Cooking Time: 8 Minutes
Ingredients:
- ½ cup radish sprouts

- 8 oz tuna, smoked, boneless and shredded
- 1 egg, beaten
- 1 tablespoon coconut flour
- ½ teaspoon ground coriander
- ½ teaspoon lemon zest, grated
- 1 tablespoon olive oil
- ½ teaspoon salt
- 1 tablespoon lemon juice
- ½ cup radish, sliced

Directions:
1. Mix up the tuna with coconut flour, ground coriander, lemon zest, and egg. Stir the mixture until homogenous. Preheat the air fryer to 400F. Then make the small tuna balls and put them in the hot air fryer. Sprinkle the tuna balls with ½ tablespoon of olive oil. Cook the tuna balls for 8 minutes. Flip the tuna balls on another side after 4 minutes of cooking. Meanwhile, mix up together radish sprouts and radish. Sprinkle the mixture with remaining olive oil, salt, and lemon juice. Shake it well. Then top the salad with tuna balls.

104.Garlic Bacon

Servings: 4
Cooking Time: 40 Minutes
Ingredients:
- 4 potatoes, peeled and cut into bite-size chunks
- 6 cloves garlic, unpeeled
- strips bacon, chopped
- 1 tbsp. fresh rosemary, finely chopped

Directions:
1. In a large bowl, thoroughly combine the potatoes, garlic, bacon, and rosemary. Place the ingredients in a baking dish.
2. Set your Air Fryer to 350°F and briefly allow to warm.
3. Cook the potatoes for 25-30 minutes until a golden brown color is achieved.

105.Breaded Pork Chops

Servings: 4
Cooking Time: 25 Minutes
Ingredients:
- 1 tsp. chili powder
- ½ tsp. garlic powder
- 1 ½ oz. pork rinds, finely ground
- 4 x 4-oz. pork chops
- 1 tbsp. coconut oil, melted

Directions:
1. Combine the chili powder, garlic powder, and ground pork rinds.
2. Coat the pork chops with the coconut oil, followed by the pork rind mixture, taking care to cover them completely. Then place the chops in the basket of the fryer.

3. Cook the chops for fifteen minutes at 400°F, turning halfway through.
4. Once they are browned, check the temperature has reached 145°F before serving with the sides of your choice.

106.Cheese & Macaroni Balls

Servings: 2
Cooking Time: 25 Minutes
Ingredients:
- 2 cups leftover macaroni
- 1 cup cheddar cheese, shredded
- 3 large eggs
- 1 cup milk
- ½ cup flour
- 1 cup bread crumbs
- ½ tsp. salt
- ¼ tsp. black pepper

Directions:
1. In a bowl, combine the leftover macaroni and shredded cheese.
2. Pour the flour in a separate bowl. Put the bread crumbs in a third bowl. Finally, in a fourth bowl, mix together the eggs and milk with a whisk.
3. With an ice-cream scoop, create balls from the macaroni mixture. Coat them the flour, then in the egg mixture, and lastly in the bread crumbs.
4. Pre-heat the Air Fryer to 365°F and cook the balls for about 10 minutes, giving them an occasional stir. Ensure they crisp up nicely.
5. Serve with the sauce of your choice.

107.Cauliflower Cheese Tater Tots

Servings: 12
Cooking Time: 25 Minutes
Ingredients:
- 1 lb. cauliflower, steamed and chopped
- ½ cup nutritional yeast
- 1 tbsp. oats
- 1 flax egg [1 tbsp. desiccated coconuts + 3 tbsp. flaxseed meal
- + 3 tbsp. water]
- 1 onion, chopped
- 1 tsp. garlic, minced
- 1 tsp. parsley, chopped
- 1 tsp. oregano, chopped
- 1 tsp. chives, chopped
- Salt and pepper to taste
- ½ cup bread crumbs

Directions:
1. Pre-heat the Air Fryer at 390°F.
2. Drain any excess water out of the cauliflower by wringing it with a paper towel.
3. In a bowl, combine the cauliflower with the remaining ingredients, save the bread

crumbs. Using your hands, shape the mixture into several small balls.
4. Coat the balls in the bread crumbs and transfer to the basket of your fryer. Allow to cook for 6 minutes, after which you should raise the temperature to 400°F and then leave to cook for an additional 10 minutes.

108.Sausage-chicken Casserole

Servings: 8
Cooking Time: 30 Minutes
Ingredients:
- 2 cloves minced garlic
- 10 eggs
- 1 cup broccoli, chopped
- ½ tbsp. salt
- 1 cup cheddar, shredded and divided
- ¼ tbsp. pepper
- ¾ cup whipping cream
- 1 x 12-oz. package cooked chicken sausage

Directions:
1. Pre-heat the Air Fryer to 400°F.
2. In a large bowl, beat the eggs with a whisk. Pour in the whipping cream and cheese. Combine well.
3. In a separate bowl, mix together the garlic, broccoli, salt, pepper and cooked sausage.
4. Place the chicken sausage mix in a casserole dish. Top with the cheese mixture.
5. Transfer to the Air Fryer and cook for about 20 minutes.

109.Salmon Skewers

Servings: 4
Cooking Time: 10 Minutes
Ingredients:
- 1-pound salmon fillet
- 4 oz bacon, sliced
- 2 mozzarella balls, sliced
- ½ teaspoon avocado oil
- ½ teaspoon chili flakes

Directions:
1. Cut the salmon into the medium size cubes (4 cubes per serving) Then sprinkle salmon cubes with chili flakes and wrap in the sliced bacon. String the wrapped salmon cubes on the skewers and sprinkle with avocado oil. After this, preheat the air fryer to 400F. Put the salmon skewers in the preheat air fryer basket and cook them at 400F for 4 minutes. Then flip the skewers on another side and cook them for 6 minutes at 385F.

110.Pork And Zucchinis

Servings: 4
Cooking Time: 30 Minutes
Ingredients:
- 2 pounds pork stew meat, cubed
- 2 zucchinis, cubed
- Salt and black pepper to the taste
- ½ cup beef stock
- ½ teaspoon smoked paprika
- A handful cilantro, chopped

Directions:
1. In a pan that fits your air fryer, mix all the ingredients, toss, introduce in your air fryer and cook at 370 degrees F for 30 minutes. Divide into bowls and serve right away.

111.Chicken Quesadillas

Servings: 4
Cooking Time: 20 Minutes
Ingredients:
- 2 soft taco shells
- 1 lb. boneless chicken breasts
- 1 large green pepper, sliced
- 1 medium-sized onion, sliced
- ½ cup Cheddar cheese, shredded
- ½ cup salsa sauce
- 2 tbsp. olive oil
- Salt and pepper, to taste

Directions:
1. Pre-heat the Air Fryer to 370°F and drizzle the basket with 1 tablespoon of olive oil.
2. Lay one taco shell into the bottom of the fryer and spread some salsa inside the taco. Slice the chicken breast into strips and put the strips into taco shell.
3. Top the chicken with the onions and peppers.
4. Season with salt and pepper. Add the shredded cheese and top with the second taco shell.
5. Drizzle with another tablespoon of olive oil. Put the rack over the taco to keep it in place.
6. Cook for 4 – 6 minutes, until it turns lightly brown and is cooked through. Serve either hot or cold.

112.Paprika Turkey Mix

Servings: 4
Cooking Time: 20 Minutes
Ingredients:
- 1 turkey breast, boneless, skinless and cubed
- 2 teaspoons olive oil
- ½ teaspoon sweet paprika
- Salt and black pepper to the taste
- 2 cups bok choy, torn and steamed
- 1 tablespoon balsamic vinegar

Directions:
1. In a bowl, mix the turkey with the oil, paprika, salt and pepper, toss, transfer them to your Air Fryer's basket and cook at 350 degrees F for 20 minutes. In a salad, mix the turkey with all the other ingredients, toss and serve for lunch.

113.Spiced Salmon And Cilantro Croquettes

Servings: 4
Cooking Time: 8 Minutes
Ingredients:
- 1-pound smoked salmon, boneless and flaked
- 1 egg, beaten
- 1 tablespoon almond flour
- ½ teaspoon ground black pepper
- ¼ teaspoon ground cumin
- ½ teaspoon ground nutmeg
- 1 tablespoon fresh cilantro, chopped
- 1 teaspoon avocado oil

Directions:
1. Put the salmon in the bowl and churn it with the help of the fork until you get the smooth mass. Then add an egg, almond flour, ground black pepper, cumin, nutmeg, and cilantro. Stir the ingredients until they are smooth. Preheat the air fryer to 365F. Wet your hands and make the croquettes. Then place them in the air fryer in one layer and sprinkle with avocado oil. Cook the croquettes for 5 minutes. Then flip them on another side and cook for 3 minutes more.

114.Corn Stew

Servings: 4
Cooking Time: 15 Minutes
Ingredients:
- 2 leeks, chopped
- 2 tablespoons butter, melted
- 2 tomatoes, cubed
- 2 garlic cloves, minced
- 4 cups corn
- ¼ cup chicken stock
- 1 teaspoon olive oil
- 4 tarragon sprigs, chopped
- Salt and black pepper to taste
- 1 tablespoon chives, chopped

Directions:
1. Grease a pan with the oil, and then add all the ingredients and toss.
2. Place the pan in the fryer and cook at 370 degrees F for 15 minutes.
3. Divide the stew between bowls and serve.

115.Sprouts And Chicken Casserole

Servings: 2
Cooking Time: 25 Minutes
Ingredients:
- 1 cup Brussels sprouts
- ½ teaspoon salt
- ½ cup ground chicken
- ½ teaspoon ground black pepper
- 1 tablespoon coconut cream
- 1 teaspoon chili powder
- 1 tablespoon butter, melted
- ½ teaspoon ground paprika

Directions:
1. Mix up ground chicken, ground black pepper, chili powder, ground paprika, and coconut cream. Add salt and stir the mixture. After this, grease the air fryer casserole mold with butter. Put Brussels sprouts in the casserole mold and flatten them in one layer. Then top the vegetables with ground chicken mixture. Cover the casserole with baking paper and secure the edges. Preheat the air fryer to 365F. Put the casserole mold in the air fryer basket and cook it for 25 minutes.

116.Leeks Stew

Servings: 4
Cooking Time: 20 Minutes
Ingredients:
- 2 big eggplants, roughly cubed
- 1 cup veggie stock
- 3 leeks, sliced
- 2 tablespoons olive oil
- 1 tablespoon hot sauce
- 1 tablespoon sweet paprika
- 1 tablespoon keto tomato sauce
- Salt and black pepper to the taste
- ½ bunch cilantro, chopped
- 2 garlic cloves, minced

Directions:
1. In a pan that fits the air fryer, mix all the ingredients, toss, introduce in the fryer and cook at 380 degrees F for 20 minutes. Divide the stew into bowls and serve for lunch.

117.Pork And Potatoes Recipe

Servings: 2
Cooking Time:35 Minutes
Ingredients:
- 2 lbs. pork loin
- 2 red potatoes; cut into medium wedges
- 1/2 tsp. garlic powder
- 1/2 tsp. red pepper flakes
- 1 tsp. parsley; dried
- A drizzle of balsamic vinegar
- Salt and black pepper to the taste

Directions:
1. In your air fryer's pan; mix pork with potatoes, salt, pepper, garlic powder, pepper flakes, parsley and vinegar; toss and cook at 390 °F, for 25 minutes. Slice pork, divide it and potatoes on plates and serve for lunch.

118.Chicken Corn Casserole

Servings: 6
Cooking Time:40 Minutes

Ingredients:
- 1 cup clean chicken stock
- 6 oz. canned coconut milk
- 1 ½ cups green lentils
- 2 lbs. chicken breasts; skinless, boneless and cubed
- 1/3 cup cilantro; chopped
- 3 cups corn
- 3 handfuls spinach
- 3 green onions; chopped
- 2 tsp. garlic powder
- Salt and black pepper to the taste

Directions:
1. In a pan that fits your air fryer; mix stock with coconut milk, salt, pepper, garlic powder, chicken and lentils. Add corn, green onions, cilantro and spinach; stir well, introduce in your air fryer and cook at 350 °F, for 30 minutes.

119.Greek Quinoa Salad

Servings: 6
Cooking Time: 15 Minutes
Ingredients:
- 1½ cups quinoa, cooked
- 1 tablespoon olive oil
- Salt and black pepper to taste
- 1 tablespoon balsamic vinegar
- 1 cup cherry tomatoes, halved
- 2 green onions, chopped
- 2 ounces feta cheese, crumbled
- ½ cup Kalamata olives, pitted and chopped
- A handful of basil leaves, chopped
- A handful of parsley leaves, chopped

Directions:
1. Add all the ingredients—except the feta cheese—to a pan that fits your air fryer and toss.
2. Sprinkle the cheese on top, and then place the pan in the air fryer and cook at 370 degrees F for 15 minutes.
3. Divide into bowls and serve.

120.Tomato And Peppers Stew

Servings: 4
Cooking Time: 15 Minutes
Ingredients:
- 4 spring onions, chopped
- 2 pound tormatoes, cubed
- 1 teaspoon sweet paprika
- Salt and black pepper to the taste
- 2 red bell peppers, cubed

- 1 tablespoon cilantro, chopped

Directions:
1. In a pan that fits your air fryer, mix all the ingredients, toss, introduce the pan in the fryer and cook at 360 degrees F for 15 minutes. Divide into bowls and serve for lunch.

121.Okra Stew

Servings: 4
Cooking Time: 20 Minutes
Ingredients:
- 1 cup okra
- 4 zucchinis, roughly cubed
- 1 teaspoon oregano, dried
- 2 green bell peppers, cut into strips
- 2 garlic cloves, minced
- Salt and black pepper to the taste
- 7 ounces keto tomato sauce
- 2 tablespoons olive oil
- 2 tablespoons cilantro, chopped

Directions:
1. In a pan that fits your air fryer, combine all the ingredients for the stew, toss, introduce the pan in the air fryer, cook the stew at 350 degrees F for 20 minutes, divide into bowls, and serve.

122.Italian Lamb Chops

Servings: 2
Cooking Time: 20 Minutes
Ingredients:
- 2 lamp chops
- 2 tsp. Italian herbs
- 2 avocados
- ½ cup mayonnaise
- 1 tbsp. lemon juice

Directions:
1. Season the lamb chops with the Italian herbs, then set aside for five minutes.
2. Pre-heat the fryer at 400°F and place the rack inside.
3. Put the chops on the rack and allow to cook for twelve minutes.
4. In the meantime, halve the avocados and open to remove the pits. Spoon the flesh into a blender.
5. Add in the mayonnaise and lemon juice and pulse until a smooth consistency is achieved.
6. Take care when removing the chops from the fryer, then plate up and serve with the avocado mayo.

VEGETABLE & SIDE DISHES

123.Cheesy Green Patties

Servings: 2
Cooking Time: 6 Minutes
Ingredients:
- 1 ½ cup fresh spinach, chopped
- 3 oz provolone cheese, shredded
- 1 egg, beaten
- ¼ cup almond flour
- ½ teaspoon salt
- Cooking spray

Directions:
1. Put the chopped spinach in the blender and blend it until you get a smooth mixture. After this, transfer the grinded spinach in the big bowl. Add shredded provolone cheese, beaten egg, almond flour, and salt. Stir the spinach mixture with the help of the spoon until it is homogenous. Then make the patties from the spinach mixture. Preheat the air fryer to 400F. Spray the air fryer basket with cooking spray from inside and put the spinach patties. Cook them for 3 minutes and then flip on another side. Cook the patties for 3 minutes more or until they are light brown.

124.Baked Cholula Cauliflower

Servings: 4
Cooking Time: 20 Minutes
Ingredients:
- 1/2 cup all-purpose flour
- 1/2 cup water
- Salt, to taste
- 1/2 teaspoon ground black pepper
- 1/2 teaspoon shallot powder
- 1/2 teaspoon garlic powder
- 1/2 teaspoon cayenne pepper
- 2 tablespoons olive oil
- 1 pound cauliflower, broken into small florets
- 1/4 cup Cholula sauce

Directions:
1. Start by preheating your Air Fryer to 400 degrees F. Lightly grease a baking pan with cooking spray.
2. In a mixing bowl, combine the flour, water, spices, and olive oil. Coat the cauliflower with the prepared batter; arrange the cauliflower on the baking pan.
3. Then, bake in the preheated Air Fryer for 8 minutes or until golden brown.
4. Brush the Cholula sauce all over the cauliflower florets and bake an additional 4 to 5 minutes. Bon appétit!

125.Roasted Broccoli With Sesame Seeds

Servings: 2
Cooking Time: 15 Minutes
Ingredients:
- 1 pound broccoli florets
- 2 tablespoons sesame oil
- 1/2 teaspoon shallot powder
- 1/2 teaspoon porcini powder
- 1 teaspoon garlic powder
- Sea salt and ground black pepper, to taste
- 1/2 teaspoon cumin powder
- 1/4 teaspoon paprika
- 2 tablespoons sesame seeds

Directions:
1. Start by preheating the Air Fryer to 400 degrees F.
2. Blanch the broccoli in salted boiling water until al dente, about 3 to 4 minutes. Drain well and transfer to the lightly greased Air Fryer basket.
3. Add the sesame oil, shallot powder, porcini powder, garlic powder, salt, black pepper, cumin powder, paprika, and sesame seeds.
4. Cook for 6 minutes, tossing halfway through the cooking time. Bon appétit!

126.Vegetable And Egg Salad

Servings: 4
Cooking Time: 35 Minutes
Ingredients:
- 1/3 pound Brussels sprouts
- 1/2 cup radishes, sliced
- 1/2 cup mozzarella cheese, crumbled
- 1 red onion, chopped
- 4 eggs, hardboiled and sliced
- Dressing:
- 1/4 cup olive oil
- 2 tablespoons champagne vinegar
- 1 teaspoon Dijon mustard
- Sea salt and ground black pepper, to taste

Directions:
1. Start by preheating your Air Fryer to 380 degrees F.
2. Add the Brussels sprouts and radishes to the cooking basket. Spritz with cooking spray and cook for 15 minutes. Let it cool to room temperature about 15 minutes.
3. Toss the vegetables with cheese and red onion.
4. Mix all ingredients for the dressing and toss to combine well. Serve topped with the hard-boiled eggs. Bon appétit!

127.Traditional Indian Kofta

Servings: 4
Cooking Time: 35 Minutes

Ingredients:

- Veggie Balls:
- 3/4 pound zucchini, grated and well drained
- 1/4 pound kohlrabi, grated and well drained
- 2 cloves garlic, minced
- 1 tablespoon Garam masala
- 1 cup paneer, crumbled
- 1/4 cup coconut flour
- 1/2 teaspoon chili powder
- Himalayan pink salt and ground black pepper, to taste
- Sauce:
- 1 tablespoon sesame oil
- 1/2 teaspoon cumin seeds
- 2 cloves garlic, roughly chopped
- 1 onion, chopped
- 1 Kashmiri chili pepper, seeded and minced
- 1 (1-inch) piece ginger, chopped
- 1 teaspoon paprika
- 1 teaspoon turmeric powder
- 2 ripe tomatoes, pureed
- 1/2 cup vegetable broth
- 1/4 full fat coconut milk

Directions:

1. Start by preheating your Air Fryer to 360 degrees F. Thoroughly combine the zucchini, kohlrabi, garlic, Garam masala, paneer, coconut flour, chili powder, salt and ground black pepper.
2. Shape the vegetable mixture into small balls and arrange them in the lightly greased cooking basket.
3. Cook in the preheated Air Fryer at 360 degrees F for 15 minutes or until thoroughly cooked and crispy. Repeat the process until you run out of ingredients.
4. Heat the sesame oil in a saucepan over medium heat and add the cumin seeds. Once the cumin seeds turn brown, add the garlic, onions, chili pepper, and ginger. Sauté for 2 to 3 minutes.
5. Add the paprika, turmeric powder, tomatoes, and broth; let it simmer, covered, for 4 to 5 minutes, stirring occasionally.
6. Add the coconut milk. Heat off; add the veggie balls and gently stir to combine. Bon appétit!

128.Lemon Fennel

Servings: 4
Cooking Time: 15 Minutes
Ingredients:

- 1 pound fennel, cut into small wedges
- A pinch of salt and black pepper
- 3 tablespoons olive oil
- Salt and black pepper to the taste
- Juice of ½ lemon

- 2 tablespoons sunflower seeds

Directions:

1. In a bowl, mix the fennel wedges with all the ingredients except the sunflower seeds, put them in your air fryer's basket and cook at 400 degrees F for 15 minutes. Divide the fennel between plates, sprinkle the sunflower seeds on top, and serve as a side dish.

129.Japanese Tempura Bowl

Servings: 3
Cooking Time: 20 Minutes
Ingredients:

- 1 cup all-purpose flour
- Kosher salt and ground black pepper, to taste
- 1/2 teaspoon paprika
- 2 eggs
- 3 tablespoons soda water
- 1 cup panko crumbs
- 2 tablespoons olive oil
- 1 cup green beans
- 1 onion, cut into rings
- 1 zucchini, cut into slices
- 2 tablespoons soy sauce
- 1 tablespoon mirin
- 1 teaspoon dashi granules

Directions:

1. In a shallow bowl, mix the flour, salt, black pepper, and paprika. In a separate bowl, whisk the eggs and soda water. In a third shallow bowl, combine the panko crumbs with olive oil.
2. Dip the vegetables in flour mixture, then in the egg mixture; lastly, roll over the panko mixture to coat evenly.
3. Cook in the preheated Air Fryer at 400 degrees F for 10 minutes, shaking the basket halfway through the cooking time. Work in batches until the vegetables are crispy and golden brown.
4. Then, make the sauce by whisking the soy sauce, mirin, and dashi granules. Bon appétit!

130.Greek-style Roasted Tomatoes With Feta

Servings: 2
Cooking Time: 20 Minutes
Ingredients:

- 3 medium-sized tomatoes, cut into four slices, pat dry
- 1 teaspoon dried basil
- 1 teaspoon dried oregano
- 1/4 teaspoon red pepper flakes, crushed
- 1/2 teaspoon sea salt
- 3 slices Feta cheese

Directions:

1. Spritz the tomatoes with cooking oil and transfer them to the Air Fryer basket. Sprinkle with seasonings.
2. Cook at 350 degrees F approximately 8 minutes turning them over halfway through the cooking time.
3. Top with the cheese and cook an additional 4 minutes. Bon appétit!

131.Colored Veggie Rice Recipe

Servings: 4
Cooking Time:35 Minutes
Ingredients:
- 1 cup mixed carrots; peas, corn and green beans
- 2 cups basmati rice
- 2 cups water
- 1/2 tsp. green chili; minced
- 1/2 tsp. ginger; grated
- 5 black peppercorns
- 2 whole cardamoms
- 3 garlic cloves; minced
- 2 tbsp. butter
- 1 tsp. cinnamon powder
- 1 tbsp. cumin seeds
- 2 bay leaves
- 3 whole cloves
- 1 tbsp. sugar
- Salt to the taste

Directions:
1. Pour the water in a heat proof dish that fits your air fryer
2. Add rice, mixed veggies, green chili, grated ginger, garlic cloves, cinnamon, cloves, butter, cumin seeds, bay leaves, cardamoms, black peppercorns, salt and sugar; stir, put in your air fryer's basket and cook at 370 °F, for 25 minutes.
3. Divide among plates and serve as a side dish.

132.Cheese Stuffed Roasted Peppers

Servings: 2
Cooking Time: 20 Minutes
Ingredients:
- 2 red bell peppers, tops and seeds removed
- 2 yellow bell peppers, tops and seeds removed
- Salt and pepper, to taste
- 1 cup cream cheese
- 4 tablespoons mayonnaise
- 2 pickles, chopped

Directions:
1. Arrange the peppers in the lightly greased cooking basket. Cook in the preheated Air Fryer at 400 degrees F for 15 minutes, turning them over halfway through the cooking time.
2. Season with salt and pepper.

3. Then, in a mixing bowl, combine the cream cheese with the mayonnaise and chopped pickles. Stuff the pepper with the cream cheese mixture and serve. Enjoy!

133.Pop Corn Broccoli

Servings: 1
Cooking Time: 10 Minutes
Ingredients:
- 4 egg yolks
- ¼ cup butter, melted
- 2 cups coconut flower
- Salt and pepper
- 2 cups broccoli florets

Directions:
1. In a bowl, whisk the egg yolks and melted butter together. Throw in the coconut flour, salt and pepper, then stir again to combine well.
2. Pre-heat the fryer at 400°F.
3. Dip each broccoli floret into the mixture and place in the fryer. Cook for six minutes, in multiple batches if necessary. Take care when removing them from the fryer and enjoy!

134.Crusted Coconut Shrimp

Servings:5
Cooking Time: 30 Minutes
Ingredients:
- ¾ cup shredded coconut
- 1 tbsp maple syrup
- ½ cup breadcrumbs
- ⅓ cup cornstarch
- ½ cup milk

Directions:
1. Pour the cornstarch and shrimp in a zipper bag and shake vigorously to coat. Mix the syrup and milk in a bowl and set aside. In a separate bowl, mix the breadcrumbs and shredded coconut. Open the zipper bag and remove shrimp while shaking off excess starch.
2. Dip shrimp in the milk mixture and then in the crumb mixture. Place in the fryer. Cook 12 minutes at 350 F, flipping once halfway through. Cook until golden brown. Serve with a coconut-based dip.

135.Classic Fried Pickles

Servings: 2
Cooking Time: 20 Minutes
Ingredients:
- 1 egg, whisked
- 2 tablespoons buttermilk
- 1/2 cup fresh breadcrumbs
- 1/4 cup Romano cheese, grated
- 1/2 teaspoon onion powder
- 1/2 teaspoon garlic powder

- 1 ½ cups dill pickle chips, pressed dry with kitchen towels
- Mayo Sauce:
- 1/4 cup mayonnaise
- 1/2 tablespoon mustard
- 1/2 teaspoon molasses
- 1 tablespoon ketchup
- 1/4 teaspoon ground black pepper

Directions:
1. In a shallow bowl, whisk the egg with buttermilk.
2. In another bowl, mix the breadcrumbs, cheese, onion powder, and garlic powder.
3. Dredge the pickle chips in the egg mixture, then, in the breadcrumb/cheese mixture.
4. Cook in the preheated Air Fryer at 400 degrees F for 5 minutes; shake the basket and cook for 5 minutes more.
5. Meanwhile, mix all the sauce ingredients until well combined. Serve the fried pickles with the mayo sauce for dipping.

136.Simple Air Fried Asparagus

Servings: 2
Cooking Time: 7 Minutes
Ingredients:
- 1 lb asparagus
- 1/4 tsp olive oil
- Pepper
- Salt

Directions:
1. Brush asparagus with olive oil and season with pepper and salt.
2. Place asparagus into the air fryer basket and cook at 400 F for 7 minutes.
3. Shake halfway through.
4. Serve and enjoy.

137.Cheese Eggplant Bites

Servings: 5
Cooking Time: 12 Minutes
Ingredients:
- 1 egg
- 1 eggplant, sliced
- 1/4 cup parmesan cheese, grated
- 1/2 tbsp dried thyme
- 1/4 cup almond flour
- 1/2 cup cheese, grated
- 1/2 tbsp dried rosemary
- Pepper
- Salt

Directions:
1. Spray air fryer basket with cooking spray.
2. Place sliced eggplants into the air fryer basket season with pepper and salt.
3. Cook eggplant at 390 F for 6 minutes.
4. In a small bowl, mix together almond flour, dried rosemary, dried thyme, and grated cheese.

5. Remove from eggplant slices from air fryer and brush with beaten egg. Sprinkle with almond flour mixture and cook until cheese is melted, about 4-6 minutes more.
6. Serve and enjoy.

138.Mozzarella Risotto

Servings: 4
Cooking Time: 20 Minutes
Ingredients:
- 1 pound white mushrooms, sliced
- ¼ cup mozzarella, shredded
- 1 cauliflower head, florets separated and riced
- 1 cup chicken stock
- 1 tablespoon thyme, chopped
- 1 teaspoon Italian seasoning
- A pinch of salt and black pepper
- 2 tablespoons olive oil

Directions:
1. Heat up a pan that fits the air fryer with the oil over medium heat, add the cauliflower rice and the mushrooms, toss and cook for a couple of minutes. Add the rest of the ingredients except the thyme, toss, put the pan in the air fryer and cook at 360 degrees F for 20 minutes. Divide the risotto between plates and serve with thyme sprinkled on top

139.Spicy Cabbage

Servings: 4
Cooking Time: 12 Minutes
Ingredients:
- 1 green cabbage head, shredded
- 1 tablespoon olive oil
- 1 teaspoon cayenne pepper
- A pinch of salt and black pepper
- 2 teaspoons sweet paprika

Directions:
1. Mix all of the ingredients in a pan that fits your fryer.
2. Place the pan in the fryer and cook at 320 degrees F for 12 minutes.
3. Divide between plates and serve right away.

140.Nutmeg Kale

Servings: 4
Cooking Time: 15 Minutes
Ingredients:
- 1 tablespoon butter, melted
- ½ cup almond milk
- Salt and black pepper to the taste
- 3 garlic cloves
- 10 cups kale, roughly chopped
- ¼ teaspoon nutmeg, ground
- 1/3 cup parmesan, grated
- ¼ cup walnuts, chopped

Directions:

1. In a pan that fits the air fryer, combine all the ingredients, toss, introduce the pan in the machine and cook at 360 degrees F for 15 minutes. Divide between plates and serve.

141.Easy Vegetable Kabobs

Servings: 4
Cooking Time: 30 Minutes
Ingredients:
- 1 medium-sized zucchini, cut into 1-inch pieces
- 2 red bell peppers, cut into 1-inch pieces
- 1 green bell pepper, cut into 1-inch pieces
- 1 red onion, cut into 1-inch pieces
- 2 tablespoons olive oil
- Sea salt, to taste
- 1/2 teaspoon black pepper, preferably freshly cracked
- 1/2 teaspoon red pepper flakes

Directions:
1. Soak the wooden skewers in water for 15 minutes.
2. Thread the vegetables on skewers; drizzle olive oil all over the vegetable skewers; sprinkle with spices.
3. Cook in the preheated Air Fryer at 400 degrees F for 13 minutes. Serve warm and enjoy!

142.Balsamic Okra

Servings: 2
Cooking Time: 6 Minutes
Ingredients:
- 1 teaspoon balsamic vinegar
- 1 teaspoon avocado oil
- 8 oz okra, sliced
- ½ teaspoon salt
- ½ teaspoon white pepper

Directions:
1. Sprinkle the sliced okra with avocado oil, salt, and white pepper. Then preheat the air fryer to 360F. Put the okra in the air fryer basket and cook it for 3 minutes. Then shake the sliced vegetables well and cook for 3 minutes more. Transfer the cooked okra in the serving bowl and sprinkle with balsamic vinegar.

143.Sweet Potato Fries With Avocado Dipping Sauce

Servings:2
Cooking Time: 15 Minutes
Ingredients:
- 2 large sweet potatoes, peeled and cut into thick strips
- 2 tablespoons olive oil
- 1 teaspoon paprika
- 1 teaspoon garlic powder
- Salt and pepper, to taste
- 1 ripe avocado, flesh scooped out
- 2 tablespoons sour cream
- 2 tablespoons fresh cilantro, chopped
- Juice from ½ lime
- ½ teaspoon garlic, minced

Directions:
1. Place the sweet potatoes in a bowl and season with oil, paprika, garlic powder, salt, and pepper.
2. Toss to coat. Place the baking dish in the air fryer and add the sweet potato.
3. Close the air fryer and cook for 15 minutes at 350 °F.
4. Halfway through the cooking time, give the baking dish a shake.
5. Meanwhile, prepare the avocado dip by combining the rest of the ingredient in a food processor.
6. Dip the sweet potato fries in the avocado dressing.

144.Chili Fried Brussels Sprouts

Servings: 5
Cooking Time: 15 Minutes
Ingredients:
- 1-pound Brussels sprouts
- 1 teaspoon chili flakes
- 3 eggs, beaten
- 3 tablespoons coconut flakes
- 1 teaspoon salt
- 1 teaspoon sesame oil

Directions:
1. Cut Brussels sprouts into halves and put them in the bowl. Add chili flakes, eggs, and salt. Shake the vegetables well and then sprinkle them with coconut flakes. Shake the vegetables well. Preheat the air fryer to 385F. Put Brussels sprouts in the air fryer and cook them for 10 minutes. Then shake the vegetables well and cook for 5 minutes more.

145.Goat Cheese Cauliflower And Bacon

Servings: 4
Cooking Time: 20 Minutes
Ingredients:
- 8 cups cauliflower florets, roughly chopped
- 4 bacon strips, chopped
- Salt and black pepper to the taste
- ½ cup spring onions, chopped
- 1 tablespoon garlic, minced
- 10 ounces goat cheese, crumbled
- ¼ cup soft cream cheese
- Cooking spray

Directions:
1. Grease a baking pan that fits the air fryer with the cooking spray and mix all the ingredients except the goat cheese into the

pan. Sprinkle the cheese on top, introduce the pan in the machine and cook at 400 degrees F for 20 minutes. Divide between plates and serve as a side dish.

146. Mushroom Bean Casserole

Servings: 6
Cooking Time: 12 Minutes
Ingredients:
- 2 cups mushrooms, sliced
- 1 tsp onion powder
- 1/2 tsp ground sage
- 1/2 tbsp garlic powder
- 1 fresh lemon juice
- 1 1/2 lbs green beans, trimmed
- 1/4 tsp pepper
- 1/2 tsp salt

Directions:
1. In a large mixing bowl, toss together green beans, onion powder, sage, garlic powder, lemon juice, mushrooms, pepper, and salt.
2. Spray air fryer basket with cooking spray.
3. Transfer green bean mixture into the air fryer basket.
4. Cook for 10-12 minutes at 400 F. Shake after every 3 minutes.
5. Serve and enjoy.

147. Turkey Garlic Potatoes

Servings: 2
Cooking Time: 45 Minutes
Ingredients:
- 3 unsmoked turkey strips
- 6 small potatoes
- 1 tsp. garlic, minced
- 2 tsp. olive oil
- Salt to taste
- Pepper to taste

Directions:
1. Peel the potatoes and cube them finely.
2. Coat in 1 teaspoon of oil and cook in the Air Fryer for 10 minutes at 350°F.
3. In a separate bowl, slice the turkey finely and combine with the garlic, oil, salt and pepper. Pour the potatoes into the bowl and mix well.
4. Lay the mixture on some silver aluminum foil, transfer to the fryer and cook for about 10 minutes.
5. Serve with raita.

148. Bacon Cabbage

Servings: 2
Cooking Time: 12 Minutes
Ingredients:
- 8 oz Chinese cabbage, roughly chopped
- 2 oz bacon, chopped
- 1 tablespoon sunflower oil
- ½ teaspoon onion powder

- ½ teaspoon salt

Directions:
1. Cook the bacon at 400F for 10 minutes. Stir it from time to time. Then sprinkle it with onion powder and salt. Add Chinese cabbage and shake the mixture well. Cook it for 2 minutes. Then add sunflower oil, stir the meal and place in the serving plates.

149. Roasted Acorn Squash

Servings: 4
Cooking Time: 25 Minutes
Ingredients:
- 1 large acorn squash, cut in half lengthwise
- 2 tbsp olive oil
- 1/4 cup parmesan cheese, grated
- 1/4 tsp pepper
- 8 fresh thyme sprigs

Directions:
1. Preheat the air fryer to 370 F.
2. Remove seed from squash and cut into 3/4-inch slices.
3. Add squash slices, olive oil, thyme, parmesan cheese, pepper, and salt in a bowl and toss to coat.
4. Add squash slices into the air fryer basket and cook for 25 minutes. Turn halfway through.
5. Serve and enjoy.

150. Asian Green Beans

Servings: 2
Cooking Time: 10 Minutes
Ingredients:
- 8 oz green beans, trimmed and cut in half
- 1 tsp sesame oil
- 1 tbsp tamari

Directions:
1. Add all ingredients into the large mixing bowl and toss well.
2. Spray air fryer basket with cooking spray.
3. Transfer green beans in air fryer basket and cook at 400 F for 10 minutes. Toss halfway through.
4. Serve and enjoy.

151. Cauliflower Falafel

Servings: 4
Cooking Time: 12 Minutes
Ingredients:
- 1 cup cauliflower, shredded
- 1 teaspoon almond flour
- ½ teaspoon ground cumin
- ¼ teaspoon ground coriander
- ½ teaspoon garlic powder
- ½ teaspoon salt
- ¼ teaspoon cayenne pepper
- 1 egg, beaten
- 1 teaspoon tahini paste

- 2 tablespoons flax meal
- ½ teaspoon sesame oil

Directions:
1. In the mixing bowl mix up shredded cauliflower, almond flour, ground cumin, coriander, garlic powder, salt, and cayenne pepper. Add egg and flax meal and stir the mixture until homogenous with the help of the spoon. After this, make the medium size balls (falafel) and press them gently. Preheat the air fryer to 375F. Put the falafel in the air fryer and sprinkle with sesame oil. Cook the falafel for 6 minutes from each side. Sprinkle the cooked falafel with tahini paste.

152.Moroccan Spice Carrots

Servings: 4
Cooking Time: 13 Minutes
Ingredients:
- 1 lb carrots, peeled and sliced
- 2 tbsp olive oil
- 1/2 tsp salt
- For the spice mix:
- 1/8 tsp cayenne pepper
- 1/8 tsp ground ginger
- 1/8 tsp ground allspice
- 1/8 tsp ground cinnamon
- 1/8 tsp paprika
- 1/4 tsp chili powder
- 1/4 tsp ground coriander
- 1/2 tsp ground cumin

Directions:
1. In a small bowl, mix together all spice ingredients.
2. Add carrots, oil, pepper, spice mix, and salt into the large bowl and toss well.
3. Transfer carrots into the air fryer basket and cook at 350 F for 8 minutes.
4. Toss well and cook for 5 minutes more.
5. Serve and enjoy.

153.Squash Noodles

Servings: 2
Cooking Time: 17 Minutes
Ingredients:
- 1 medium butternut squash, peel and spiralized
- 3 tbsp cream
- 1/4 cup parmesan cheese
- 1 tsp thyme, chopped
- 1 tbsp sage, chopped
- 1 tsp garlic powder
- 2 tbsp cream cheese

Directions:
1. Preheat the air fryer to 370 F.
2. In a bowl, mix together cream cheese, parmesan, thyme, sage, cream, and garlic powder.

3. Add noodles into the air fryer baking pan.
4. Place pan in the air fryer and cook for 15 minutes.
5. Spread cream cheese mixture over noodles and cook for 2-3 minutes more.
6. Serve and enjoy.

154.Parmesan Cherry Tomatoes

Servings: 4
Cooking Time: 15 Minutes
Ingredients:
- 1 tablespoon ghee, melted
- 2 cups cherry tomatoes, halved
- 3 tablespoons scallions, chopped
- 1 teaspoon lemon zest, grated
- 2 tablespoons parsley, chopped
- ¼ cup parmesan, grated

Directions:
1. In a pan that fits the air fryer, combine all the ingredients except the parmesan, and toss. Sprinkle the parmesan on top, introduce the pan in the machine and cook at 360 degrees F for 10 minutes. Divide between plates and serve.

155.Italian Pork Sausage Pizza

Servings:1
Cooking Time: 15 Minutes
Ingredients:
- ½ tsp oregano
- ¼ cup tomato sauce
- ¼ cup mozzarella cheese
- 1 shallot, thinly sliced
- 1 Italian pork sausage, sliced
- 4 fresh basil leaves
- 4 black olives

Directions:
1. Preheat air fryer to 390 F. Grease the pizza dough with cooking spray and transfer it to the air fryer basket. Spread tomato sauce over pizza crust and sprinkle with oregano. Top with mozzarella cheese, shallot, and sausage slices. Cook the pizza for 8 minutes. Scatter over basil leaves and olives to serve.

156.Paprika Beef Fajitas

Servings:4
Cooking Time: 35 Minutes
Ingredients:
- 2 garlic cloves, minced
- 1 tbsp paprika
- 1 red bell pepper, sliced
- 1 orange bell pepper, sliced
- 2 shallots, sliced
- 2 tbsp cajun seasoning
- 2 tbsp olive oil
- 8 tortilla wraps
- ½ cup cheddar cheese, shredded
- Salt and black pepper to taste

Directions:
1. Preheat your Air Fryer to 360 F.
2. In a bowl, combine the beef, shallots, bell peppers, and garlic. Season with cajun seasoning, paprika, salt, and black pepper; toss to combine. Transfer the mixture to the air fryer basket. Cook for 10 minutes, shaking once halfway through cooking. Serve on tortillas topped with cheddar cheese.

157.Scallion & Ricotta Potatoes

Servings: 4
Cooking Time: 15 Minutes
Ingredients:
- 4 baking potatoes
- 2 tbsp. olive oil
- ½ cup Ricotta cheese, room temperature
- 2 tbsp. scallions, chopped
- 1 heaped tbsp. fresh parsley, roughly chopped
- 1 heaped tbsp. coriander, minced
- 2 oz. Cheddar cheese, preferably freshly grated
- 1 tsp. celery seeds
- ½ tsp. salt
- ½ tsp. garlic pepper

Directions:
1. Pierce the skin of the potatoes with a knife.
2. Cook in the Air Fryer basket for roughly 13 minutes at 350°F. If they are not cooked through by this time, leave for 2 – 3 minutes longer.
3. In the meantime, make the stuffing by combining all the other ingredients.
4. Cut halfway into the cooked potatoes to open them.
5. Spoon equal amounts of the stuffing into each potato and serve hot.

158.Tasty Okra

Servings: 2
Cooking Time: 12 Minutes
Ingredients:
- 1/2 lb okra, ends trimmed and sliced
- 1 tsp olive oil
- 1/2 tsp mango powder
- 1/2 tsp chili powder
- 1/2 tsp ground coriander
- 1/2 tsp ground cumin
- 1/8 tsp pepper
- 1/4 tsp salt

Directions:
1. Preheat the air fryer to 350 F.
2. Add all ingredients into the large bowl and toss well.
3. Spray air fryer basket with cooking spray.
4. Transfer okra mixture into the air fryer basket and cook for 10 minutes. Shake basket halfway through.
5. Toss okra well and cook for 2 minutes more.
6. Serve and enjoy.

159.Fava Beans Mix

Servings: 4
Cooking Time: 15 Minutes
Ingredients:
- 3 pounds fava beans, shelled
- 1 teaspoon olive oil
- Salt and black pepper to taste
- 4 ounces bacon, cooked and crumbled
- ½ cup white wine
- 1 tablespoon parsley, chopped

Directions:
1. Place all of the ingredients into a pan that fits your air fryer and mix well.
2. Put the pan in the air fryer and cook at 380 degrees F for 15 minutes.
3. Divide between plates and serve as a side dish.

160.Pita Pizzas

Servings:5
Cooking Time: 25 Minutes
Ingredients:
- 5 tbsp marinara sauce
- 10 rounds of chorizo
- 10 button mushrooms, sliced
- 10 fresh basil leaves
- 2 cups grated cheddar cheese
- 1 tsp chili flakes
- Cooking spray

Directions:
1. Spray the pitas with oil and scatter the sauce over. Top with chorizo, mushrooms, basil, cheddar and chili flakes. Cook for 14 minutes at 360 F, checking it at least once halfway through. Serve.

161.Perfect Crispy Tofu

Servings: 4
Cooking Time: 20 Minutes
Ingredients:
- 1 block firm tofu, pressed and cut into 1-inch cubes
- 1 tbsp arrowroot flour
- 2 tsp sesame oil
- 1 tsp vinegar
- 2 tbsp soy sauce

Directions:
1. In a bowl, toss tofu with oil, vinegar, and soy sauce and let sit for 15 minutes.
2. Toss marinated tofu with arrowroot flour.
3. Spray air fryer basket with cooking spray.
4. Add tofu in air fryer basket and cook for 20 minutes at 370 F. Shake basket halfway through.
5. Serve and enjoy.

162.Shallots Almonds Green Beans

Servings: 6
Cooking Time: 15 Minutes

Ingredients:
- 1/4 cup almonds, toasted
- 1 1/2 lbs green beans, trimmed and steamed
- 2 tbsp olive oil
- 1/2 lb shallots, chopped
- Pepper
- Salt

Directions:
1. Add all ingredients into the large bowl and toss well.
2. Transfer green bean mixture into the air fryer basket and cook at 400 F for 15 minutes.
3. Serve and enjoy.

163.Mint-butter Stuffed Mushrooms

Servings:3
Cooking Time:19 Minutes
Ingredients:
- 3 garlic cloves, minced
- 1 teaspoon ground black pepper, or more to taste
- 1/3 cup seasoned breadcrumbs
- 1½ tablespoons fresh mint, chopped
- 1 teaspoon salt, or more to taste
- 1½ tablespoons melted butter
- 14 medium-sized mushrooms, cleaned, stalks removed

Directions:
1. Mix all of the above ingredients, minus the mushrooms, in a mixing bowl to prepare the filling.
2. Then, stuff the mushrooms with the prepared filling.
3. Air-fry stuffed mushrooms at 375 degrees F for about 12 minutes. Taste for doneness and serve at room temperature as a vegetarian appetizer.

164.Beetroot Chips

Servings: 4
Cooking Time: 15 Minutes
Ingredients:
- 2 medium beetroot, wash, peeled, and sliced thinly
- 1 tsp olive oil
- 1 sprig rosemary, chopped
- Salt

Directions:
1. Sprinkle rosemary and salt on the beetroot slices.
2. Preheat the air fryer to 300 F.
3. Add beetroot slices into the air fryer basket. Drizzle beetroot slices with olive oil.
4. Cook for 15 minutes. Shake basket after every 5 minutes while cooking.
5. Serve and enjoy.

165.Green Celery Puree

Servings: 6
Cooking Time: 6 Minutes

Ingredients:
- 1-pound celery stalks, chopped
- ½ cup spinach, chopped
- 2 oz Parmesan, grated
- ¼ cup chicken broth
- ½ teaspoon cayenne pepper

Directions:
1. In the air fryer pan, mix celery stalk with chopped spinach, chicken broth, and cayenne pepper. Blend the mixture until homogenous. After this, top the puree with Parmesan. Preheat the air fryer to 400F. Put the pan with puree in the air fryer basket and cook the meal for 6 minutes.

166.Cajun Peppers

Servings: 4
Cooking Time: 12 Minutes
Ingredients:
- 1 tablespoon olive oil
- ½ pound mixed bell peppers, sliced
- 1 cup black olives, pitted and halved
- ½ tablespoon Cajun seasoning

Directions:
1. In a pan that fits the air fryer, combine all the ingredients. Put the pan it in your air fryer and cook at 390 degrees F for 12 minutes. Divide the mix between plates and serve.

167.Crispy Cauliflower Bites

Servings:4
Cooking Time: 20 Minutes
Ingredients:
- 1 cup flour
- 1 cup milk
- 1 egg, beaten
- 1 head cauliflower, cut into florets

Directions:
1. Preheat the Air fryer to 390 F. Grease the air fryer basket with cooking spray. In a bowl, mix flour, milk, egg, and Italian seasoning. Coat the cauliflower in the mixture, then drain the excess liquid.
2. Place the florets in the air fryer cooking basket, spray them with cooking spray, and cook for 7 minutes, shake and continue cooking for another 5 minutes. Allow to cool before serving.

168.Garlic Bread

Servings: 4
Cooking Time: 8 Minutes
Ingredients:
- 1 oz Mozzarella, shredded
- 2 tablespoons almond flour
- 1 teaspoon cream cheese
- ¼ teaspoon garlic powder
- ¼ teaspoon baking powder
- 1 egg, beaten
- 1 teaspoon coconut oil, melted
- ¼ teaspoon minced garlic

- 1 teaspoon dried dill
- 1 oz Provolone cheese, grated

Directions:
1. In the mixing bowl mix up Mozzarella, almond flour, cream cheese, garlic powder, baking powder, egg, minced garlic, dried dill, and Provolone cheese. When the mixture is homogenous, transfer it on the baking paper and spread it in the shape of the bread. Sprinkle the garlic bread with coconut oil. Preheat the air fryer to 400F. Transfer the baking paper with garlic bread in the air fryer and cook for 8 minutes or until it is light brown. When the garlic bread is cooked, cut it on 4 servings and place it in the serving plates.

169. Prawn & Cabbage In Egg Rolls

Servings:4
Cooking Time: 50 Minutes
Ingredients:
- 1-inch piece fresh ginger, grated
- 1 tbsp minced garlic
- 1 carrot, cut into strips
- ¼ cup chicken broth
- 2 tbsp reduced-sodium soy sauce
- 1 tbsp sugar
- 1 cup shredded Napa cabbage
- 1 tbsp sesame oil
- 8 cooked prawns, minced
- 1 egg
- 8 egg roll wrappers

Directions:
1. In a skillet over high heat, heat oil, and cook ginger, carrot, and garlic for 2 minutes. Pour in chicken broth, soy sauce, and sugar and bring to a boil. Add cabbage and let simmer until softened, for 4 minutes. Remove skillet from the heat and stir in sesame oil. Let cool for 15 minutes.
2. Strain cabbage mixture, and fold in minced prawns. Whisk an egg in a small bowl. Fill wrappers with prawn mixture. Fold the bottom part over the filling and tuck under. Fold in both sides and tightly roll-up. Use the whisked egg to seal the wrapper. Place the rolls into a greased air fryer basket, spray them with oil and cook for 12 minutes at 370 F, turning once halfway through.

170. Cauliflower And Goat Cheese Croquettes

Servings: 2
Cooking Time: 30 Minutes
Ingredients:
- 1/2 pound cauliflower florets
- 2 garlic cloves, minced
- 1 cup goat cheese, shredded
- Sea salt and ground black pepper, to taste
- 1/2 teaspoon shallot powder
- 1/4 teaspoon cumin powder
- 1 cup sour cream

- 1 teaspoon Dijon mustard

Directions:
1. Place the cauliflower florets in a saucepan of water; bring to the boil; reduce the heat and cook for 10 minutes or until tender.
2. Mash the cauliflower using your blender; add the garlic, cheese, and spices; mix to combine well.
3. Form the cauliflower mixture into croquettes shapes.
4. Cook in the preheated Air Fryer at 375 degrees F for 16 minutes, shaking halfway through the cooking time. Serve with the sour cream and mustard. Bon appétit!

171. Buttery Cauliflower Mix

Servings: 4
Cooking Time: 15 Minutes
Ingredients:
- 1 pound cauliflower florets, roughly grated
- 3 eggs, whisked
- 3 tablespoons butter, melted
- Salt and black pepper to the taste
- 1 tablespoon sweet paprika

Directions:
1. Heat up a pan that fits the air fryer with the butter over high heat, add the cauliflower and brown for 5 minutes. Add whisked eggs, salt, pepper and the paprika, toss, introduce the pan in the fryer and cook at 400 degrees F for 10 minutes. Divide between plates and serve.

172. Cauliflower And Tomato Bake

Servings: 2
Cooking Time: 20 Minutes
Ingredients:
- 1 cup heavy whipping cream
- 2 tablespoons basil pesto
- Salt and black pepper to the taste
- Juice of ½ lemon
- 1 pound cauliflower, florets separated
- 4 ounces cherry tomatoes, halved
- 3 tablespoons ghee, melted
- 7 ounces cheddar cheese, grated

Directions:
1. Grease a baking pan that fits the air fryer with the ghee. Add the cauliflower, lemon juice, salt, pepper, the pesto and the cream and toss gently. Add the tomatoes, sprinkle the cheese on top, introduce the pan in the fryer and cook at 380 degrees F for 20 minutes. Divide between plates and serve as a side dish.

173. Paprika Asparagus

Servings: 4
Cooking Time: 10 Minutes
Ingredients:
- 1 pound asparagus, trimmed
- 3 tablespoons olive oil
- A pinch of salt and black pepper

- 1 tablespoon sweet paprika

Directions:
1. In a bowl, mix the asparagus with the rest of the ingredients and toss. Put the asparagus in your air fryer's basket and cook at 400 degrees F for 10 minutes. Divide between plates and serve.

174. Brussels Sprouts With Garlic

Servings: 8
Cooking Time: 30 Minutes
Ingredients:
- 2 lbs Brussels sprouts, trimmed and quartered
- 2 tbsp coconut oil, melted
- 5 garlic cloves, sliced
- 1/8 tsp pepper
- 1 tsp salt

Directions:
1. Preheat the air fryer to 370 F.
2. In a bowl, mix together Brussels sprouts, coconut oil, and garlic.
3. Transfer Brussels sprouts into the air fryer basket and cooks for 30 minutes. Shake basket halfway through.
4. Season with pepper and salt.
5. Serve and enjoy.

175. Mustard Endives

Servings: 4
Cooking Time: 15 Minutes
Ingredients:
- 4 endives, trimmed
- 3 tablespoons olive oil
- A pinch of salt and black pepper
- 1 teaspoon mustard
- 2 tablespoons white vinegar
- ½ cup walnuts, chopped

Directions:
1. In a bowl, mix the oil with salt, pepper, mustard and vinegar and whisk really well. Add the endives, toss and transfer them to your air fryer's basket. Cook at 350 degrees F for 15 minutes, divide between plates and serve with walnuts sprinkled on top.

176. Dill Bok Choy

Servings: 2
Cooking Time: 5 Minutes
Ingredients:
- 6 oz bok choy
- 1 teaspoon sesame seeds
- 1 garlic clove, diced
- 1 tablespoon olive oil
- 1 teaspoon fresh dill, chopped
- 1 teaspoon apple cider vinegar

Directions:
1. Preheat the air fryer to 350F. Then chop the bok choy roughly and sprinkle with olive oil, diced garlic, olive oil, fresh dill, and apple cider vinegar. Mix up the bok choy and leave to marinate for 15 minutes. Then

transfer the marinated bok choy in the air fryer basket and cook for 5 minutes. Shake it after 3 minutes of cooking. Transfer the cooked vegetables in the bowl and sprinkle with sesame seeds. Shake the meal gently before serving.

177. Paprika Chicken Nuggets

Servings: 4
Cooking Time: 20 Minutes
Ingredients:
- 2 tbsp paprika
- 2 cups milk
- 2 eggs
- 4 tsp onion powder
- 1 ½ tsp garlic powder
- Salt and pepper to taste
- 1 cups flour
- 2 cups breadcrumbs
- Cooking spray

Directions:
1. In a bowl, mix paprika, onion, garlic, salt, pepper, flour, and breadcrumbs. In another bowl, beat eggs with milk. Dip chicken in the egg mixtureand refrigerate for 1 hour.
2. Preheat air fryer to 370 F. Roll each chunk in the crumb mixture. Place the chicken in the fryer's basket. Spray with cooking spray. Cook for 8 minutes at 360 F, flipping once halfway through. Yum!

178. Balsamic Asparagus And Tomatoes

Servings: 4
Cooking Time: 10 Minutes
Ingredients:
- 1 pound asparagus, trimmed
- 2 cups cherry tomatoes, halved
- ¼ cup parmesan, grated
- ½ cup balsamic vinegar
- 2 tablespoons olive oil
- A pinch of salt and black pepper

Directions:
1. In a bowl, mix the asparagus with the rest of the ingredients except the parmesan, and toss. Put the asparagus and tomatoes in your air fryer's basket and cook at 400 degrees F for 10 minutes Divide between plates and serve with the parmesan sprinkled on top.

179. Butter Green Beans

Servings: 4
Cooking Time: 20 Minutes
Ingredients:
- 10 ounces green beans, trimmed
- A pinch of salt and black pepper
- 3 ounces butter, melted
- 1 cup coconut cream
- Zest of ½ lemon, grated
- ¼ cup parsley, chopped
- 2 garlic cloves, minced

Directions:

1. In a bowl, the butter with all the ingredients except the green beans and whisk really well. Put the green beans in a pan that fits the air fryer, drizzle the buttery sauce all over, introduce the pan in the machine and cook at 370 degrees F for 20 minutes. Divide between plates and serve as a side dish.

180.Roasted Beet Salad

Servings: 2
Cooking Time: 20 Minutes + Chilling Time
Ingredients:
- 2 medium-sized beets, peeled and cut into wedges
- 2 tablespoons extra virgin olive oil
- 1 tablespoon balsamic vinegar
- 1 teaspoon yellow mustard
- 1 garlic clove, minced
- 1/4 teaspoon cumin powder
- Coarse sea salt and ground black pepper, to taste
- 1 tablespoon fresh parsley leaves, roughly chopped

Directions:
1. Place the beets in a single layer in the lightly greased cooking basket.
2. Cook at 370 degrees F for 13 minutes, shaking the basket halfway through the cooking time.
3. Let it cool to room temperature; toss the beets with the remaining ingredients. Serve well chilled. Enjoy!

181.Balsamic Garlic Kale

Servings: 6
Cooking Time: 12 Minutes
Ingredients:
- 2 tablespoons olive oil
- 3 garlic cloves, minced
- 2 and ½ pounds kale leaves
- Salt and black pepper to the taste
- 2 tablespoons balsamic vinegar

Directions:
1. In a pan that fits the air fryer, combine all the ingredients and toss. Put the pan in your air fryer and cook at 300 degrees F for 12 minutes. Divide between plates and serve.

182.Asparagus Salad With Boiled Eggs

Servings: 4
Cooking Time: 10 Minutes + Chilling Time

Ingredients:
- 1/4 cup olive oil
- 1 pound asparagus, trimmed
- 1 cup cherry tomatoes, halved
- 1/4 cup balsamic vinegar
- 2 garlic cloves, minced
- 2 scallion stalks, chopped
- 1/2 teaspoon oregano
- Coarse sea salt and ground black pepper, to your liking
- 2 hard-boiled eggs, sliced

Directions:
1. Start by preheating your Air Fryer to 400 degrees F. Brush the cooking basket with 1 tablespoon of olive oil.
2. Add the asparagus and cherry tomatoes to the cooking basket. Drizzle 1 tablespoon of olive oil all over your veggies.
3. Cook for 5 minutes, shaking the basket halfway through the cooking time. Let it cool slightly.
4. Toss with the remaining olive oil, balsamic vinegar, garlic, scallions, oregano, salt, and black pepper.
5. Afterwards, add the hard-boiled eggs on the top of your salad and serve.

183.Crispy Wax Beans With Almonds And Blue Cheese

Servings: 3
Cooking Time: 15 Minutes
Ingredients:
- 1 pound wax beans, cleaned
- 2 tablespoons peanut oil
- 4 tablespoons seasoned breadcrumbs
- Sea salt and ground black pepper, to taste
- 1/2 teaspoon red pepper flakes, crushed
- 2 tablespoons almonds, sliced
- 1/3 cup blue cheese, crumbled

Directions:
1. Toss the wax beans with the peanut oil, breadcrumbs, salt, black pepper, and red pepper.
2. Place the wax beans in the lightly greased cooking basket.
3. Cook in the preheated Air Fryer at 400 degrees F for 5 minutes. Shake the basket once or twice.
4. Add the almonds and cook for 3 minutes more or until lightly toasted. Serve topped with blue cheese and enjoy!

VEGAN & VEGETARIAN RECIPES

184.Grilled 'n Glazed Strawberries

Servings:2
Cooking Time: 20 Minutes
Ingredients:
- 1 tbsp honey
- 1 tsp lemon zest
- 1-lb large strawberries
- 3 tbsp melted butter
- Lemon wedges
- Pinch kosher salt

Directions:
1. Thread strawberries in 4 skewers.
2. In a small bowl, mix well remaining Ingredients except for lemon wedges. Brush all over strawberries.
3. Place skewer on air fryer skewer rack.
4. For 10 minutes, cook on 360°F. Halfway through cooking time, brush with honey mixture and turnover skewer.
5. Serve and enjoy with a squeeze of lemon.

185.Pesto Tomatoes

Servings:4
Cooking Time: 16 Minutes
Ingredients:
- For Pesto:
- ½ cup plus 1 tablespoon olive oil, divided
- 3 tablespoons pine nuts
- Salt, to taste
- ½ cup fresh basil, chopped
- ½ cup fresh parsley, chopped
- 1 garlic clove, chopped
- ½ cup Parmesan cheese, grated
- For Tomatoes:
- 2 heirloom tomatoes, cut into ½ inch thick slices
- 8 ounces feta cheese, cut into ½ inch thick slices.
- ½ cup red onions, thinly sliced
- 1 tablespoon olive oil
- Salt, to taste

Directions:
1. Set the temperature of air fryer to 390 degrees F. Grease an air fryer basket.
2. In a bowl, mix together one tablespoon of oil, pine nuts and pinch of salt.
3. Arrange pine nuts into the prepared air fryer basket.
4. Air fry for about 1-2 minutes.
5. Remove from air fryer and transfer the pine nuts onto a paper towel-lined plate.
6. In a food processor, add the toasted pine nuts, fresh herbs, garlic, Parmesan, and salt and pulse until just combined.
7. While motor is running, slowly add the remaining oil and pulse until smooth.

8. Transfer into a bowl, covered and refrigerate until serving.
9. Spread about one tablespoon of pesto onto each tomato slice.
10. Top each tomato slice with one feta and onion slice and drizzle with oil.
11. Arrange tomato slices into the prepared air fryer basket in a single layer.
12. Air fry for about 12-14 minutes.
13. Remove from air fryer and transfer the tomato slices onto serving plates.
14. Sprinkle with a little salt and serve with the remaining pesto.

186.Sweet 'n Nutty Marinated Cauliflower-tofu

Servings:2
Cooking Time: 20 Minutes
Ingredients:
- ¼ cup brown sugar
- ¼ cup low sodium soy sauce
- ½ teaspoon chili garlic sauce
- 1 package extra firm tofu, pressed to release extra water and cut into cubes
- 1 small head cauliflower, cut into florets
- 1 tablespoon sesame oil
- 2 ½ tablespoons almond butter
- 2 cloves of garlic, minced

Directions:
1. Place the garlic, sesame oil, soy sauce, sugar, chili garlic sauce, and almond butter in a mixing bowl. Whisk until well combined.
2. Place the tofu cubes and cauliflower in the marinade and allow to soak up the sauce for at least 30 minutes.
3. Preheat the air fryer to 400 °F. Add tofu and cauliflower. Coo for 20 minutes. Shake basket halfway through cooking time.
4. Meanwhile, place the remaining marinade in a saucepan and bring to a boil over medium heat. Adjust the heat to low once boiling and stir until the sauce thickens.
5. Pour the sauce over the tofu and cauliflower.
6. Serve with rice or noodles.

187.Ooey-gooey Dessert Quesadilla

Servings: 2
Cooking Time: 25 Minutes
Ingredients:
- 1/4 cup blueberries
- 1/4 cup fresh orange juice
- 1/2 tablespoon maple syrup
- 1/2 cup vegan cream cheese
- 1 teaspoon vanilla extract
- 2 (6-inch tortillas
- 2 teaspoons coconut oil
- 1/4 cup vegan dark chocolate

Directions:

1. Bring the blueberries, orange juice, and maple syrup to a boil in a saucepan. Reduce the heat and let it simmer until the sauce thickens, about 10 minutes.
2. In a mixing dish, combine the cream cheese with the vanilla extract; spread on the tortillas. Add the blueberry filling on top. Fold in half.
3. Place the quesadillas in the greased Air Fryer basket. Cook at 390 degrees F for 10 minutes, until tortillas are golden brown and filling is melted. Make sure to turn them over halfway through the cooking.
4. Heat the coconut oil in a small pan and add the chocolate; whisk to combine well. Drizzle the chocolate sauce over the quesadilla and serve. Enjoy!

188. Okra With Green Beans

Servings:2
Cooking Time:20 Minutes
Ingredients:

- ½ (10-ounces) bag frozen cut okra
- ½ (10-ounces) bag frozen cut green beans
- ¼ cup nutritional yeast
- 3 tablespoons balsamic vinegar
- Salt and black pepper, to taste

Directions:

1. Preheat the Air fryer to 400 °F and grease an Air fryer basket.
2. Mix the okra, green beans, nutritional yeast, vinegar, salt, and black pepper in a bowl and toss to coat well.
3. Arrange the okra mixture into the Air fryer basket and cook for about 20 minutes.
4. Dish out in a serving dish and serve hot.

189. Three Veg Bake

Servings:3
Cooking Time: 30 Minutes
Ingredients:

- 1 large red onion, cut into rings
- 1 large zucchini, sliced
- Salt and pepper to taste
- 2 cloves garlic, crushed
- 1 bay leaf, cut in 6 pieces
- 1 tbsp olive oil
- Cooking spray

Directions:

1. Place the turnips, onion, and zucchini in a bowl. Toss with olive oil and season with salt and pepper.
2. Preheat the air fryer to 330 F, and place the veggies into a baking pan that fits in the air fryer. Slip the bay leaves in the different parts of the slices and tuck the garlic cloves in between the slices. Insert the pan in the

air fryer's basket and cook for 15 minutes. Serve warm with salad.

190. Stuffed Tomatoes

Servings:4
Cooking Time: 22 Minutes
Ingredients:

- 4 tomatoes
- 1 teaspoon olive oil
- 1 carrot, peeled and finely chopped
- 1 onion, chopped
- 1 cup frozen peas, thawed
- 1 garlic clove, minced
- 2 cups cold cooked rice
- 1 tablespoon soy sauce

Directions:

1. Cut the top of each tomato and scoop out pulp and seeds.
2. In a skillet, heat oil over low heat and sauté the carrot, onion, garlic, and peas for about 2 minutes.
3. Stir in the soy sauce and rice and remove from heat.
4. Set the temperature of air fryer to 355 degrees F. Grease an air fryer basket.
5. Stuff each tomato with the rice mixture.
6. Arrange tomatoes into the prepared air fryer basket.
7. Air fry for about 20 minutes.
8. Remove from air fryer and transfer the tomatoes onto a serving platter.
9. Set aside to cool slightly.
10. Serve warm.

191. Warm Farro Salad With Roasted Tomatoes

Servings: 2
Cooking Time: 40 Minutes
Ingredients:

- 3/4 cup farro
- 3 cups water
- 1 tablespoon sea salt
- 1 pound cherry tomatoes
- 2 spring onions, chopped
- 2 carrots, grated
- 2 heaping tablespoons fresh parsley leaves
- 2 tablespoons champagne vinegar
- 2 tablespoons white wine
- 2 tablespoons extra-virgin olive oil
- 1 teaspoon red pepper flakes

Directions:

1. Place the farro, water, and salt in a saucepan and bring it to a rapid boil. Turn the heat down to medium-low, and simmer, covered, for 30 minutes or until the farro has softened.
2. Drain well and transfer to an air fryer-safe pan.

3. Meanwhile, place the cherry tomatoes in the lightly greased Air Fryer basket. Roast at 400 degrees F for 4 minutes.
4. Add the roasted tomatoes to the pan with the cooked farro, Toss the salad ingredients with the spring onions, carrots, parsley, vinegar, white wine, and olive oil.
5. Bake at 360 degrees F an additional 5 minutes. Serve garnished with red pepper flakes and enjoy!

192.Avocado Rolls

Servings:5
Cooking Time: 15 Minutes
Ingredients:
- 10 egg roll wrappers
- 1 tomato, diced
- ¼ tsp pepper
- ½ tsp salt

Directions:
1. Place all filling ingredients in a bowl; mash with a fork until somewhat smooth. There should be chunks left. Divide the feeling between the egg wrappers. Wet your finger and brush along the edges, so the wrappers can seal well. Roll and seal the wrappers.
2. Arrange them on a baking sheet lined dish, and place in the air fryer. Cook at 350 F for 5 minutes. Serve with sweet chili dipping and enjoy.

193.Quick Beetroot Chips

Servings:2
Cooking Time: 9 Minutes
Ingredients:
- 2 tbsp olive oil
- 1 tbsp yeast flakes
- 1 tsp vegan seasoning
- salt to taste

Directions:
1. In a bowl, add the oil, beetroot, the vegan seasoning, and the yeast and mix well. Dump the coated chips in the basket. Set the heat to 370 F and fry for a total of 6 minutes, shaking once halfway through cooking.

194.Spicy Veggie Recipe From Thailand

Servings:4
Cooking Time: 15 Minutes
Ingredients:
- 1 ½ cups packed cilantro leaves
- 1 tablespoon black pepper
- 1 tablespoon chili garlic sauce
- 1/3 cup vegetable oil
- 2 pounds vegetable of your choice, sliced into cubes
- 2 tablespoons fish sauce
- 8 cloves of garlic, minced

Directions:

1. Preheat the air fryer to 330 °F.
2. Place the grill pan accessory in the air fryer.
3. Place all Ingredients in a mixing bowl and toss to coat all Ingredients.
4. Put in the grill pan and cook for 15 minutes.

195.Crispy Green Beans With Pecorino Romano

Servings: 3
Cooking Time: 15 Minutes
Ingredients:
- 2 tablespoons buttermilk
- 1 egg
- 4 tablespoons almond meal
- 4 tablespoons golden flaxseed meal
- 4 tablespoons Pecorino Romano cheese, finely grated
- Coarse salt and crushed black pepper, to taste
- 1 teaspoon smoked paprika
- 6 ounces green beans, trimmed

Directions:
1. In a shallow bowl, whisk together the buttermilk and egg.
2. In a separate bowl, combine the almond meal, golden flaxseed meal, Pecorino Romano cheese, salt, black pepper, and paprika.
3. Dip the green beans in the egg mixture, then, in the cheese mixture. Place the green beans in the lightly greased cooking basket.
4. Cook in the preheated Air Fryer at 390 degrees F for 4 minutes. Shake the basket and cook for a further 3 minutes.
5. Taste, adjust the seasonings, and serve with the dipping sauce if desired. Bon appétit!

196.Honey Glazed Carrots

Servings:4
Cooking Time: 12 Minutes
Ingredients:
- 3 cups carrots, peeled and cut into large chunks
- 1 tablespoon olive oil
- 1 tablespoon honey
- 1 tablespoon fresh thyme, finely chopped
- Salt and ground black pepper, as required

Directions:
1. Set the temperature of air fryer to 390 degrees F. Grease an air fryer basket.
2. In a bowl, mix well carrot, oil, honey, thyme, salt, and black pepper.
3. Arrange carrot chunks into the prepared air fryer basket in a single layer.
4. Air fry for about 12 minutes.
5. Remove from air fryer and transfer the carrot chunks onto serving plates.
6. Serve hot.

197.Garlic 'n Basil Crackers

Servings:6
Cooking Time: 15 Minutes
Ingredients:
- ¼ teaspoon dried basil powder
- ½ teaspoon baking powder
- 1 ¼ cups almond flour
- 1 clove of garlic, minced
- 3 tablespoons coconut oil
- A pinch of cayenne pepper powder
- Salt and pepper to taste

Directions:
1. Preheat the air fryer for 5 minutes.
2. Mix everything in a mixing bowl to create a dough.
3. Transfer the dough on a clean and flat working surface and spread out until 2mm thick. Cut into squares.
4. Place gently in the air fryer basket. Do this in batches if possible.
5. Cook for 15 minutes at 325 °F.

198.Mozzarella Cabbage With Blue Cheese

Servings:4
Cooking Time: 25 Minutes
Ingredients:
- 2 cups Parmesan cheese, chopped
- 4 tbsp melted butter
- Salt and pepper to taste
- ½ cup blue cheese sauce

Directions:
1. Preheat your air fryer to 380 F, and cover cabbage wedges with melted butter; coat with mozzarella. Place the coated cabbage in the cooking basket and cook for 20 minutes. Serve with blue cheese.

199.Simple Brown Carrot Roast With Cumin

Servings:6
Cooking Time: 15 Minutes
Ingredients:
- 1 tbsp olive oil
- 1 tsp cumin seeds
- A handful of fresh coriander

Directions:
1. Preheat the fryer to 350 F, and in a bowl, mix oil, carrots, and cumin seeds. Gently stir to coat the carrots well. Place the carrots in your air fryer basket and cook for 12 minutes. Scatter fresh coriander over the carrots.

200.Sweet Potato French Fries

Servings:4
Cooking Time: 30 Minutes
Ingredients:
- ½ tsp garlic powder
- ½ tsp chili powder
- ¼ tsp cumin
- 3 tbsp olive oil
- 3 sweet potatoes, cut into thick strips

Directions:
1. In a bowl, mix salt, garlic powder, chili powder, and cumin, and whisk in oil. Coat the strips well in this mixture and arrange them on the air fryer's basket. Cook for 20 minutes at 380 F until crispy. Serve.

201.Marinated Tofu Bowl With Pearl Onions

Servings: 4
Cooking Time: 1 Hour 20 Minutes
Ingredients:
- 16 ounces firm tofu, pressed and cut into 1-inch pieces
- 2 tablespoons vegan Worcestershire sauce
- 1 tablespoon apple cider vinegar
- 1 tablespoon maple syrup
- 1/2 teaspoon shallot powder
- 1/2 teaspoon porcini powder
- 1/2 teaspoon garlic powder
- 2 tablespoons peanut oil
- 1 cup pearl onions, peeled

Directions:
1. Place the tofu, Worcestershire sauce, vinegar, maple syrup, shallot powder, porcini powder, and garlic powder in a ceramic dish. Let it marinate in your refrigerator for 1 hour.
2. Transfer the tofu to the lightly greased Air Fryer basket. Add the peanut oil and pearl onions; toss to combine.
3. Cook the tofu with the pearl onions in the preheated Air Fryer at 380 degrees F for 6 minutes; pause and brush with the reserved marinade; cook for a further 5 minutes.
4. Serve immediately. Bon appétit!

202.Spicy Pepper, Sweet Potato Skewers

Servings:1
Cooking Time: 20 Minutes
Ingredients:
- 1 beetroot
- 1 green bell pepper
- 1 tsp chili flakes
- ¼ tsp black pepper
- ½ tsp turmeric
- ¼ tsp garlic powder
- ¼ tsp paprika
- 1 tbsp olive oil

Directions:
1. Preheat air fryer to 350 F. Peel the veggies and cut them into bite-sized chunks. Place the chunks in a bowl, along with the remaining ingredients; mix until fully coated. Thread the veggies onto skewers in this order: potato, pepper, beetroot. Place in

the air fryer and cook for 15 minutes, shaking once.

203.Sweet & Sour Brussel Sprouts

Servings:2
Cooking Time: 10 Minutes
Ingredients:
- 2 cups Brussels sprouts, trimmed and halved lengthwise
- 1 tablespoon balsamic vinegar
- 1 tablespoon maple syrup
- Salt, as required

Directions:
1. Set the temperature of air fryer to 400 degrees F. Grease an air fryer basket.
2. In a bowl, add all the ingredients and toss to coat well.
3. Arrange Brussels sprouts into the prepared air fryer basket in a single layer.
4. Air fry for about 8-10 minutes, shaking once halfway through.
5. Remove from air fryer and transfer the Brussels sprouts onto serving plates.
6. Serve hot.

204.Cheesy Mushroom Pizza

Servings:2
Cooking Time: 6 Minutes
Ingredients:
- 2 Portobello mushroom caps, stemmed
- 2 tablespoons olive oil
- 1/8 teaspoon dried Italian seasonings
- Salt, to taste
- 2 tablespoons canned tomatoes, chopped
- 2 tablespoons mozzarella cheese, shredded
- 2 Kalamata olives, pitted and sliced
- 2 tablespoons Parmesan cheese, grated freshly
- 1 teaspoon red pepper flakes, crushed

Directions:
1. Set the temperature of air fryer to 320 degrees F. Grease an air fryer basket.
2. With a spoon, scoop out the center of each mushroom cap.
3. Coat each mushroom cap with oil from both sides.
4. Sprinkle the inside of caps with Italian seasoning and salt.
5. Place the canned tomato evenly over both caps, followed by the olives and mozzarella cheese.
6. Arrange mushroom caps into the prepared air fryer basket.
7. Air fry for about 5-6 minutes.
8. Remove from air fryer and immediately sprinkle with the Parmesan cheese and red pepper flakes.
9. Serve.

205.Crispy Bacon-wrapped Asparagus Bundles

Servings:4
Cooking Time:8 Minutes
Ingredients:
- 1 pound asparagus
- 4 bacon slices
- ½ tablespoon sesame seeds, toasted
- 1 garlic clove, minced
- 1½ tablespoons brown sugar
- 1½ tablespoons olive oil
- ½ tablespoon sesame oil, toasted

Directions:
1. Preheat the Air fryer to 355 °F and grease an Air fryer basket.
2. Mix garlic, brown sugar, olive oil and sesame oil in a bowl till sugar is dissolved.
3. Divide asparagus into 4 equal bunches and wrap a bacon slice around each bunch.
4. Rub the asparagus bunch with garlic mixture and arrange in the Air fryer basket.
5. Sprinkle with sesame seeds and cook for about 8 minutes.
6. Dish out and serve hot.

206.Cheesy Kale

Servings: 2
Cooking Time: 15 Minutes
Ingredients:
- lb. kale
- 8 oz. parmesan cheese, shredded
- 1 onion, diced
- 1 tsp. butter
- 1 cup heavy cream

Directions:
1. Dice up the kale, discarding any hard stems. In a baking dish small enough to fit inside the fryer, combine the kale with the parmesan, onion, butter and cream.
2. Pre-heat the fryer at 250°F.
3. Set the baking dish in the fryer and cook for twelve minutes. Make sure to give it a good stir before serving.

207.Eggplant Salad

Servings:2
Cooking Time:15 Minutes
Ingredients:
- 1 eggplant, cut into ½-inch-thick slices crosswise
- 1 avocado, peeled, pitted and chopped
- 2 tablespoons canola oil
- Salt and ground black pepper, as required
- 1 teaspoon fresh lemon juice
- For Dressing
- 1 tablespoon extra-virgin olive oil
- 1 tablespoon red wine vinegar
- 1 tablespoon honey

- 1 tablespoon fresh oregano leaves, chopped
- 1 teaspoon fresh lemon zest, grated
- 1 teaspoon Dijon mustard
- Salt and ground black pepper, as required

Directions:
1. Preheat the Air fryer to 400 °F and grease an Air fryer basket.
2. Mix eggplant, oil, salt, and black pepper in a bowl and toss to coat well.
3. Arrange the eggplants pieces in the Air fryer basket and cook for about 15 minutes, flipping twice in between.
4. Dish out the Brussel sprouts in a serving bowl and keep aside to cool.
5. Add avocado and lemon juice and mix well.
6. Mix all the ingredients for dressing in a bowl and pour over the salad.
7. Toss to coat well and serve immediately.

208. Beans & Veggie Burgers

Servings:4
Cooking Time: 22 Minutes
Ingredients:
- 1 cup cooked black beans
- 2 cups boiled potatoes, peeled and mashed
- 1 cup fresh spinach, chopped
- 1 cup fresh mushrooms, chopped
- 2 teaspoons Chile lime seasoning
- Olive oil cooking spray
- 6 cups fresh baby greens

Directions:
1. In a large bowl, add the beans, potatoes, spinach, mushrooms, and seasoning and with your hands, mix until well combined.
2. Make 4 equal-sized patties from the mixture.
3. Set the temperature of air fryer to 370 degrees F. Grease an air fryer basket.
4. Arrange patties into the prepared air fryer basket in a single layer and spray with the cooking spray.
5. Air fry for about 12 minutes, shaking once halfway through.
6. Flip the patties and air fry for another 6-7 minutes.
7. Now, set the temperature of air fryer to 90 degrees F and air fry for 3 more minutes.
8. Remove from air fryer and transfer the burgers onto serving plates.
9. Serve warm alongside the baby greens.

209. Garden Fresh Veggie Medley

Servings:4
Cooking Time:15 Minutes
Ingredients:
- 2 yellow bell peppers seeded and chopped
- 1 eggplant, chopped
- 1 zucchini, chopped
- 3 tomatoes, chopped
- 2 small onions, chopped

- 2 garlic cloves, minced
- 2 tablespoons herbs de Provence
- 1 tablespoon olive oil
- 1 tablespoon balsamic vinegar
- Salt and black pepper, to taste

Directions:
1. Preheat the Air fryer to 355 °F and grease an Air fryer basket.
2. Mix all the ingredients in a bowl and toss to coat well.
3. Transfer into the Air fryer basket and cook for about 15 minutes.
4. Keep in the Air fryer for about 5 minutes and dish out to serve hot.

210. Healthy Breakfast Casserole

Servings:2
Cooking Time: 30 Minutes
Ingredients:
- ½ cup cooked quinoa
- ½ cup diced bell pepper
- ½ cup shiitake mushrooms, diced
- ½ tsp black pepper
- ½ tsp dill
- ½ tsp ground cumin
- ½ tsp red pepper flakes
- ½ tsp salt
- 1 large carrot, peeled and chopped
- 1 small onion, diced
- 1 tbsp lemon juice
- 1 tsp dried oregano
- 1 tsp garlic, minced
- 1 tsp olive oil
- 2 small celery stalks, chopped
- 2 tbsp soy yogurt, plain
- 2 tbsp water
- 2 tbsp yeast
- 7-oz extra firm tofu, drained

Directions:
1. Lightly grease baking pan of air fryer with olive oil. Add garlic and onion.
2. For 2 minutes, cook on 390°F.
3. Remove basket, stir in bell pepper, celery, and carrots. Cook for 3 minutes.
4. Remove basket, give a quick stir. Then add cumin, red pepper flakes, dill, pepper, salt, oregano, and mushrooms. Mix well. Cook for 5 minutes. Mixing halfway through cooking time.
5. Meanwhile, in a food processor pulse lemon juice, water, yogurt, yeast, and tofu. Process until creamy.
6. Transfer creamy tofu mixture into air fryer basket. Add quinoa and give a good stir.
7. Cook for another 15 minutes at 330°F or until golden brown.
8. Let it rest for 5 minutes.
9. Serve and enjoy.

211.Paprika Vegetable Kabobs

Servings: 4
Cooking Time: 20 Minutes
Ingredients:
- 1 celery, cut into thick slices
- 1 parsnip, cut into thick slices
- 1 fennel bulb, diced
- 1 teaspoon whole grain mustard
- 2 cloves garlic, pressed
- 1 red onion, cut into wedges
- 2 tablespoons dry white wine
- 1/4 cup sesame oil
- 1 teaspoon sea salt flakes
- 1/2 teaspoon ground black pepper
- 1 teaspoon smoked paprika

Directions:
1. Place all of the above ingredients in a mixing dish; toss to coat well. Alternately thread vegetables onto the bamboo skewers.
2. Cook on the Air Fryer grill pan for 15 minutes at 380 degrees F. Flip them over halfway through the cooking time.
3. Taste, adjust the seasonings and serve warm.

212.Cheese Stuffed Zucchini With Scallions

Servings: 4
Cooking Time: 20 Minutes
Ingredients:
- 1 large zucchini, cut into four pieces
- 2 tablespoons olive oil
- 1 cup Ricotta cheese, room temperature
- 2 tablespoons scallions, chopped
- 1 heaping tablespoon fresh parsley, roughly chopped
- 1 heaping tablespoon coriander, minced
- 2 ounces Cheddar cheese, preferably freshly grated
- 1 teaspoon celery seeds
- 1/2 teaspoon salt
- 1/2 teaspoon garlic pepper

Directions:
1. Cook your zucchini in the Air Fryer cooking basket for approximately 10 minutes at 350 degrees F. Check for doneness and cook for 2-3 minutes longer if needed.
2. Meanwhile, make the stuffing by mixing the other items.
3. When your zucchini is thoroughly cooked, open them up. Divide the stuffing among all zucchini pieces and bake an additional 5 minutes.

213.Mushrooms With Tahini Sauce

Servings: 5
Cooking Time: 22 Minutes
Ingredients:
- 1/2 cup tahini
- 1/2 teaspoon turmeric powder
- 1/3 teaspoon cayenne pepper
- 2 tablespoons lemon juice, freshly squeezed
- 1 teaspoon kosher salt
- 1/3 teaspoon freshly cracked black pepper
- 1 1/2 tablespoons vermouth
- 1 ½ tablespoons olive oil
- 1 ½ pounds Cremini mushrooms

Directions:
1. Grab a mixing dish and toss the mushrooms with the olive oil, turmeric powder, salt, black pepper, and cayenne pepper.
2. Cook them in your air fryer for 9 minutes at 355 degrees F.
3. Pause your Air Fryer, give it a good stir and cook for 10 minutes longer.
4. Meanwhile, thoroughly combine lemon juice, vermouth, and tahini. Serve warm mushrooms with tahini sauce. Bon appétit!

214.Broccoli With Olives

Servings:4
Cooking Time:19 Minutes
Ingredients:
- 2 pounds broccoli, stemmed and cut into 1-inch florets
- 1/3 cup Kalamata olives, halved and pitted
- ¼ cup Parmesan cheese, grated
- 2 tablespoons olive oil
- Salt and ground black pepper, as required
- 2 teaspoons fresh lemon zest, grated

Directions:
1. Preheat the Air fryer to 400 °F and grease an Air fryer basket.
2. Boil the broccoli for about 4 minutes and drain well.
3. Mix broccoli, oil, salt, and black pepper in a bowl and toss to coat well.
4. Arrange broccoli into the Air fryer basket and cook for about 15 minutes.
5. Stir in the olives, lemon zest and cheese and dish out to serve.

215.Herbed Eggplant

Servings:2
Cooking Time:15 Minutes
Ingredients:
- 1 large eggplant, cubed
- ½ teaspoon dried marjoram, crushed
- ½ teaspoon dried oregano, crushed
- ½ teaspoon dried thyme, crushed
- ½ teaspoon garlic powder
- Salt and black pepper, to taste
- Olive oil cooking spray

Directions:
1. Preheat the Air fryer to 390 °F and grease an Air fryer basket.

2. Mix herbs, garlic powder, salt, and black pepper in a bowl.
3. Spray the eggplant cubes with cooking spray and rub with the herb mixture.
4. Arrange the eggplant cubes in the Air fryer basket and cook for about 15 minutes, flipping twice in between.
5. Dish out onto serving plates and serve hot.

216.Mediterranean-style Potato Chips With Vegveeta Dip

Servings: 4
Cooking Time: 1 Hour
Ingredients:
- 1 large potato, cut into 1/8 inch thick slices
- 1 tablespoon olive oil
- Sea salt, to taste
- 1/2 teaspoon red pepper flakes, crushed
- 1 teaspoon fresh rosemary
- 1/2 teaspoon fresh sage
- 1/2 teaspoon fresh basil
- Dipping Sauce:
- 1/3 cup raw cashews
- 1 tablespoon tahini
- 1 ½ tablespoons olive oil
- 1/4 cup raw almonds
- 1/4 teaspoon prepared yellow mustard

Directions:
1. Soak the potatoes in a large bowl of cold water for 20 to 30 minutes. Drain the potatoes and pat them dry with a kitchen towel.
2. Toss with olive oil and seasonings.
3. Place in the lightly greased cooking basket and cook at 380 degrees F for 30 minutes. Work in batches.
4. Meanwhile, puree the sauce ingredients in your food processor until smooth. Serve the potato chips with the Vegveeta sauce for dipping. Bon appétit!

217.Eggplant Caviar

Servings:3
Cooking Time: 20 Minutes
Ingredients:
- ½ red onion, chopped and blended
- 2 tbsp balsamic vinegar
- 1 tbsp olive oil
- salt

Directions:
1. Arrange the eggplants in the basket and cook them for 15 minutes at 380 F. Remove them and let them cool. Then cut the eggplants in half, lengthwise, and empty their insides with a spoon.
2. Blend the onion in a blender. Put the inside of the eggplants in the blender and process everything. Add the vinegar, olive oil and

salt, then blend again. Serve cool with bread and tomato sauce or ketchup.

218.Sesame Seeds Bok Choy(1)

Servings:4
Cooking Time:6 Minutes
Ingredients:
- 4 bunches baby bok choy, bottoms removed and leaves separated
- 1 teaspoon sesame seeds
- Olive oil cooking spray
- 1 teaspoon garlic powder

Directions:
1. Preheat the Air fryer to 325 °F and grease an Air fryer basket.
2. Arrange the bok choy leaves into the Air fryer basket and spray with the cooking spray.
3. Sprinkle with garlic powder and cook for about 6 minutes, shaking twice in between.
4. Dish out in the bok choy onto serving plates and serve garnished with sesame seeds.

219.Teriyaki Cauliflower4

Servings:4
Cooking Time: 20 Minutes
Ingredients:
- ½ cup soy sauce
- 3 tbsp brown sugar
- 1 tsp sesame oil
- ⅓ cup water
- ½ chili powder
- 2 cloves garlic, chopped
- 1 tsp cornstarch

Directions:
1. In a bowl, whisk soy sauce, sugar, sesame oil, water, chili powder, garlic and cornstarch, until smooth. In a bowl, add cauliflower, and pour teriyaki sauce over the top, toss with hands until well-coated.
2. Take the cauliflower to the air fryer's basket and cook for 14 minutes at 340 F, turning once halfway through. When ready, check if the cauliflower is cooked but not too soft. Serve with rice.

220.Family Favorite Potatoes

Servings:4
Cooking Time:20 Minutes
Ingredients:
- 1¾ pound waxy potatoes, cubed and boiled
- ½ cup Greek plain yoghurt
- 2 tablespoons olive oil, divided
- 1 tablespoon paprika, divided
- Salt and black pepper, to taste

Directions:
1. Preheat the Air fryer to 355 °F and grease an Air fryer basket.

2. Mix 1 tablespoon olive oil, 1/3 tablespoon of paprika and black pepper in a bowl and toss to coat well.
3. Transfer into the Air fryer basket and cook for about 20 minutes.
4. Mix yogurt, remaining oil, salt and black pepper in a bowl and serve with potatoes.

221.Garlic-roasted Brussels Sprouts With Mustard

Servings: 3
Cooking Time: 20 Minutes
Ingredients:
- 1 pound Brussels sprouts, halved
- 2 tablespoons olive oil
- Sea salt and freshly ground black pepper, to taste
- 2 garlic cloves, minced
- 1 tablespoon Dijon mustard

Directions:
1. Toss the Brussels sprouts with the olive oil, salt, black pepper, and garlic.
2. Roast in the preheated Air Fryer at 380 degrees F for 15 minutes, shaking the basket occasionally.
3. Serve with Dijon mustard and enjoy!

222.Paneer Cheese Balls

Servings:2
Cooking Time: 12 Minutes
Ingredients:
- 2 tbsp flour
- 2 medium onions, chopped
- 1 tbsp cornflour
- 1 green chili, chopped
- 1-inch ginger piece, chopped
- 1 tsp red chili powder
- A few leaves of coriander, chopped
- oil and salt

Directions:
1. Mix all ingredients, except the oil and cheese. Take a small part of the mixture, roll it up and slowly press it to flatten. Stuff in 1 cube of cheese and seal the edges. Repeat with the rest of the mixture. Fry the balls in the fryer for 12 minutes and at 370 F. Serve hot with ketchup!

223.Classic Baked Banana

Servings: 2
Cooking Time: 20 Minutes
Ingredients:
- 2 just-ripe bananas
- 2 teaspoons lime juice
- 2 tablespoons honey
- 1/4 teaspoon grated nutmeg
- 1/2 teaspoon ground cinnamon
- A pinch of salt

Directions:
1. Toss the banana with all ingredients until well coated. Transfer your bananas to the parchment-lined cooking basket.
2. Bake in the preheated Air Fryer at 370 degrees F for 12 minutes, turning them over halfway through the cooking time. Enjoy!

224.Crispy Vegie Tempura Style

Servings:3
Cooking Time:15 Minutes
Ingredients:
- ¼ teaspoon salt
- ¾ cup club soda
- 1 ½ cups panko break crumbs
- 1 cup broccoli florets
- 1 egg, beaten
- 1 red bell pepper, cut into strips
- 1 small sweet potato, peeled and cut into thick slices
- 1 small zucchini, cut into thick slices
- 1/3 cup all-purpose flour
- 2/3 cup cornstarch
- Non-stick cooking spray

Directions:
1. Dredge the vegetables in a cornstarch and all-purpose flour mixture.
2. Once all vegetables are dusted with flour, dip each vegetable in a mixture of egg and club soda before dredging in bread crumbs.
3. Place the vegetables on the double layer rack accessory and spray with cooking oil.
4. Place inside the air fryer.
5. Close and cook for 20 minutes at 330 °F.

225.Barbecue Tofu With Green Beans

Servings: 3
Cooking Time: 1 Hour
Ingredients:
- 12 ounces super firm tofu, pressed and cubed
- 1/4 cup ketchup
- 1 tablespoon white vinegar
- 1 tablespoon coconut sugar
- 1 tablespoon mustard
- 1/4 teaspoon ground black pepper
- 1/2 teaspoon sea salt
- 1/4 teaspoon smoked paprika
- 1/2 teaspoon freshly grated ginger
- 2 cloves garlic, minced
- 2 tablespoons olive oil
- 1 pound green beans

Directions:
1. Toss the tofu with the ketchup, white vinegar, coconut sugar, mustard, black pepper, sea salt, paprika, ginger, garlic, and olive oil. Let it marinate for 30 minutes.
2. Cook at 360 degrees F for 10 minutes; turn them over and cook for 12 minutes more. Reserve.

3. Place the green beans in the lightly greased Air Fryer basket. Roast at 400 degrees F for 5 minutes. Bon appétit!

226.Mushrooms Marinated In Garlic Coco-aminos

Servings:8
Cooking Time: 20 Minutes
Ingredients:
- ¼ cup coconut aminos
- 2 cloves of garlic, minced
- 2 pounds mushrooms, sliced
- 3 tablespoons olive oil

Directions:
1. Place all ingredients in a dish and mix until well-combined.
2. Allow to marinate for 2 hours in the fridge.
3. Preheat the air fryer for 5 minutes.
4. Place the mushrooms in a heat-proof dish that will fit in the air fryer.
5. Cook for 20 minutes at 350 °F.

227.Indian Aloo Tikka

Servings:2
Cooking Time: 20 Minutes
Ingredients:
- 3 tbsp lemon juice
- 1 bell pepper, sliced
- Salt and pepper to taste
- 2 onions, chopped
- 4 tbsp fennel
- 5 tbsp flour
- 2 tbsp ginger-garlic paste
- ½ cup mint leaves, chopped
- 2 cups cilantro, chopped

Directions:
1. Preheat your air fryer to 360 F.
2. In a bowl, mix cilantro, mint, fennel, ginger garlic paste, flour, salt and lemon juice. Blend to form a paste and add potato. In another bowl, mix bell pepper, onions and fennel mixture. Blend the mixture until you have a thick mix. Divide the mixture evenly into 5-6 cakes. Add the prepared potato cakes into your air fryer and cook for 15 minutes. Serve with ketchup.

228.Creamy 'n Cheese Broccoli Bake

Servings:2
Cooking Time: 30 Minutes
Ingredients:
- 1-pound fresh broccoli, coarsely chopped
- 2 tablespoons all-purpose flour
- salt to taste
- 1 tablespoon dry bread crumbs, or to taste
- 1/2 large onion, coarsely chopped
- 1/2 (14 ounce) can evaporated milk, divided
- 1/2 cup cubed sharp Cheddar cheese

- 1-1/2 teaspoons butter, or to taste
- 1/4 cup water

Directions:
1. Lightly grease baking pan of air fryer with cooking spray. Mix in half of the milk and flour in pan and for 5 minutes, cook on 360°F. Halfway through cooking time, mix well. Add broccoli and remaining milk. Mix well and cook for another 5 minutes.
2. Stir in cheese and mix well until melted.
3. In a small bowl mix well, butter and bread crumbs. Sprinkle on top of broccoli.
4. Cook for 20 minutes at 360°F until tops are lightly browned.
5. Serve and enjoy.

229.Cabbage Steaks

Servings:3
Cooking Time: 25 Minutes
Ingredients:
- 1 tbsp garlic stir-in paste
- 1 tsp salt
- 2 tbsp olive oil
- ½ tsp black pepper
- 2 tsp fennel seeds

Directions:
1. Preheat the air fryer to 350 F, and slice the cabbage into 1 ½-inch slice. In a small bowl, combine all the other ingredients; brush cabbage with the mixture. Arrange the cabbage steaks in the air fryer and cook for 15 minutes.

230.Zucchini Gratin

Servings: 2
Cooking Time: 15 Minutes
Ingredients:
- 5 oz. parmesan cheese, shredded
- 1 tbsp. coconut flour
- 1 tbsp. dried parsley
- 2 zucchinis
- 1 tsp. butter, melted

Directions:
1. Mix the parmesan and coconut flour together in a bowl, seasoning with parsley to taste.
2. Cut the zucchini in half lengthwise and chop the halves into four slices.
3. Pre-heat the fryer at 400°F.
4. Pour the melted butter over the zucchini and then dip the zucchini into the parmesan-flour mixture, coating it all over. Cook the zucchini in the fryer for thirteen minutes.

231.Roasted Vegetable Salad

Servings:1
Cooking Time: 25 Minutes
Ingredients:

- ¼ onion, sliced
- 1 carrot, sliced diagonally
- ½ small beetroot, sliced
- 1 cup cherry tomatoes
- Juice of 1 lemon
- A handful of rocket salad
- A handful of baby spinach
- 3 tbsp canned chickpeas
- ½ tsp cumin
- ½ tsp turmeric
- ¼ tsp sea salt
- 2 tbsp olive oil
- Parmesan shavings

Directions:
1. Preheat air fryer to 370 F.
2. In a bowl, combine onion, potato, cherry tomatoes, carrot, beetroot, cumin, sea salt, turmeric, and 1 tbsp. olive oil, in a bowl. Place in the fryer and cook for 20 minutes; let cool for 2 minutes.
3. Place the rocket salad, spinach, lemon juice, and 1 tbsp. olive oil, into a serving bowl; mix to combine. Stir in the roasted veggies. Top with chickpeas and Parmesan shavings.

232.The Best Crispy Tofu

Servings: 4
Cooking Time: 55 Minutes
Ingredients:
- 16 ounces firm tofu, pressed and cubed
- 1 tablespoon vegan oyster sauce
- 1 tablespoon tamari sauce
- 1 teaspoon cider vinegar
- 1 teaspoon pure maple syrup
- 1 teaspoon sriracha
- 1/2 teaspoon shallot powder
- 1/2 teaspoon porcini powder
- 1 teaspoon garlic powder
- 1 tablespoon sesame oil
- 5 tablespoons cornstarch

Directions:
1. Toss the tofu with the oyster sauce, tamari sauce, vinegar, maple syrup, sriracha, shallot powder, porcini powder, garlic powder, and sesame oil. Let it marinate for 30 minutes.
2. Toss the marinated tofu with the cornstarch.
3. Cook at 360 degrees F for 10 minutes; turn them over and cook for 12 minutes more. Bon appétit!

233.Tofu With Orange Sauce

Servings:4
Cooking Time:20 Minutes
Ingredients:
- 1 pound extra-firm tofu, pressed and cubed
- ½ cup water
- 4 teaspoons cornstarch, divided
- 2 scallions (green part), chopped

- 1 tablespoon tamari
- 1/3 cup fresh orange juice
- 1 tablespoon honey
- 1 teaspoon orange zest, grated
- 1 teaspoon garlic, minced
- 1 teaspoon fresh ginger, minced
- ¼ teaspoon red pepper flakes, crushed

Directions:
1. Preheat the Air fryer to 390 °F and grease an Air fryer basket.
2. Mix the tofu, cornstarch, and tamari in a bowl and toss to coat well.
3. Arrange half of the tofu pieces in the Air fryer pan and cook for about 10 minutes.
4. Repeat with the remaining tofu and dish out in a bowl.
5. Put all the ingredients except scallions in a small pan over medium-high heat and bring to a boil.
6. Pour this sauce over the tofu and garnish with scallions to serve.

234.Ultimate Vegan Calzone

Servings: 1
Cooking Time: 25 Minutes
Ingredients:
- 1 teaspoon olive oil
- 1/2 small onion, chopped
- 2 sweet peppers, seeded and sliced
- Sea salt, to taste
- 1/4 teaspoon ground black pepper
- 1/4 teaspoon dried oregano
- 4 ounces prepared Italian pizza dough
- 1/4 cup marinara sauce
- 2 ounces plant-based cheese Mozzarella-style, shredded

Directions:
1. Heat the olive oil in a nonstick skillet. Once hot, cook the onion and peppers until tender and fragrant, about 5 minutes. Add salt, black pepper, and oregano.
2. Sprinkle some flour on a kitchen counter and roll out the pizza dough.
3. Spoon the marinara sauce over half of the dough; add the sautéed mixture and sprinkle with the vegan cheese. Now, gently fold over the dough to create a pocket; make sure to seal the edges.
4. Use a fork to poke the dough in a few spots. Add a few drizzles of olive oil and place in the lightly greased cooking basket.
5. Bake in the preheated Air Fryer at 330 degrees F for 12 minutes, turning the calzones over halfway through the cooking time. Bon appétit!

235.Baked Zucchini Recipe From Mexico

Servings:4
Cooking Time: 30 Minutes

Ingredients:
- 1 tablespoon olive oil
- 1-1/2 pounds zucchini, cubed
- 1/2 cup chopped onion
- 1/2 teaspoon garlic salt
- 1/2 teaspoon paprika
- 1/2 teaspoon dried oregano
- 1/2 teaspoon cayenne pepper, or to taste
- 1/2 cup cooked long-grain rice
- 1/2 cup cooked pinto beans
- 1-1/4 cups salsa
- 3/4 cup shredded Cheddar cheese

Directions:
1. Lightly grease baking pan of air fryer with olive oil. Add onions and zucchini and for 10 minutes, cook on 360°F. Halfway through cooking time, stir.
2. Season with cayenne, oregano, paprika, and garlic salt. Mix well.
3. Stir in salsa, beans, and rice. Cook for 5 minutes.
4. Stir in cheddar cheese and mix well.
5. Cover pan with foil.
6. Cook for 15 minutes at 390°F until bubbly.
7. Serve and enjoy.

236.Garden Fresh Green Beans

Servings:4
Cooking Time:12 Minutes
Ingredients:
- 1 pound green beans, washed and trimmed
- 1 teaspoon butter, melted
- 1 tablespoon fresh lemon juice
- ¼ teaspoon garlic powder
- Salt and freshly ground pepper, to taste

Directions:
1. Preheat the Air fryer to 400 °F and grease an Air fryer basket.
2. Put all the ingredients in a large bowl and transfer into the Air fryer basket.
3. Cook for about 8 minutes and dish out in a bowl to serve warm.

237.Layered Tortilla Bake

Servings:6
Cooking Time: 30 Minutes
Ingredients:
- 1 (15 ounce) can black beans, rinsed and drained
- 1 cup salsa
- 1 cup salsa, divided
- 1/2 cup chopped tomatoes
- 1/2 cup sour cream
- 2 (15 ounce) cans pinto beans, drained and rinsed
- 2 cloves garlic, minced
- 2 cups shredded reduced-fat Cheddar cheese
- 2 tablespoons chopped fresh cilantro

- 7 (8 inch) flour tortillas

Directions:
1. Mash pinto beans in a large bowl and mix in garlic and salsa.
2. In another bowl whisk together tomatoes, black beans, cilantro, and ¼ cup salsa.
3. Lightly grease baking pan of air fryer with cooking spray. Spread 1 tortilla, spread ¾ cup pinto bean mixture evenly up to ½-inch away from the edge of tortilla, spread ¼ cup cheese on top. Cover with another tortilla, spread 2/3 cup black bean mixture, and then ¼ cup cheese. Repeat twice the layering process. Cover with the last tortilla, top with pinto bean mixture and then cheese.
4. Cover pan with foil.
5. Cook for 25 minutes at 390°F, remove foil and cook for 5 minutes or until tops are lightly browned.
6. Serve and enjoy.

238.Green Beans And Mushroom Casserole

Servings:6
Cooking Time:12 Minutes
Ingredients:
- 24 ounces fresh green beans, trimmed
- 2 cups fresh button mushrooms, sliced
- 1/3 cup French fried onions
- 3 tablespoons olive oil
- 2 tablespoons fresh lemon juice
- 1 teaspoon ground sage
- 1 teaspoon garlic powder
- 1 teaspoon onion powder
- Salt and black pepper, to taste

Directions:
1. Preheat the Air fryer to 400 °F and grease an Air fryer basket.
2. Mix the green beans, mushrooms, oil, lemon juice, sage, and spices in a bowl and toss to coat well.
3. Arrange the green beans mixture into the Air fryer basket and cook for about 12 minutes.
4. Dish out in a serving dish and top with fried onions to serve.

239.Classic Vegan Chili

Servings: 3
Cooking Time: 40 Minutes
Ingredients:
- 1 tablespoon olive oil
- 1/2 yellow onion, chopped
- 2 garlic cloves, minced
- 2 red bell peppers, seeded and chopped
- 1 red chili pepper, seeded and minced
- Sea salt and ground black pepper, to taste
- 1 teaspoon ground cumin

- 1 teaspoon cayenne pepper
- 1 teaspoon Mexican oregano
- 1/2 teaspoon mustard seeds
- 1/2 teaspoon celery seeds
- 1 can (28-ounces) diced tomatoes with juice
- 1 cup vegetable broth
- 1 (15-ounce) can black beans, rinsed and drained
- 1 bay leaf
- 1 teaspoon cider vinegar
- 1 avocado, sliced

Directions:
1. Start by preheating your Air Fryer to 365 degrees F.
2. Heat the olive oil in a baking pan until sizzling. Then, sauté the onion, garlic, and peppers in the baking pan. Cook for 4 to 6 minutes.
3. Now, add the salt, black pepper, cumin, cayenne pepper, oregano, mustard seeds, celery seeds, tomatoes, and broth. Cook for 20 minutes, stirring every 4 minutes.
4. Stir in the canned beans, bay leaf, cider vinegar; let it cook for a further 8 minutes, stirring halfway through the cooking time.
5. Serve in individual bowls garnished with the avocado slices. Enjoy!

240.Breadcrumbs Stuffed Mushrooms

Servings:4
Cooking Time:10 Minutes
Ingredients:
- 1½ spelt bread slices
- 1 tablespoon flat-leaf parsley, finely chopped
- 16 small button mushrooms, stemmed and gills removed
- 1½ tablespoons olive oil
- 1 garlic clove, crushed
- Salt and black pepper, to taste

Directions:
1. Preheat the Air fryer to 390 °F and grease an Air fryer basket.
2. Put the bread slices in a food processor and pulse until fine crumbs form.
3. Transfer the crumbs into a bowl and stir in the olive oil, garlic, parsley, salt, and black pepper.
4. Stuff the breadcrumbs mixture in each mushroom cap and arrange the mushrooms in the Air fryer basket.
5. Cook for about 10 minutes and dish out in a bowl to serve warm.

241.Air-fried Falafel

Servings:6
Cooking Time: 25 Minutes
Ingredients:
- ½ cup chickpea flour

- 1 cup fresh parsley, chopped
- Juice of 1 lemon
- 4 garlic cloves, chopped
- 1 onion, chopped
- 2 tsp ground cumin
- 2 tsp ground coriander
- 1 tsp chili powder
- Salt and black pepper

Directions:
1. In a blender, add chickpeas, flour, parsley, lemon juice, garlic, onion, cumin, coriander, chili, turmeric, salt and pepper, and blend until well-combined but not too battery; there should be some lumps. Shape the mixture into 15 balls and press them with hands, making sure they are still around.
2. Spray with oil and arrange them in a paper-lined air fryer basket; work in batches if needed. Cook at 360 F for 14 minutes, turning once halfway through. They should be crunchy and golden.

242.Mushrooms With Peas

Servings:4
Cooking Time:15 Minutes
Ingredients:
- 16 ounces cremini mushrooms, halved
- ½ cup frozen peas
- ½ cup soy sauce
- 4 tablespoons maple syrup
- 4 tablespoons rice vinegar
- 4 garlic cloves, finely chopped
- 2 teaspoons Chinese five spice powder
- ½ teaspoon ground ginger

Directions:
1. Preheat the Air fryer to 350 °F and grease an Air fryer pan.
2. Mix soy sauce, maple syrup, vinegar, garlic, five spice powder, and ground ginger in a bowl.
3. Arrange the mushrooms in the Air fryer basket and cook for about 10 minutes.
4. Stir in the soy sauce mixture and peas and cook for about 5 more minutes.
5. Dish out the mushroom mixture in plates and serve hot.

243.Stuffed Eggplant

Servings: 2
Cooking Time: 35 Minutes
Ingredients:
- large eggplant
- ¼ medium yellow onion, diced
- 2 tbsp. red bell pepper, diced
- 1 cup spinach
- ¼ cup artichoke hearts, chopped

Directions:

1. Cut the eggplant lengthwise into slices and spoon out the flesh, leaving a shell about a half-inch thick. Chop it up and set aside.
2. Set a skillet over a medium heat and spritz with cooking spray. Cook the onions for about three to five minutes to soften. Then add the pepper, spinach, artichokes, and the flesh of eggplant. Fry for a further five minutes, then remove from the heat.
3. Scoop this mixture in equal parts into the eggplant shells and place each one in the fryer.
4. Cook for twenty minutes at 320°F until the eggplant shells are soft. Serve warm.

244.Herb Roasted Potatoes And Peppers

Servings: 4
Cooking Time: 30 Minutes
Ingredients:

- 1 pound russet potatoes, cut into 1-inch chunks
- 2 bell peppers, seeded and cut into 1-inch chunks
- 2 tablespoons olive oil
- 1 teaspoon dried rosemary
- 1 teaspoon dried basil
- 1 teaspoon dried oregano
- 1 teaspoon dried parsley flakes
- Sea salt and ground black pepper, to taste
- 1/2 teaspoon smoked paprika

Directions:
1. Toss all ingredients in the Air Fryer basket.
2. Roast at 400 degrees F for 15 minutes, tossing the basket occasionally. Work in batches.
3. Serve warm and enjoy!

POULTRY RECIPES

245. Honey, Lime, And Garlic Chicken Bbq

Servings:4
Cooking Time: 40 Minutes
Ingredients:
- ¼ cup lime juice, freshly squeezed
- ½ cup cilantro, chopped finely
- ½ cup honey
- 1 tablespoon olive oil
- 2 cloves of garlic, minced
- 2 pounds boneless chicken breasts
- 2 tablespoons soy sauce
- Salt and pepper to taste

Directions:
1. Place all Ingredients in a Ziploc bag and give a good shake. Allow to marinate in the fridge for at least 2 hours.
2. Preheat the air fryer to 390 °F.
3. Place the grill pan accessory in the air fryer.
4. Grill the chicken for 40 minutes making sure to flip the chicken every 10 minutes to grill evenly on all sides.

246. Ethiopian-style Chicken With Cauliflower

Servings: 6
Cooking Time: 30 Minutes
Ingredients:
- 2 handful fresh Italian parsleys, roughly chopped
- ½ cup fresh chopped chives
- 2 sprigs thyme
- 6 chicken drumsticks
- 1 ½ small-sized head cauliflower, broken into large-sized florets
- For the Berbere Spice Rub Mix:
- 2 teaspoons mustard powder
- 1/3 teaspoon porcini powder
- 1 ½ teaspoons berbere spice
- 1/3teaspoon sweet paprika
- 1/2 teaspoon shallot powder
- 1teaspoon granulated garlic
- 1 teaspoon freshly cracked pink peppercorns
- 1/2 teaspoon sea salt

Directions:
1. Simply combine all items for the berbere spice rub mix. After that, coat the chicken drumsticks with this rub mix on all sides. Transfer them to the baking dish.
2. Now, lower the cauliflower onto the chicken drumsticks. Add thyme, chives and Italian parsley and spritz everything with a pan spray. Transfer the baking dish to the preheated Air Fryer.

3. Next step, set the timer for 28 minutes; roast at 355 degrees F, turning occasionally. Bon appétit!

247. Grilled Chicken Pesto

Servings:8
Cooking Time: 30 Minutes
Ingredients:
- 1 ¾ cup commercial pesto
- 8 chicken thighs
- Salt and pepper to taste

Directions:
1. Place all Ingredients in the Ziploc bag and allow to marinate in the fridge for at least 2 hours.
2. Preheat the air fryer to 390 °F.
3. Place the grill pan accessory in the air fryer.
4. Grill the chicken for at least 30 minutes.
5. Make sure to flip the chicken every 10 minutes for even grilling.

248. Lemon-parsley Chicken Packets

Servings:4
Cooking Time: 45 Minutes
Ingredients:
- ¼ cup smoked paprika
- ½ cup parsley leaves
- ½ teaspoon liquid smoke seasoning
- 1 ½ tablespoon cayenne pepper
- 2 pounds chicken thighs
- 4 lemons, halved
- Salt and pepper to taste

Directions:
1. Preheat the air fryer to 390 °F.
2. Place the grill pan accessory in the air fryer.
3. In a large foil, place the chicken and season with paprika, liquid smoke seasoning, salt, pepper, and cayenne pepper.
4. Top with lemon and parsley.
5. Place on the grill and cook for 45 minutes.

249. Spinach Stuffed Chicken Breasts

Servings:2
Cooking Time:29 Minutes
Ingredients:
- 1¾ ounces fresh spinach
- ¼ cup ricotta cheese, shredded
- 2 (4-ounces) skinless, boneless chicken breasts
- 2 tablespoons cheddar cheese, grated
- 1 tablespoon olive oil
- Salt and ground black pepper, as required
- ¼ teaspoon paprika

Directions:
1. Preheat the Air fryer to 390 °F and grease an Air fryer basket.

2. Heat olive oil in a medium skillet over medium heat and cook spinach for about 4 minutes.
3. Add the ricotta and cook for about 1 minute.
4. Cut the slits in each chicken breast horizontally and stuff with the spinach mixture.
5. Season each chicken breast evenly with salt and black pepper and top with cheddar cheese and paprika.
6. Arrange chicken breasts into the Air fryer basket in a single layer and cook for about 25 minutes.
7. Dish out and serve hot.

250. Chicken Breasts With Sweet Chili Adobo

Servings:3
Cooking Time: 20 Minutes
Ingredients:
- Salt to season
- ¼ cup sweet chili sauce
- 3 tbsp turmeric

Directions:
1. Preheat air fryer to 390 F. In a bowl, add salt, sweet chili sauce, and turmeric; mix with a spoon. Place the chicken on a clean flat surface and with a brush, apply the turmeric sauce lightly on the chicken.
2. Place in the fryer basket and grill for 18 minutes; turn them halfway through. Serve with a side of steamed greens.

251. Meat-covered Boiled Eggs

Servings:7
Cooking Time: 25 Minutes
Ingredients:
- ¼ cup coconut flour
- 1-pound ground beef
- 2 eggs, beaten
- 2 tablespoons butter, melted
- 7 large eggs, boiled and peeled
- Cooking spray
- Salt and pepper to taste

Directions:
1. Preheat the air fryer for 5 minutes.
2. Place the beaten eggs, ground beef, butter, and coconut flour in a mixing bowl. Season with salt and pepper to taste.
3. Coat the boiled eggs with the meat mixture and place in the fridge to set for 2 hours.
4. Grease with cooking spray.
5. Place in the air fryer basket.
6. Cook at 350 °F for 25 minutes.

252. Authentic Mexican Mole

Servings: 4
Cooking Time: 35 Minutes
Ingredients:

- 8 chicken thighs, skinless, bone-in
- 1 tablespoon peanut oil
- Sea salt and ground black pepper, to taste
- Mole sauce:
- 1 tablespoon peanut oil
- 1 onion, chopped
- 1 ounce dried negro chiles, stemmed, seeded, and chopped
- 2 garlic cloves, peeled and halved
- 1 large-sized fresh tomatoes, pureed
- 1 ½ ounces sugar-free bakers' chocolate, chopped
- 1 teaspoon dried Mexican oregano
- 1/2 teaspoon ground cumin
- 1 teaspoon coriander seeds
- A pinch of ground cloves
- 1/4 cup almonds, slivered and toasted

Directions:
1. Start by preheating your Air Fryer to 380 degrees F. Toss the chicken thighs with the peanut oil, salt, and black pepper.
2. Cook in the preheated Air Fryer for 12 minutes; flip them and cook an additional 10 minutes; reserve.
3. To make the sauce, heat 1 tablespoon of peanut oil in a saucepan over medium-high heat. Now, sauté the onion, chiles and garlic until fragrant or about 2 minutes.
4. Next, stir in the tomatoes, chocolate, oregano, cumin, coriander seeds, and cloves. Let it simmer until the sauce has slightly thickened.
5. Add the reserved chicken to the baking pan; add the sauce and cook in the preheated Air Fryer at 360 degrees F for 10 minutes or until thoroughly warmed.
6. Serve garnished with slivered almonds. Enjoy!

253. Tarragon Chicken

Servings: 4
Cooking Time: 40 Minutes
Ingredients:
- 2 cups roasted vegetable broth
- 2 chicken breasts, cut into halves
- ¾ tsp. fine sea salt
- ¼ tsp. mixed peppercorns, freshly cracked
- 1 tsp. cumin powder
- 1 ½ teaspoons sesame oil
- 1 ½ tbsp. Worcester sauce
- ½ cup of spring onions, chopped
- 1 Serrano pepper, deveined and chopped
- 1 bell pepper, deveined and chopped
- 1 tbsp. tamari sauce
- ½ chopped fresh tarragon

Directions:
1. Cook the vegetable broth and chicken breasts in a large saucepan for 10 minutes.

2. Lower the heat and simmer for another 10 minutes.
3. Let the chicken cool briefly. Then tear the chicken into shreds with a stand mixer or two forks.
4. Coat the shredded chicken with the salt, cracked peppercorns, cumin, sesame oil and the Worcester sauce.
5. Transfer to the Air Fryer and air fry at 380°F for 18 minutes, or longer as needed.
6. In the meantime, cook the remaining ingredients over medium heat in a skillet, until the vegetables are tender and fragrant.
7. Take the skillet off the heat. Stir in the shredded chicken, incorporating all the ingredients well.
8. Serve immediately.

254.Sweet Chili Chicken Wings

Servings:4
Cooking Time: 20 Minutes
Ingredients:
- 1 tsp garlic powder
- 1 tbsp tamarind powder
- ¼ cup sweet chili sauce

Directions:
1. Preheat your Air Fryer to 390 F. Spray the air fryer basket with cooking spray.
2. Rub the chicken wings with tamarind and garlic powders. Spray with cooking spray and place in the cooking basket. Cook for 6 minutes, Slide out the fryer basket and cover with sweet chili sauce; cook for 8 more minutes. Serve cooled.

255.Creamy Chicken-veggie Pasta

Servings:3
Cooking Time: 30 Minutes
Ingredients:
- 3 chicken tenderloins, cut into chunks
- salt and pepper to taste
- garlic powder to taste
- 1 cup frozen mixed vegetables
- 1 tablespoon grated Parmesan cheese
- 1 tablespoon butter, melted
- 1/2 (10.75 ounce) can condensed cream of chicken soup
- 1/2 (10.75 ounce) can condensed cream of mushroom soup
- 1/2 cup dry fusilli pasta, cooked according to manufacturer's Directions:
- 1 tablespoon and 1-1/2 teaspoons olive oil
- 1-1/2 teaspoons dried minced onion
- 1-1/2 teaspoons dried basil
- 1-1/2 teaspoons dried parsley
- 1/2 cup dry bread crumbs

Directions:
1. Lightly grease baking pan of air fryer with oil. Add chicken and season with parsley,

basil, garlic powder, pepper, salt, and minced onion. For 10 minutes, cook on 360°F. Stirring halfway through cooking time.
2. Then stir in mixed vegetables, mushroom soup, chicken soup, and cooked pasta. Mix well.
3. Mix well butter, Parmesan cheese, and bread crumbs in a small bowl and spread on top of casserole.
4. Cook for 20 minutes or until tops are lightly browned.
5. Serve and enjoy.

256.Chicken With Golden Roasted Cauliflower

Servings: 4
Cooking Time: 30 Minutes
Ingredients:
- 2 pounds chicken legs
- 2 tablespoons olive oil
- 1 teaspoon sea salt
- 1/2 teaspoon ground black pepper
- 1 teaspoon smoked paprika
- 1 teaspoon dried marjoram
- 1 (1-pound head cauliflower, broken into small florets
- 2 garlic cloves, minced
- 1/3 cup Pecorino Romano cheese, freshly grated
- 1/2 teaspoon dried thyme
- Salt, to taste

Directions:
1. Toss the chicken legs with the olive oil, salt, black pepper, paprika, and marjoram.
2. Cook in the preheated Air Fryer at 380 degrees F for 11 minutes. Flip the chicken legs and cook for a further 5 minutes.
3. Toss the cauliflower florets with garlic, cheese, thyme, and salt.
4. Increase the temperature to 400 degrees F; add the cauliflower florets and cook for 12 more minutes. Serve warm.

257.Simple Turkey Breast

Servings:10
Cooking Time:40 Minutes
Ingredients:
- 1 (8-pounds) bone-in turkey breast
- Salt and black pepper, as required
- 2 tablespoons olive oil

Directions:
1. Preheat the Air fryer to 360 °F and grease an Air fryer basket.
2. Season the turkey breast with salt and black pepper and drizzle with oil.
3. Arrange the turkey breast into the Air Fryer basket, skin side down and cook for about 20 minutes.

4. Flip the side and cook for another 20 minutes.
5. Dish out in a platter and cut into desired size slices to serve.

258. Must-serve Roasted Turkey Thighs With Vegetables

Servings:4
Cooking Time:1 Hour 15 Minutes
Ingredients:
- 1 red onion, cut into wedges
- 1 carrot, trimmed and sliced
- 1 celery stalk, trimmed and sliced
- 1 cup Brussel sprouts, trimmed and halved
- 1 cup roasted vegetable broth
- 1 tablespoon apple cider vinegar
- 1 teaspoon maple syrup
- 2 turkey thighs
- 1/2 teaspoon mixed peppercorns, freshly cracked
- 1 teaspoon fine sea salt
- 1 teaspoon cayenne pepper
- 1 teaspoon onion powder
- 1/2 teaspoon garlic powder
- 1/3 teaspoon mustard seeds

Directions:
1. Take a baking dish that easily fits into your device; place the vegetables on the bottom of the baking dish and pour in roasted vegetable broth.
2. In a large-sized mixing dish, place the remaining ingredients; let them marinate for about 30 minutes. Lay them on the top of the vegetables.
3. Roast at 330 degrees F for 40 to 45 minutes. Bon appétit!

259. Chicken & Potatoes

Servings: 6
Cooking Time: 45 Minutes
Ingredients:
- 1 lb. potatoes
- 2 lb. chicken
- 2 tbsp. olive oil
- Pepper and salt to taste

Directions:
1. Pre-heat the Air Fryer to 350°F.
2. Place the chicken in Air Fryer basket along with the potatoes. Sprinkle on the pepper and salt.
3. Add a drizzling of the olive oil, making sure to cover the chicken and potatoes well.
4. Cook for 40 minutes.

260. Beer Coated Duck Breast

Servings:2
Cooking Time:20 Minutes
Ingredients:
- 1 tablespoon fresh thyme, chopped
- 1 cup beer
- 1 (10½-ounces) duck breast
- 6 cherry tomatoes
- 1 tablespoon olive oil
- 1 teaspoon mustard
- Salt and ground black pepper, as required
- 1 tablespoon balsamic vinegar

Directions:
1. Preheat the Air fryer to 390 °F and grease an Air fryer basket.
2. Mix the olive oil, mustard, thyme, beer, salt, and black pepper in a bowl.
3. Coat the duck breasts generously with marinade and refrigerate, covered for about 4 hours.
4. Cover the duck breasts and arrange into the Air fryer basket.
5. Cook for about 15 minutes and remove the foil from breast.
6. Set the Air fryer to 355 °F and place the duck breast and tomatoes into the Air Fryer basket.
7. Cook for about 5 minutes and dish out the duck breasts and cherry tomatoes.
8. Drizzle with vinegar and serve immediately.

261. Red Thai Turkey Drumsticks In Coconut Milk

Servings: 2
Cooking Time: 25 Minutes
Ingredients:
- 1 tablespoon red curry paste
- 1/2 teaspoon cayenne pepper
- 1 ½ tablespoons minced ginger
- 2 turkey drumsticks
- 1/4 cup coconut milk
- 1 teaspoon kosher salt, or more to taste
- 1/3 teaspoon ground pepper, to more to taste

Directions:
1. First of all, place turkey drumsticks with all ingredients in your refrigerator; let it marinate overnight.
2. Cook turkey drumsticks at 380 degrees F for 23 minutes; make sure to flip them over at half-time. Serve with the salad on the side.

262. Turkey With Paprika And Tarragon

Servings: 6
Cooking Time: 40 Minutes
Ingredients:
- 2 pounds turkey tenderloins
- 2 tablespoons olive oil
- Salt and ground black pepper, to taste
- 1 teaspoon smoked paprika
- 2 tablespoons dry white wine
- 1 tablespoon fresh tarragon leaves, chopped

Directions:

1. Brush the turkey tenderloins with olive oil. Season with salt, black pepper, and paprika.
2. Afterwards, add the white wine and tarragon.
3. Cook the turkey tenderloins at 350 degrees F for 30 minutes, flipping them over halfway through. Let them rest for 5 to 9 minutes before slicing and serving. Enjoy!

263. Easy How-to Hard Boil Egg In Air Fryer

Servings:6
Cooking Time: 15 Minutes
Ingredients:
- 6 eggs

Directions:
1. Preheat the air fryer for 5 minutes.
2. Place the eggs in the air fryer basket.
3. Cook for 15 minutes at 360 °F.
4. Remove from the air fryer basket and place in cold water.

264. Buffalo Chicken Wings

Servings: 3
Cooking Time: 37 Minutes
Ingredients:
- 2 lb. chicken wings
- 1 tsp. salt
- ¼ tsp. black pepper
- 1 cup buffalo sauce

Directions:
1. Wash the chicken wings and pat them dry with clean kitchen towels.
2. Place the chicken wings in a large bowl and sprinkle on salt and pepper.
3. Pre-heat the Air Fryer to 380°F.
4. Place the wings in the fryer and cook for 15 minutes, giving them an occasional stir throughout.
5. Place the wings in a bowl. Pour over the buffalo sauce and toss well to coat.
6. Put the chicken back in the Air Fryer and cook for a final 5 – 6 minutes.

265. Chicken, Rice & Vegetables

Servings: 4
Cooking Time: 30 Minutes
Ingredients:
- 1 lb. skinless, boneless chicken breasts
- ½ lb. button mushrooms, sliced
- 1 medium onion, chopped
- 1 package [10 oz.] Alfredo sauce
- 2 cups cooked rice
- ½ tsp. dried thyme
- 1 tbsp. olive oil
- Salt and black pepper to taste

Directions:
1. Slice up the chicken breasts into 1-inch cubes.

2. In a large bowl, combine all of the ingredients. Sprinkle on salt and dried thyme and mix again.
3. Pre-heat the Air Fryer to 370°F and drizzle the basket with the olive oil.
4. Place the chicken and vegetables in the fryer and cook for 10 – 12 minutes. Stir the contents now and again.
5. Pour in the Alfredo sauce and allow to cook for an additional 3 – 4 minutes.
6. Serve with rice if desired.

266. Chicken Fajita Casserole

Servings: 4
Cooking Time: 12 Minutes
Ingredients:
- 1 lb cooked chicken, shredded
- 1 onion, sliced
- 1 bell pepper, sliced
- 1/3 cup mayonnaise
- 7 oz cream cheese
- 7 oz cheese, shredded
- 2 tbsp tex-mex seasoning
- Pepper
- Salt

Directions:
1. Preheat the air fryer to 370 F.
2. Spray air fryer baking dish with cooking spray.
3. Mix all ingredients except 2 oz shredded cheese in a prepared dish.
4. Spread remaining cheese on top.
5. Place dish in the air fryer and cook for 12 minutes.
6. Serve and enjoy.

267. Coconut Turkey And Spinach Mix

Servings: 4
Cooking Time: 15 Minutes
Ingredients:
- 1 pound turkey meat, ground and browned
- 1 tablespoon garlic, minced
- 1 tablespoon ginger, grated
- 2 tablespoons coconut aminos
- 4 cups spinach leaves
- A pinch of salt and black pepper

Directions:
1. In a pan that fits your air fryer, combine all the ingredients and toss. Put the pan in the air fryer and cook at 380 degrees F for 15 minutes Divide everything into bowls and serve.

268. Mixed Vegetable Breakfast Frittata

Servings:6
Cooking Time: 45 Minutes
Ingredients:
- ½-pound breakfast sausage
- 1 cup cheddar cheese shredded

- 1 teaspoon kosher salt
- 1/2 cup milk or cream
- 1/2 teaspoon black pepper
- 6 eggs
- 8-ounces frozen mixed vegetables (bell peppers, broccoli, etc.), thawed

Directions:
1. Lightly grease baking pan of air fryer with cooking spray. For 10 minutes, cook on 360°F the breakfast sausage and crumble. Halfway through cooking time, crumble sausage some more until it looks like ground meat. Once done cooking, discard excess fat.
2. Stir in thawed mixed vegetables and cook for 7 minutes or until heated through, stirring halfway through cooking time.
3. Meanwhile, in a bowl, whisk well eggs, cream, salt, and pepper.
4. Remove basket, evenly spread vegetable mixture, and pour in egg mixture. Cover pan with foil.
5. Cook for another 15 minutes, remove foil and continue cooking for another 5-10 minutes or until eggs are set to desired doneness.
6. Serve and enjoy.

269.Paprika Duck And Eggplant Mix

Servings: 4
Cooking Time: 25 Minutes
Ingredients:
- 1 pound duck breasts, skinless, boneless and cubed
- 2 eggplants, cubed
- A pinch of salt and black pepper
- 2 tablespoons olive oil
- 1 tablespoon sweet paprika
- ½ cup keto tomato sauce

Directions:
1. Heat up a pan that fits your air fryer with the oil over medium heat, add the duck pieces and brown for 5 minutes. Add the rest of the ingredients, toss, introduce the pan in the fryer and cook at 370 degrees F for 20 minutes. Divide between plates and serve.

270.Chicken Bbq Recipe From Italy

Servings:2
Cooking Time: 40 Minutes
Ingredients:
- 1 tablespoon fresh Italian parsley
- 1 tablespoon minced garlic
- 1-pound boneless chicken breasts
- 2 tablespoons tomato paste
- Salt and pepper to taste

Directions:

1. Place all Ingredients in a Ziploc bag except for the corn. Allow to marinate in the fridge for at least 2 hours.
2. Preheat the air fryer to 390 °F.
3. Place the grill pan accessory in the air fryer.
4. Grill the chicken for 40 minutes.

271.Chicken In Packets Southwest Style

Servings:4
Cooking Time: 40 Minutes
Ingredients:
- 1 can black beans, rinsed and drained
- 1 cup cilantro, chopped
- 1 cup commercial salsa
- 1 cup corn kernels, frozen
- 1 cup Mexican cheese blend, shredded
- 4 chicken breasts
- 4 lime wedges
- 4 teaspoons taco seasoning
- Salt and pepper to taste

Directions:
1. Preheat the air fryer to 390 °F.
2. Place the grill pan accessory in the air fryer.
3. On a big aluminum foil, place the chicken breasts and season with salt and pepper to taste.
4. Add the corn, commercial salsa beans, and taco seasoning.
5. Close the foil and crimp the edges.
6. Place on the grill pan and cook for 40 minutes.
7. Before serving, top with cheese, cilantro and lime wedges.

272.Middle Eastern Chicken Bbq With Tzatziki Sauce

Servings:6
Cooking Time: 24 Minutes
Ingredients:
- 1 1/2 pounds skinless, boneless chicken breast halves - cut into bite-sized pieces
- 1 teaspoon dried oregano
- 1/2 teaspoon salt
- 1/4 cup olive oil
- 2 cloves garlic, minced
- 2 tablespoons lemon juice
- Tzatziki Dip Ingredients
- 1 (6 ounce) container plain Greek-style yogurt
- 1 tablespoon olive oil
- 2 teaspoons white vinegar
- 1 clove garlic, minced
- 1 pinch salt
- 1/2 cucumber - peeled, seeded, and grated

Directions:
1. In a medium bowl mix well, all Tzatziki dip Ingredients. Refrigerate for at least 2 hours to allow flavors to blend.

2. In a resealable bag, mix well salt, oregano, garlic, lemon juice, and olive oil. Add chicken, squeeze excess air, seal, and marinate for at least 2 hours.
3. Thread chicken into skewers and place on skewer rack. Cook in batches.
4. For 12 minutes, cook on 360°F. Halfway through cooking time, turnover skewers and baste with marinade from resealable bag.
5. Serve and enjoy with Tzatziki dip.

273.Provençal Chicken

Servings: 4
Cooking Time: 25 Minutes
Ingredients:
- 4 medium-sized skin-on chicken drumsticks
- 1 ½ tsp. herbs de Provence
- Salt and pepper to taste
- 1 tbsp. rice vinegar
- 2 tbsp. olive oil
- 2 garlic cloves, crushed
- 12 oz. crushed canned tomatoes
- 1 small-size leek, thinly sliced
- 2 slices smoked bacon, chopped

Directions:
1. Season the chicken drumsticks with herbs de Provence, salt and pepper. Pour over a light drizzling of the rice vinegar and olive oil.
2. Cook in the baking pan at 360°F for 8 - 10 minutes.
3. Pause the fryer. Add in the rest of the ingredients, give them a stir, and resume cooking for 15 more minutes, checking them occasionally to ensure they don't overcook.
4. Serve with rice and lemon wedges.

274.Chicken & Prawn Paste

Servings:2
Cooking Time: 30 Minutes
Ingredients:
- 2 tbsp cornflour
- ½ tbsp wine
- 1 tbsp shrimp paste
- 1 tbsp ginger
- ½ tbsp olive oil

Directions:
1. Preheat your air fryer to 360 F. In a bowl, mix oil, ginger, and wine. Cover the chicken wings with the prepared marinade and top with flour. Add the floured chicken to shrimp paste and coat it. Place the chicken in your air fryer's cooking basket and cook for 20 minutes, until crispy on the outside.

275.Peppery Lemon-chicken Breast

Servings:1

Cooking Time:
Ingredients:
- 1 chicken breast
- 1 teaspoon minced garlic
- 2 lemons, rinds and juice reserved
- Salt and pepper to taste

Directions:
1. Preheat the air fryer.
2. Place all ingredients in a baking dish that will fit in the air fryer.
3. Place in the air fryer basket.
4. Close and cook for 20 minutes at 400 °F.

276.Texas Bbq Chicken Thighs

Servings:4
Cooking Time: 30 Minutes
Ingredients:
- Salt and black pepper to taste
- 2 tsp Texas BBQ Jerky seasoning
- 1 tbsp olive oil
- 2 tbsp cilantro, chopped

Directions:
1. Preheat the Air fryer to 380 F. Grease the air fryer basket with cooking spray.
2. Drizzle the chicken with olive oil, season with salt and pepper, and sprinkle over BBQ seasoning. Place in the air fryer basket. Cook for 20 minutes. Serve sprinkled with cilantro.

277.Chicken With Rice

Servings:4
Cooking Time: 40 Minutes
Ingredients:
- 1 cup rice
- 2 cups water
- 2 tomatoes, cubed
- 3 tbsp butter
- 1 tbsp tomato paste
- Salt and black pepper
- 1 onion
- 3 minced cloves garlic

Directions:
1. Rub the chicken legs with butter. Sprinkle with salt and pepper and fry in a preheated air fryer for 30 minutes at 380 F. Then, add small onion and a little bit of oil; keep stirring. Add the tomatoes, the tomato paste, and the garlic, and cook for 5 more minutes.
2. Meanwhile, in a pan, boil the rice in 2 cups of water for around 20 minutes. In a baking tray, place the rice and top it with the air fried chicken and cook in the air fryer for 5 minutes. Serve and enjoy!

278.Duck And Blackberry Mix

Servings: 4
Cooking Time: 25 Minutes
Ingredients:

- 4 duck breasts, boneless and skin scored
- A pinch of salt and black pepper
- 2 tablespoons olive oil
- 1 and ½ cups chicken stock
- 2 spring onions, chopped
- 4 garlic cloves, minced
- 1 and ½ cups blackberries, pureed
- 2 tablespoons butter, melted

Directions:
1. Heat up a pan that fits the air fryer with the oil and the butter over medium-high heat, add the duck breasts skin side down and sear for 5 minutes. Add the remaining ingredients, toss, put the pan in the air fryer and cook at 370 degrees F for 20 minutes. Divide the duck and sauce between plates and serve.

279.Spicy Green Crusted Chicken

Servings:6
Cooking Time:40 Minutes
Ingredients:
- 6 eggs, beaten
- 6 teaspoons parsley
- 4 teaspoons thyme
- 1 pound chicken pieces
- 6 teaspoons oregano
- Salt and freshly ground black pepper, to taste
- 4 teaspoons paprika

Directions:
1. Preheat the Air fryer to 360 °F and grease an Air fryer basket.
2. Whisk eggs in a bowl and mix all the ingredients in another bowl except chicken pieces.
3. Dip the chicken in eggs and then coat generously with the dry mixture.
4. Arrange half of the chicken pieces in the Air fryer basket and cook for about 20 minutes.
5. Repeat with the remaining mixture and dish out to serve hot.

280.Marrod's Meatballs

Servings: 6
Cooking Time: 15 Minutes
Ingredients:
- 1 lb. ground turkey
- 1 tbsp. fresh mint leaves, finely chopped
- 1 tsp. onion powder
- 1 ½ teaspoons garlic paste
- 1 tsp. crushed red pepper flakes
- ¼ cup melted butter
- ¾ tsp. fine sea salt
- ¼ cup grated Pecorino Romano

Directions:
1. In a bowl, combine all of the ingredients well. Using an ice cream scoop, mold the meat into balls.

2. Air fry the meatballs at 380°F for about 7 minutes, in batches if necessary. Shake the basket frequently throughout the cooking time for even results.
3. Serve with basil leaves and tomato sauce if desired.

281.Quick & Easy Meatballs

Servings: 4
Cooking Time: 10 Minutes
Ingredients:
- 1 lb ground chicken
- 1 egg, lightly beaten
- 1/2 cup mozzarella cheese, shredded
- 1 1/2 tbsp taco seasoning
- 3 garlic cloves, minced
- 3 tbsp fresh parsley, chopped
- 1 small onion, minced
- Pepper
- Salt

Directions:
1. Add all ingredients into the large mixing bowl and mix until well combined.
2. Make small balls from mixture and place in the air fryer basket.
3. Cook meatballs for 10 minutes at 400 F.
4. Serve and enjoy.

282.Chicken Wings And Vinegar Sauce

Servings: 4
Cooking Time: 12 Minutes
Ingredients:
- 4 chicken wings
- 1 teaspoon Erythritol
- 1 teaspoon water
- 1 teaspoon apple cider vinegar
- 1 teaspoon salt
- ¼ teaspoon ground paprika
- ½ teaspoon dried oregano
- Cooking spray

Directions:
1. Sprinkle the chicken wings with salt and dried oregano. Then preheat the air fryer to 400F. Place the chicken wings in the air fryer basket and cook them for 8 minutes. Flip the chicken wings on another side after 4 minutes of cooking. Meanwhile, mix up Erythritol, water, apple cider vinegar, and ground paprika in the saucepan and bring the liquid to boil. Stir the liquid well and cook it until Erythritol is dissolved. After this, generously brush the chicken wings with sweet Erythritol liquid and cook them in the air fryer at 400F for 4 minutes more.

283.Spice-rubbed Jerk Chicken Wings

Servings:4
Cooking Time: 40 Minutes
Ingredients:

- 1 tbsp olive oil
- 3 cloves garlic, minced
- 1 tbsp chili powder
- ½ tbsp cinnamon powder
- ½ tsp allspice
- 1 habanero pepper, seeded
- 1 tbsp soy sauce
- ½ tbsp white pepper
- ¼ cup red wine vinegar
- 3 tbsp lime juice
- 2 Scallions, chopped
- ½ tbsp grated ginger
- ½ tbsp chopped fresh thyme
- ⅓ tbsp sugar
- ½ tbsp salt

Directions:
1. In a bowl, add the olive oil, soy sauce, garlic, habanero pepper, allspice, cinnamon powder, cayenne pepper, white pepper, salt, sugar, thyme, ginger, scallions, lime juice, and red wine vinegar; mix well.
2. Add the chicken wings to the marinade mixture and coat it well with the mixture. Cover the bowl with cling film and refrigerate the chicken to marinate for 16 hours. Preheat the air fryer to 400 F. Remove the chicken from the fridge, drain all the liquid, and pat each wing dry using a paper towel.
3. Place half of the wings in the basket and cook for 16 minutes. Shake halfway through. Remove onto a serving platter. Serve with blue cheese dip or ranch dressing.

284.Indian Chicken Tenders
Servings: 4
Cooking Time: 15 Minutes
Ingredients:
- 1 lb chicken tenders, cut in half
- ¼ cup parsley, chopped
- 1/2 tbsp garlic, minced
- 1/2 tbsp ginger, minced
- ¼ cup yogurt
- 3/4 tsp paprika
- 1 tsp garam masala
- 1 tsp turmeric
- 1/2 tsp cayenne pepper
- 1 tsp salt

Directions:
1. Preheat the air fryer to 350 F.
2. Add all ingredients into the large bowl and mix well. Place in refrigerator for 30 minutes.
3. Spray air fryer basket with cooking spray.
4. Add marinated chicken into the air fryer basket and cook for 10 minutes.
5. Turn chicken to another side and cook for 5 minutes more.
6. Serve and enjoy.

285.Creamy Asiago Chicken
Servings:4
Cooking Time: 20 Minutes
Ingredients:
- 1 tbsp garlic powder
- 1 cup mayonnaise
- ½ tsp pepper
- ½ cup soft cheese
- ½ tbsp salt
- Chopped basil for garnish

Directions:
1. Preheat your air fryer to 380 F. In a bowl, mix cheese, mayonnaise, garlic powder and salt to form a marinade. Cover your chicken with the marinade. Place the marinated chicken in your air fryer's cooking basket and cook for 15 minutes. Serve with a garnish of chopped basil.

286.Asian Chicken Filets With Cheese
Servings: 2
Cooking Time: 50 Minutes
Ingredients:
- 4 rashers smoked bacon
- 2 chicken filets
- 1/2 teaspoon coarse sea salt
- 1/4 teaspoon black pepper, preferably freshly ground
- 1 teaspoon garlic, minced
- 1 (2-inch) piece ginger, peeled and minced
- 1 teaspoon black mustard seeds
- 1 teaspoon mild curry powder
- 1/2 cup coconut milk
- 1/3 cup tortilla chips, crushed
- 1/2 cup Pecorino Romano cheese, freshly grated

Directions:
1. Start by preheating your Air Fryer to 400 degrees F. Add the smoked bacon and cook in the preheated Air Fryer for 5 to 7 minutes. Reserve.
2. In a mixing bowl, place the chicken fillets, salt, black pepper, garlic, ginger, mustard seeds, curry powder, and milk. Let it marinate in your refrigerator about 30 minutes.
3. In another bowl, mix the crushed chips and grated Pecorino Romano cheese.
4. Dredge the chicken fillets through the chips mixture and transfer them to the cooking basket. Reduce the temperature to 380 degrees F and cook the chicken for 6 minutes.
5. Turn them over and cook for a further 6 minutes. Repeat the process until you have run out of ingredients.
6. Serve with reserved bacon. Enjoy!

287.Chicken Sausage With Nestled Eggs

Servings: 6
Cooking Time: 20 Minutes
Ingredients:

- 6 eggs
- 2 bell peppers, seeded and sliced
- 1 teaspoon dried oregano
- 1 teaspoon hot paprika
- 1 teaspoon freshly cracked black pepper
- 6 chicken sausages
- 1 teaspoon sea salt
- 1 1/2 shallots, cut into wedges
- 1 teaspoon dried basil

Directions:

1. Take four ramekins and divide chicken sausages, shallot, and bell pepper among those ramekins. Cook at 315 degrees F for about 12 minutes.
2. Now, crack an egg into each ramekin. Sprinkle the eggs with hot paprika, basil, oregano, salt, and cracked black pepper. Cook for 5 more minutes at 405 degrees F.
3. Bon appétit!

288.Charcoal Chicken

Servings: 2
Cooking Time: 20 Minutes
Ingredients:

- 2 medium skinless, boneless chicken breasts
- ½ tsp. salt
- 3 tbsp. Cajun spice
- 1 tbsp. olive oil

Directions:

1. Massage the salt and Cajun spice into the chicken breasts. Drizzle with olive oil.
2. Pre-heat the Air Fryer to 370°F.
3. Place the chicken in the fryer and cook for 7 minutes.
4. Flip both chicken breasts over and cook for an additional 3 – 4 minutes.
5. Slice up before serving.

289.Ranch Parmesan Chicken Wings

Servings: 3
Cooking Time: 25 Minutes
Ingredients:

- 1/2 cup seasoned breadcrumbs
- 2 tablespoons butter, melted
- 6 tablespoons parmesan cheese, preferably freshly grated
- 1 tablespoon Ranch seasoning mix
- 2 tablespoons oyster sauce
- 6 chicken wings, bone-in

Directions:

1. Start by preheating your Air Fryer to 370 degrees F.
2. In a resealable bag, place the breadcrumbs, butter, parmesan, Ranch seasoning mix, and oyster sauce. Add the chicken wings and shake to coat on all sides.
3. Arrange the chicken wings in the Air Fryer basket. Spritz the chicken wings with a nonstick cooking spray.
4. Cook for 11 minutes. Turn them over and cook an additional 11 minutes. Serve warm with your favorite dipping sauce, if desired. Enjoy!

290.Simple Paprika Duck

Servings: 4
Cooking Time: 25 Minutes
Ingredients:

- 1 pound duck breasts, skinless, boneless and cubed
- Salt and black pepper to the taste
- 1 tablespoon olive oil
- ½ teaspoon sweet paprika
- ¼ cup chicken stock
- 1 teaspoon thyme, chopped

Directions:

1. Heat up a pan that fits your air fryer with the oil over medium heat, add the duck pieces, and brown them for 5 minutes. Add the rest of the ingredients, toss, put the pan in the machine and cook at 380 degrees F for 20 minutes. Divide between plates and serve.

291.Moroccan Chicken

Servings: 2
Cooking Time: 25 Minutes
Ingredients:

- ½ lb. shredded chicken
- 1 cup broth
- 1 carrot
- 1 broccoli, chopped
- Pinch of cinnamon
- Pinch of cumin
- Pinch of red pepper
- Pinch of sea salt

Directions:

1. In a bowl, cover the shredded chicken with cumin, red pepper, sea salt and cinnamon.
2. Chop up the carrots into small pieces. Put the carrot and broccoli into the bowl with the chicken.
3. Add the broth and stir everything well. Set aside for about 30 minutes.
4. Transfer to the Air Fryer. Cook for about 15 minutes at 390°F. Serve hot.

292.Peppery Turkey Sandwiches

Servings: 4
Cooking Time: 25 Minutes
Ingredients:

- 1 cup leftover turkey, cut into bite-sized chunks

- 2 bell peppers, deveined and chopped
- 1 Serrano pepper, deveined and chopped
- 1 leek, sliced
- ½ cup sour cream
- 1 tsp. hot paprika
- ¾ tsp. kosher salt
- ½ tsp. ground black pepper
- 1 heaping tbsp. fresh cilantro, chopped
- Dash of Tabasco sauce
- 4 hamburger buns

Directions:
1. Combine all of the ingredients except for the hamburger buns, ensuring to coat the turkey well.
2. Place in an Air Fryer baking pan and roast for 20 minutes at 385°F.
3. Top the hamburger buns with the turkey, and serve with mustard or sour cream as desired.

293.Parmesan-crusted Chicken Fingers

Servings:2
Cooking Time: 30 Minutes
Ingredients:
- 1 tbsp salt
- 1 tbsp black pepper
- 2 cloves garlic, crushed
- 3 tbsp cornstarch
- 4 tbsp breadcrumbs, like flour bread
- 4 tbsp grated Parmesan cheese
- 2 eggs, beaten
- Cooking spray

Directions:
1. Mix salt, garlic, and pepper in a bowl. Add the chicken and stir to coat. Marinate for 1 hour in the fridge.
2. Mix the breadcrumbs with cheese evenly; set aside. Remove the chicken from the fridge, lightly toss in cornstarch, dip in egg and coat them gently in the cheese mixture. Preheat the air fryer to 350 F. Lightly spray the air fryer basket with cooking spray and place the chicken inside; cook for 15 minutes, until nice and crispy. Serve the chicken with a side of vegetable fries and cheese dip. Yum!

294.Pizza Spaghetti Casserole

Servings: 4
Cooking Time: 30 Minutes
Ingredients:
- 8 ounces spaghetti
- 1 pound smoked chicken sausage, sliced
- 2 tomatoes, pureed
- 1/2 cup Asiago cheese, shredded
- 1 tablespoon Italian seasoning mix
- 3 tablespoons Romano cheese, grated
- 1 tablespoon fresh basil leaves, chiffonade

Directions:

1. Bring a large pot of lightly salted water to a boil. Cook your spaghetti for 10 minutes or until al dente; drain and reserve, keeping warm.
2. Stir in the chicken sausage, tomato puree, Asiago cheese, and Italian seasoning mix.
3. Then, spritz a baking pan with cooking spray; add the spaghetti mixture to the pan. Bake in the preheated Air Fryer at 325 degrees F for 11 minutes.
4. Top with the grated Romano cheese. Turn the temperature to 390 degrees F and cook an additional 5 minutes or until everything is thoroughly heated and the cheese is melted.
5. Garnish with fresh basil leaves. Bon appétit!

295.Chili, Lime & Corn Chicken Bbq

Servings:4
Cooking Time: 40 Minutes
Ingredients:
- ½ teaspoon cumin
- 1 tablespoon lime juice
- 1 teaspoon chili powder
- 2 chicken breasts
- 2 chicken thighs
- 2 cups barbecue sauce
- 2 teaspoon grated lime zest
- 4 ears of corn, cleaned
- Salt and pepper to taste

Directions:
1. Place all Ingredients in a Ziploc bag except for the corn. Allow to marinate in the fridge for at least 2 hours.
2. Preheat the air fryer to 390 °F.
3. Place the grill pan accessory in the air fryer.
4. Grill the chicken and corn for 40 minutes.
5. Meanwhile, pour the marinade in a saucepan over medium heat until it thickens.
6. Before serving, brush the chicken and corn with the glaze.

296.Chicken Breasts & Spiced Tomatoes

Servings: 1
Cooking Time: 40 Minutes
Ingredients:
- 1 lb. boneless chicken breast
- Salt and pepper
- 1 cup butter
- 1 cup tomatoes, diced
- 1 ½ tsp. paprika
- 1 tsp. pumpkin pie spices

Directions:
1. Preheat your fryer at 375°F.
2. Cut the chicken into relatively thick slices and put them in the fryer. Sprinkle with salt and pepper to taste. Cook for fifteen minutes.

3. In the meantime, melt the butter in a saucepan over medium heat, before adding the tomatoes, paprika, and pumpkin pie spices. Leave simmering while the chicken finishes cooking.
4. When the chicken is cooked through, place it on a dish and pour the tomato mixture over. Serve hot.

297.Beastly Bbq Drumsticks

Servings: 4
Cooking Time: 45 Minutes
Ingredients:
- 4 chicken drumsticks
- ½ tbsp. mustard
- 1 clove garlic, crushed
- 1 tsp. chili powder
- 2 tsp. sugar
- 1 tbsp. olive oil
- Freshly ground black pepper

Directions:
1. Pre-heat the Air Fryer to 390°F.
2. Mix together the garlic, sugar, mustard, a pinch of salt, freshly ground pepper, chili powder and oil.
3. Massage this mixture into the drumsticks and leave to marinate for a minimum of 20 minutes.
4. Put the drumsticks in the fryer basket and cook for 10 minutes.
5. Bring the temperature down to 300°F and continue to cook the drumsticks for a further10 minutes. When cooked through, serve with bread and corn salad.

298.Crunchy Munchy Chicken Tenders With Peanuts

Servings: 4
Cooking Time: 25 Minutes
Ingredients:
- 1 ½ pounds chicken tenderloins
- 2 tablespoons peanut oil
- 1/2 cup tortilla chips, crushed
- Sea salt and ground black pepper, to taste
- 1/2 teaspoon garlic powder
- 1 teaspoon red pepper flakes
- 2 tablespoons peanuts, roasted and roughly chopped

Directions:
1. Start by preheating your Air Fryer to 360 degrees F.
2. Brush the chicken tenderloins with peanut oil on all sides.
3. In a mixing bowl, thoroughly combine the crushed chips, salt, black pepper, garlic powder, and red pepper flakes. Dredge the chicken in the breading, shaking off any residual coating.

4. Lay the chicken tenderloins into the cooking basket. Cook for 12 to 13 minutes or until it is no longer pink in the center. Work in batches; an instant-read thermometer should read at least 165 degrees F.
5. Serve garnished with roasted peanuts. Bon appétit!

299.Authentic Chicken-fajitas With Salsa

Servings: 4
Cooking Time: 30 Minutes
Ingredients:
- 1 pound chicken tenderloins, chopped
- Sea salt and ground black pepper, to your liking
- 1 teaspoon shallot powder
- 1 teaspoon fajita seasoning
- 2 bell peppers, seeded and diced
- 4 flour tortillas
- Salsa
- 1 ancho chili pepper, seeded and finely chopped
- 2 ripe tomatoes, crushed
- 1 bunch fresh coriander, roughly chopped
- 1 lime
- 2 tablespoons extra-virgin olive oil

Directions:
1. Toss the chicken with salt, pepper, shallot powder, and fajita seasoning mix.
2. Roast in the preheated Air Fryer at 390 degrees F for 9 minutes. Add the bell peppers and roast an additional 8 minutes.
3. For the salsa, mix the chilli, tomatoes and coriander. Squeeze over the juice of 1 lime; add olive oil and stir to combine well.
4. Warm the tortillas in your Air Fryer at 200 degrees F for 10 minutes.
5. Serve the chicken fajitas with tortilla and salsa. Enjoy!

300.Agave Mustard Glazed Chicken

Servings: 4
Cooking Time: 30 Minutes
Ingredients:
- 1 tablespoon avocado oil
- 2 pounds chicken breasts, boneless, skin-on
- 1 tablespoon Jamaican Jerk Rub
- 1/2 teaspoon salt
- 3 tablespoons agave syrup
- 1 tablespoon mustard
- 2 tablespoons scallions, chopped

Directions:
1. Start by preheating your Air Fryer to 370 degrees F.
2. Drizzle the avocado oil all over the chicken breast. Then, rub the chicken breast with the Jamaican Jerk rub.

3. Cook in the preheated Air Fryer approximately 15 minutes. Turn them over and cook an additional 8 minutes.
4. While the chicken breasts are roasting, combine the salt, agave syrup, and mustard in a pan over medium heat. Let it simmer until the glaze thickens.
5. After that, brush the glaze all over the chicken breast. Air-fry for a further 6 minutes or until the surface is crispy. Serve garnished with fresh scallions. Bon appétit!

301.Pretzel Crusted Chicken With Spicy Mustard Sauce

Servings: 6
Cooking Time: 20 Minutes
Ingredients:
- 2 eggs
- 1 ½ pound chicken breasts, boneless, skinless, cut into bite-sized chunks
- 1/2 cup crushed pretzels
- 1 teaspoon shallot powder
- 1 teaspoon paprika
- Sea salt and ground black pepper, to taste
- 1/2 cup vegetable broth
- 1 tablespoon cornstarch
- 3 tablespoons Worcestershire sauce
- 3 tablespoons tomato paste
- 1 tablespoon apple cider vinegar
- 2 tablespoons olive oil
- 2 garlic cloves, chopped
- 1 jalapeno pepper, minced
- 1 teaspoon yellow mustard

Directions:
1. Start by preheating your Air Fryer to 390 degrees F.
2. In a mixing dish, whisk the eggs until frothy; toss the chicken chunks into the whisked eggs and coat well.
3. In another dish, combine the crushed pretzels with shallot powder, paprika, salt and pepper. Then, lay the chicken chunks in the pretzel mixture; turn it over until well coated.
4. Place the chicken pieces in the air fryer basket. Cook the chicken for 12 minutes, shaking the basket halfway through.
5. Meanwhile, whisk the vegetable broth with cornstarch, Worcestershire sauce, tomato paste, and apple cider vinegar.
6. Preheat a cast-iron skillet over medium flame. Heat the olive oil and sauté the garlic with jalapeno pepper for 30 to 40 seconds, stirring frequently.
7. Add the cornstarch mixture and let it simmer until the sauce has thickened a little. Now, add the air-fried chicken and mustard; let it simmer for 2 minutes more or until heated through.

8. Serve immediately and enjoy!

302.Almond Turkey And Shallots

Servings: 2
Cooking Time: 25 Minutes
Ingredients:
- 1 big turkey breast, skinless, boneless and halved
- 1/3 cup almonds, chopped
- Salt and black pepper to the taste
- 2 tablespoons olive oil
- 1 tablespoon sweet paprika
- 2 shallots, chopped

Directions:
1. In a pan that fits the air fryer, combine the turkey with all the other ingredients, toss, put the pan in the machine and cook at 370 degrees F for 25 minutes. Divide everything between plates and serve.

303.Crispy Chicken Drumsticks

Servings:2
Cooking Time:20 Minutes
Ingredients:
- 4 (4-ounces) chicken drumsticks
- ½ cup buttermilk
- ½ cup all-purpose flour
- ½ cup panko breadcrumbs
- 3 tablespoons butter, melted
- ¼ teaspoon baking powder
- ¼ teaspoon dried oregano
- ¼ teaspoon dried thyme
- ¼ teaspoon celery salt
- ¼ teaspoon garlic powder
- ¼ teaspoon ground ginger
- ¼ teaspoon cayenne pepper
- ¼ teaspoon paprika
- Salt and ground black pepper, as required

Directions:
1. Preheat the Air fryer to 390 °F and grease an Air fryer basket.
2. Put the chicken drumsticks and buttermilk in a resealable plastic bag.
3. Seal the bag tightly and refrigerate for about 3 hours.
4. Mix the flour, breadcrumbs, baking powder, herbs and spices in a bowl.
5. Remove the chicken drumsticks from bag and coat chicken drumsticks evenly with the seasoned flour mixture.
6. Transfer the chicken drumsticks into the Air fryer basket and cook for about 20 minutes, flipping once in between.
7. Dish out and serve hot.

304.Jalapeno Chicken Breasts

Servings: 2
Cooking Time: 25 Minutes
Ingredients:

74

- 2 oz. full-fat cream cheese, softened
- 4 slices sugar-free bacon, cooked and crumbled
- ¼ cup pickled jalapenos, sliced
- ½ cup sharp cheddar cheese, shredded and divided
- 2 x 6-oz. boneless skinless chicken breasts

Directions:
1. In a bowl, mix the cream cheese, bacon, jalapeno slices, and half of the cheddar cheese until well-combined.
2. Cut parallel slits in the chicken breasts of about ¾ the length – make sure not to cut all the way down. You should be able to make between six and eight slices, depending on the size of the chicken breast.
3. Insert evenly sized dollops of the cheese mixture into the slits of the chicken breasts. Top the chicken with sprinkles of the rest of the cheddar cheese. Place the chicken in the basket of your air fryer.
4. Set the fryer to 350°F and cook the chicken breasts for twenty minutes.
5. Test with a meat thermometer. The chicken should be at 165°F when fully cooked. Serve hot and enjoy!

305.Spiced Roasted Chicken

Servings:2
Cooking Time:14 Minutes
Ingredients:
- 1 (5-pounds) whole chicken, necks and giblets removed
- 2 teaspoons dried thyme
- 2 teaspoons paprika
- 1 teaspoon cayenne pepper
- 1 teaspoon ground white pepper
- 1 teaspoon onion powder
- 1 teaspoon garlic powder
- Salt and ground black pepper, as required
- 3 tablespoons olive oil

Directions:
1. Preheat the Air fryer to 350 °F and grease an Air fryer basket.
2. Mix the thyme and spices in a bowl.
3. Coat the chicken generously with olive oil and rub with spice mixture.
4. Arrange the chicken into the Air Fryer basket, breast side down and cook for about 30 minutes.
5. Flip the chicken and cook for 30 more minutes.
6. Dish out the chicken in a platter and cut into desired size pieces to serve.

BEEF,PORK & LAMB RECIPES

306.Capers 'n Olives Topped Flank Steak

Servings:4
Cooking Time: 45 Minutes
Ingredients:
- 1 anchovy fillet, minced
- 1 clove of garlic, minced
- 1 cup pitted olives
- 1 tablespoon capers, minced
- 1/3 cup olive oil
- 2 pounds flank steak, pounded
- 2 tablespoons fresh oregano
- 2 tablespoons garlic powder
- 2 tablespoons onion powder
- 2 tablespoons smoked paprika
- Salt and pepper to taste

Directions:
1. Preheat the air fryer to 390 °F.
2. Place the grill pan accessory in the air fryer.
3. Season the steak with salt and pepper. Rub the oregano, paprika, onion powder, and garlic powder all over the steak.
4. Place on the grill pan and cook for 45 minutes. Make sure to flip the meat every 10 minutes for even cooking.
5. Meanwhile, mix together the olive oil, olives, capers, garlic, and anchovy fillets.
6. Serve the steak with the tapenade.

307.Roasted Cilantro Lamb Chops

Servings: 6
Cooking Time: 24 Minutes
Ingredients:
- 12 lamb chops
- A pinch of salt and black pepper
- ½ cup cilantro, chopped
- 1 green chili pepper, chopped
- 1 garlic clove, minced
- Juice of 1 lime
- 3 tablespoons olive oil

Directions:
1. In a bowl, mix the lamb chops with the rest of the ingredients and rub well. Put the chops in your air fryer's basket and cook at 400 degrees F for 12 minutes on each side. Divide between plates and serve.

308.Beef And Zucchini Sauté

Servings: 4
Cooking Time: 25 Minutes
Ingredients:
- 1 pound beef meat, cut into thin strips
- 1 zucchini, roughly cubed
- 2 tablespoons coconut aminos
- 2 garlic cloves, minced
- ¼ cup cilantro, chopped
- 2 tablespoons avocado oil

Directions:
1. Heat up a pan that fits your air fryer with the oil over medium heat, add the meat and brown for 5 minutes. Add the rest of the ingredients, toss, put the pan in the fryer and cook at 380 degrees F for 20 minutes. Divide everything into bowls and serve.

309.Easy Beef Medallions With Parsley And Peppers

Servings: 4
Cooking Time: 30 Minutes
Ingredients:
- 2 tablespoons olive oil
- 2 small bunch parsley, roughly chopped
- 1 ½ pounds beef medallions
- 3 bell peppers, seeded and sliced
- 2 sprigs thyme
- 1 sprig rosemary
- Umami dust seasoning, to taste
- Salt and ground black pepper, to taste

Directions:
1. Firstly, arrange the vegetables on the bottom of the air fry Air Fryer basket; add seasonings and drizzle with olive oil. Roast for 8 minutes and pause the machine.
2. Now, place beef medallions on top of the vegetables.
3. Roast for 18 minutes longer at 375 degrees, stirring once halfway through. To serve, sprinkle with umami dust seasoning and enjoy!

310.Garlic-cumin'n Orange Juice Marinated Steak

Servings:4
Cooking Time: 60 Minutes
Ingredients:
- ¼ cup orange juice
- 1 teaspoon ground cumin
- 2 pounds skirt steak, trimmed from excess fat
- 2 tablespoons lime juice
- 2 tablespoons olive oil
- 4 cloves of garlic, minced
- Salt and pepper to taste

Directions:
1. Place all ingredients in a mixing bowl and allow to marinate in the fridge for at least 2 hours
2. Preheat the air fryer to 390 °F.
3. Place the grill pan accessory in the air fryer.
4. Grill for 15 minutes per batch and flip the beef every 8 minutes for even grilling.
5. Meanwhile, pour the marinade on a saucepan and allow to simmer for 10 minutes or until the sauce thickens.

6. Slice the beef and pour over the sauce.

311.Ribeye Steak With Classis Garlic Mayonnaise

Servings: 3
Cooking Time: 20 Minutes
Ingredients:
- 1 ½ pounds ribeye, bone-in
- 1 tablespoon butter, room temperature
- Salt, to taste
- 1/2 teaspoon crushed black pepper
- 1/2 teaspoon dried dill
- 1/2 teaspoon cayenne pepper
- 1/2 teaspoon garlic powder
- 1/2 teaspoon onion powder
- 1 teaspoon ground coriander
- 3 tablespoons mayonnaise
- 1 teaspoon garlic, minced

Directions:
1. Start by preheating your Air Fryer to 400 degrees F.
2. Pat dry the ribeye and rub it with softened butter on all sides. Sprinkle with seasonings and transfer to the cooking basket.
3. Cook in the preheated Air Fryer for 15 minutes, flipping them halfway through the cooking time.
4. In the meantime, simply mix the mayonnaise with garlic and place in the refrigerator until ready to serve. Bon appétit!

312.Pork With Buttery Broccoli

Servings: 4
Cooking Time: 30 Minutes
Ingredients:
- 1 ½ pounds blade steaks skinless, boneless
- Kosher salt and ground black pepper, to taste
- 2 garlic cloves, crushed
- 2 tablespoons coconut aminos
- 1 tablespoon oyster sauce
- 2 tablespoon lemon juice
- 1 pound broccoli, broken into florets
- 2 tablespoons butter, melted
- 1 teaspoon dried dill weed
- 2 tablespoons sunflower seeds, lightly toasted

Directions:
1. Start by preheating your Air Fryer to 385 degrees F. Spritz the bottom and sides of the cooking basket with cooking spray.
2. Now, season the pork with salt and black pepper. Add the garlic, coconut aminos, oyster sauce, and lemon juice.
3. Cook for 20 minutes; turning over halfway through the cooking time.
4. Toss the broccoli with the melted butter and dill. Add the broccoli to the cooking

basket and cook at 400 degrees F for 6 minutes, shaking the basket periodically.
5. Serve the warm pork with broccoli and garnish with sunflower seeds. Bon appétit!

313.Air Fried Roast Beef

Servings:8
Cooking Time: 2 Hours
Ingredients:
- 1 large onion, quartered
- 1 tablespoon fresh rosemary
- 1 tablespoon fresh thyme
- 2 tablespoons Worcestershire sauce
- 3 cups beef broth
- 3 pounds bone-in beef roast
- 4 tablespoons olive oil
- Salt and pepper to taste

Directions:
1. Preheat the air fryer for 5 minutes.
2. Place all ingredients in a baking dish that will fit in the air fryer.
3. Place the dish in the air fryer and cook for 2 hours at 325 °F.

314.Beef Cheeseburgers

Servings:2
Cooking Time:12 Minutes
Ingredients:
- ½ pound ground beef
- 2 tablespoons fresh cilantro, minced
- 2 slices cheddar cheese
- 2 salad leaves
- 2 dinner rolls, cut into half
- 1 garlic clove, minced
- Salt and black pepper, to taste

Directions:
1. Preheat the Air fryer to 390 °F and grease an Air fryer basket.
2. Mix the beef, garlic, cilantro, salt, and black pepper in a bowl.
3. Make 2 equal-sized patties from the beef mixture and arrange in the Air fryer basket.
4. Cook for about 11 minutes and top each patty with 1 cheese slice.
5. Cook for about 1 more minute and dish out in a platter.
6. Place dinner rolls in a serving platter and arrange salad leaf between each dinner roll.
7. Top with 1 patty and immediately serve.

315.Herbed Beef Roast

Servings:5
Cooking Time:45 Minutes
Ingredients:
- 2 pounds beef roast
- 1 tablespoon olive oil
- 1 teaspoon dried rosemary, crushed
- 1 teaspoon dried thyme, crushed
- Salt, to taste

Directions:
1. Preheat the Air fryer to 360 °F and grease an Air fryer basket.
2. Rub the roast generously with herb mixture and coat with olive oil.
3. Arrange the roast in the Air fryer basket and cook for about 45 minutes.
4. Dish out the roast and cover with foil for about 10 minutes.
5. Cut into desired size slices and serve.

316.Smoky Flavored Pork Ribs

Servings:6
Cooking Time:13 Minutes
Ingredients:
- 1¾ pound pork ribs
- ¼ cup honey, divided
- ¾ cup BBQ sauce
- 2 tablespoons tomato ketchup
- 1 tablespoon Worcestershire sauce
- 1 tablespoon soy sauce
- ½ teaspoon garlic powder
- Freshly ground white pepper, to taste

Directions:
1. Preheat the Air fryer to 355 °F and grease an Air fryer basket.
2. Mix 3 tablespoons of honey and remaining ingredients in a large bowl except the ribs.
3. Coat the pork ribs with marinade generously and cover to refrigerate for about 30 minutes.
4. Transfer the ribs into the Air fryer basket and cook for about 13 minutes.
5. Coat with remaining honey and serve hot.

317.Marinated Beef

Servings: 4
Cooking Time: 35 Minutes
Ingredients:
- 2 tablespoons olive oil
- 3 garlic cloves, minced
- Salt and black pepper to the taste
- 4 medium beef steaks
- 1 cup balsamic vinegar

Directions:
1. In a bowl, mix steaks with the rest of the ingredients, and toss. Transfer the steaks to your air fryer's basket and cook at 390 degrees F for 35 minutes, flipping them halfway. Divide between plates and serve with a side salad.

318.Beef And Veggie Spring Rolls

Servings:8
Cooking Time:14 Minutes
Ingredients:
- 2-ounce Asian rice noodles, soaked in warm water, drained and cut into small lengths
- 7-ounce ground beef
- 1 small onion, chopped
- 1 cup fresh mixed vegetables
- 1 packet spring roll skins
- 2 tablespoons olive oil
- Salt and black pepper, to taste

Directions:
1. Preheat the Air fryer to 350 °F and grease an Air fryer basket.
2. Heat olive oil in a pan and add the onion and garlic.
3. Sauté for about 5 minutes and stir in the beef.
4. Cook for about 5 minutes and add vegetables and soy sauce.
5. Cook for about 7 minutes and stir in the noodles.
6. Place the spring rolls skin onto a smooth surface and put the filling mixture diagonally in it.
7. Fold in both sides to seal properly and brush with oil.
8. Arrange the rolls in batches in the Air fryer basket and cook for about 14 minutes, tossing in between.
9. Cook for about 15 minutes, flipping once in between and dish out in a platter.

319.Chili Tomato Pork

Servings: 3
Cooking Time: 15 Minutes
Ingredients:
- 12 oz pork tenderloin
- 1 tablespoon grain mustard
- 1 tablespoon swerve
- 1 tablespoon keto tomato sauce
- 1 teaspoon chili pepper, grinded
- ¼ teaspoon garlic powder
- 1 tablespoon olive oil

Directions:
1. In the mixing bowl mix up grain mustard, swerve, tomato sauce, chili pepper, garlic powder, and olive oil. Rub the pork tenderloin with mustard mixture generously and leave for 5-10 minutes to marinate. Meanwhile, preheat the air fryer to 370F. Put the marinated pork tenderloin in the air fryer baking pan. Then insert the baking pan in the preheated air fryer and cook the meat for 15 minutes. Cool the cooked meat to the room temperature and slice it into the servings.

320.Leg Of Lamb With Brussels Sprout

Servings:6
Cooking Time:1 Hour 30 Minutes
Ingredients:
- 2¼ pounds leg of lamb
- 1 tablespoon fresh rosemary, minced
- 1 tablespoon fresh lemon thyme

- 1½ pounds Brussels sprouts, trimmed
- 3 tablespoons olive oil, divided
- 1 garlic clove, minced
- Salt and ground black pepper, as required
- 2 tablespoons honey

Directions:
1. Preheat the Air fryer to 300 °F and grease an Air fryer basket.
2. Make slits in the leg of lamb with a sharp knife.
3. Mix 2 tablespoons of oil, herbs, garlic, salt, and black pepper in a bowl.
4. Coat the leg of lamb with oil mixture generously and arrange in the Air fryer basket.
5. Cook for about 75 minutes and set the Air fryer to 390 °F.
6. Coat the Brussels sprout evenly with the remaining oil and honey and arrange them in the Air fryer basket with leg of lamb.
7. Cook for about 15 minutes and dish out to serve warm.

321.Almond Meatloaf

Servings: 4
Cooking Time: 25 Minutes
Ingredients:
- 1 pound beef meat, ground
- 3 tablespoons almond meal
- Cooking spray
- 1 egg, whisked
- Salt and black pepper to the taste
- 1 tablespoon parsley, chopped
- 1 tablespoon oregano, chopped
- 2 spring onions, chopped

Directions:
1. In a bowl, mix all the ingredients except the cooking spray, stir well and put in a loaf pan that fits the air fryer. Put the pan in the fryer and cook at 390 degrees F for 25 minutes. Slice and serve hot.

322.Bavarian Beef Schnitzel

Servings: 2
Cooking Time: 13 Minutes
Ingredients:
- 2 medium-sized eggs
- 1 teaspoon cayenne pepper, or more to taste
- 1/4 cup coconut flour
- 1/4 cup parmesan cheese
- 1/3 freshly ground black pepper, or more to taste
- Wedges of 1 fresh lemon, to serve
- 2 beef schnitzels
- 1 teaspoon fine sea salt
- 1 ½ tablespoons canola oil

Directions:

1. Season beef schnitzel with salt, cayenne pepper, and ground black pepper.
2. In a mixing dish, whisk the oil with coconut flour and parmesan cheese. In another bowl, whisk the eggs until pale and frothy.
3. Firstly, coat beef schnitzels with the whisked eggs; then, coat it with the parmesan mixture.
4. Air-fry for 10 minutes at 355 degrees F. Serve warm, garnished with lemon wedges and enjoy!

323.Bbq Skirt Steak

Servings: 5
Cooking Time: 20 Minutes + Marinating Time
Ingredients:
- 2 pounds skirt steak
- 2 tablespoons tomato paste
- 1 tablespoon olive oil
- 1 tablespoon coconut aminos
- 1/4 cup rice vinegar
- 1 tablespoon fish sauce
- Sea salt, to taste
- 1/2 teaspoon dried dill
- 1/2 teaspoon dried rosemary
- 1/4 teaspoon black pepper, freshly cracked

Directions:
1. Place all ingredients in a large ceramic dish; let it marinate for 3 hours in your refrigerator.
2. Coat the sides and bottom of the Air Fryer with cooking spray.
3. Add your steak to the cooking basket; reserve the marinade. Cook the skirt steak in the preheated Air Fryer at 400 degrees F for 12 minutes, turning over a couple of times, basting with the reserved marinade.
4. Bon appétit!

324.Keto-approved Cheeseburger Bake

Servings:4
Cooking Time: 35 Minutes
Ingredients:
- 1 clove garlic, minced
- 1/2 cup heavy whipping cream
- 1/2-pound bacon, cut into small pieces
- 1/4 teaspoon onion powder
- 1/4 teaspoon salt
- 1/8 teaspoon ground black pepper
- 1-pound ground beef
- 4 eggs
- 6-ounce shredded Cheddar cheese, divided

Directions:
1. Lightly grease baking pan of air fryer with cooking spray. Add beef, onion powder, and garlic. For 10 minutes, cook on 360°F. stirring and crumbling halfway through cooking time.

2. Discard excess fat and evenly spread ground beef on bottom of pan. Top with evenly spread bacon slices. Sprinkle half of the cheese on top.
3. In a bowl, whisk well pepper, salt, heavy cream, and eggs. Pour over bacon.
4. Sprinkle remaining cheese on top of eggs.
5. Cover pan with foil and cook for 15 minutes.
6. Uncover and cook for another 10 minutes until tops are browned and eggs are set.
7. Serve and enjoy.

325.Roast Beef With Buttered Garlic-celery

Servings:8
Cooking Time: 1 Hour
Ingredients:
- 1 bulb of garlic, peeled and crushed
- 1 tablespoon butter
- 2 medium onions, chopped
- 2 pounds topside of beef
- 2 sticks of celery, sliced
- 3 tablespoons olive oil
- A bunch of fresh herbs of your choice
- Salt and pepper to taste

Directions:
1. Preheat the air fryer for 5 minutes.
2. In a baking dish that will fit in the air fryer, place all the ingredients and give a good stir.
3. Place the dish in the air fryer and bake for 1 hour at 350 °F.

326.Beef Patties And Mushroom Sauce Recipe

Servings: 6
Cooking Time:35 Minutes
Ingredients:
- 2 lbs. beef; ground
- 1/2 tsp. garlic powder
- 1 tbsp. soy sauce
- 1/4 cup beef stock
- 3/4 cup flour
- 1 tbsp. parsley; chopped
- 1 tbsp. onion flakes
- Salt and black pepper to the taste
- For the sauce:
- 1 cup yellow onion; chopped.
- 1/2 tsp. soy sauce
- 1/4 cup sour cream
- 1/2 cup beef stock
- 2 cups mushrooms; sliced
- 2 tbsp. bacon fat
- 2 tbsp. butter
- Salt and black pepper to the taste

Directions:
1. In a bowl; mix beef with salt, pepper, garlic powder, 1 tbsp. soy sauce, 1/4 cup beef stock, flour, parsley and onion flakes; stir

well, shape 6 patties, place them in your air fryer and cook at 350 °F, for 14 minutes.
2. Meanwhile; heat up a pan with the butter and the bacon fat over medium heat, add mushrooms; stir and cook for 4 minutes.
3. Add onions; stir and cook for 4 minutes more.
4. Add 1/2 tsp. soy sauce, sour cream and 1/2 cup stock; stir well, bring to a simmer and take off heat. Divide beef patties on plates and serve with mushroom sauce on top.

327.Classic Keto Cheeseburgers

Servings: 4
Cooking Time: 15 Minutes
Ingredients:
- 1 ½ pounds ground chuck
- 1 envelope onion soup mix
- Kosher salt and freshly ground black pepper, to taste
- 1 teaspoon paprika
- 4 slices Monterey-Jack cheese

Directions:
1. In a mixing dish, thoroughly combine ground chuck, onion soup mix, salt, black pepper, and paprika.
2. Then, set your Air Fryer to cook at 385 degrees F. Shape the mixture into 4 patties. Air-fry them for 10 minutes.
3. Next step, place the slices of cheese on the top of the warm burgers. Air-fry for one minute more.
4. Serve with mustard and pickled salad of choice. Bon appétit!

328.Coriander, Mustard 'n Cumin Rubbed Flank Steak

Servings:3
Cooking Time: 45 Minutes
Ingredients:
- ½ teaspoon coriander
- ½ teaspoon ground cumin
- 1 ½ pounds flank steak
- 1 tablespoon chili powder
- 1 tablespoon paprika
- 1 teaspoon garlic powder
- 1 teaspoon mustard powder
- 2 tablespoons sugar
- 2 teaspoons black pepper
- 2 teaspoons salt

Directions:
1. Preheat the air fryer to 390 °F.
2. Place the grill pan accessory in the air fryer.
3. In a small bowl, combine all the spices and rub all over the flank steak.
4. Place on the grill and cook for 15 minutes per batch.
5. Make sure to flip the meat every 8 minutes for even grilling.

329.Top Round Roast With Mustard-rosemary-thyme Blend

Servings:10
Cooking Time: 1 Hour
Ingredients:
- 1 teaspoon dry mustard
- 2 teaspoons dried rosemary
- 3 tablespoons olive oil
- 4 pounds beef top round roast
- 4 teaspoons dried oregano
- 4 teaspoons dried thyme
- Salt and pepper to taste

Directions:
1. Preheat the air fryer for 5 minutes.
2. Place all ingredients in a baking dish that will fit in the air fryer.
3. Place the dish in the air fryer and cook for 1 hour at 325 °F.

330.Sweet Pork Belly

Servings: 6
Cooking Time: 55 Minutes
Ingredients:
- 1-pound pork belly
- 1 teaspoon Splenda
- 1 teaspoon salt
- 1 teaspoon white pepper
- 1 teaspoon butter, softened
- ½ teaspoon onion powder

Directions:
1. Sprinkle the pork belly with salt, white pepper, and onion powder. Then preheat the air fryer to 385F. Put the pork belly in the air fryer and cook it for 45 minutes. Then turn the pork belly on another side and spread it with butter. After this, top the pork belly with Splenda and cook it at 400F for 10 minutes.

331.Crispy Roast Garlic-salt Pork

Servings:4
Cooking Time: 45 Minutes
Ingredients:
- 1 teaspoon Chinese five spice powder
- 1 teaspoon white pepper
- 2 pounds pork belly
- 2 teaspoons garlic salt

Directions:
1. Preheat the air fryer to 390 °F.
2. Mix all the spices in a bowl to create the dry rub.
3. Score the skin of the pork belly with a knife and season the entire pork with the spice rub.
4. Place in the air fryer basket and cook for 40 to 45 minutes until the skin is crispy.
5. Chop before serving.

332.Champagne-vinegar Marinated Skirt Steak

Servings:2
Cooking Time: 40 Minutes
Ingredients:
- ¼ cup Dijon mustard
- 1 tablespoon rosemary leaves
- 1-pound skirt steak, trimmed
- 2 tablespoons champagne vinegar
- Salt and pepper to taste

Directions:
1. Place all ingredients in a Ziploc bag and marinate in the fridge for 2 hours.
2. Preheat the air fryer to 390 °F.
3. Place the grill pan accessory in the air fryer.
4. Grill the skirt steak for 20 minutes per batch.
5. Flip the beef halfway through the cooking time.

333.Beefy'n Cheesy Spanish Rice Casserole

Servings:3
Cooking Time: 50 Minutes
Ingredients:
- 2 tablespoons chopped green bell pepper
- 1 tablespoon chopped fresh cilantro
- 1/2-pound lean ground beef
- 1/2 cup water
- 1/2 teaspoon salt
- 1/2 teaspoon brown sugar
- 1/2 pinch ground black pepper
- 1/3 cup uncooked long grain rice
- 1/4 cup finely chopped onion
- 1/4 cup chile sauce
- 1/4 teaspoon ground cumin
- 1/4 teaspoon Worcestershire sauce
- 1/4 cup shredded Cheddar cheese
- 1/2 (14.5 ounce) can canned tomatoes

Directions:
1. Lightly grease baking pan of air fryer with cooking spray. Add ground beef. For 10 minutes, cook on 360°F. Halfway through cooking time, stir and crumble beef. Discard excess fat,
2. Stir in pepper, Worcestershire sauce, cumin, brown sugar, salt, chile sauce, rice, water, tomatoes, green bell pepper, and onion. Mix well. Cover pan with foil and cook for 25 minutes. Stirring occasionally.
3. Give it one last good stir, press down firmly and sprinkle cheese on top.
4. Cook uncovered for 15 minutes at 390°F until tops are lightly browned.
5. Serve and enjoy with chopped cilantro.

334.Ham Rolls

Servings:4

Cooking Time:15 Minutes
Ingredients:
- 12-ounce refrigerated pizza crust, rolled into ¼ inch thickness
- 1/3 pound cooked ham, sliced
- ¾ cup Mozzarella cheese, shredded
- 3 cups Colby cheese, shredded
- 3-ounce roasted red bell peppers
- 1 tablespoon olive oil

Directions:
1. Preheat the Air fryer to 360 °F and grease an Air fryer basket.
2. Arrange the ham, cheeses and roasted peppers over one side of dough and fold to seal.
3. Brush the dough evenly with olive oil and cook for about 15 minutes, flipping twice in between.
4. Dish out in a platter and serve warm.

335.Hungarian Beef Goulash

Servings: 4
Cooking Time: 1 Hour 10 Minutes
Ingredients:
- Sea salt and cracked black pepper, to taste
- 1 teaspoon Hungarian paprika
- 1 ½ pounds beef chuck roast, boneless, cut into bite-sized cubes
- 2 teaspoons sunflower oil
- 1 medium-sized leek, chopped
- 2 garlic cloves, minced
- 2 bay leaves
- 1 teaspoon caraway seeds.
- 2 cups roasted vegetable broth
- 1 ripe tomato, pureed
- 2 tablespoons red wine
- 2 bell peppers, chopped
- 1 celery stalk, peeled and diced

Directions:
1. Add the salt, black pepper, Hungarian paprika, and beef to a resealable bag; shake to coat well.
2. Heat the oil in a Dutch oven over medium-high flame; sauté the leeks, garlic, bay leaves, and caraway seeds about 4 minutes or until fragrant. Transfer to a lightly greased baking pan.
3. Then, brown the beef, stirring occasionally, working in batches. Add to the baking pan.
4. Add the vegetable broth, tomato, and red wine. Lower the pan onto the Air Fryer basket. Bake at 325 degrees F for 40 minutes.
5. Add the bell peppers and celery. Cook an additional 20 minutes. Serve immediately and enjoy!

336.Spiced Hot Ribs

Servings: 4

Cooking Time: 35 Minutes
Ingredients:
- 1-pound pork baby back ribs
- ½ teaspoon fennel seeds
- ½ teaspoon ground cumin
- ½ teaspoon ground coriander
- ½ teaspoon smoked paprika
- ½ teaspoon garlic powder
- ½ teaspoon onion powder
- ¼ teaspoon ground nutmeg
- 1 teaspoon cayenne pepper
- 1 teaspoon dried oregano
- 1 tablespoon coconut oil, melted
- 4 tablespoons apple cider vinegar

Directions:
1. In the mixing bowl mix up fennel seeds, cumin, coriander, smoked paprika, garlic powder, onion powder, ground nutmeg, cayenne pepper, and dried oregano. Then rub the pork baby back ribs with spice mixture well and sprinkle with apple cider vinegar. Then brush the ribs with coconut oil and leave for 15 minutes to marinate. Then preheat the air fryer to 355F. Put the pork baby back ribs in the air fryer and cook them for 35 minutes. Flip the ribs on another side after 15 minutes of cooking.

337.Perfect Thai Meatballs

Servings:4
Cooking Time:20 Minutes
Ingredients:
- 1 pound ground beef
- 1 teaspoon red Thai curry paste
- 1/2 lime, rind and juice
- 1 teaspoon Chinese spice
- 2 teaspoons lemongrass, finely chopped
- 1 tablespoon sesame oil

Directions:
1. Thoroughly combine all ingredients in a mixing dish.
2. Shape into 24 meatballs and place them into the Air Fryer cooking basket. Cook at 380 degrees F for 10 minutes; pause the machine and cook for a further 5 minutes, or until cooked through.
3. Serve accompanied by the dipping sauce. Bon appétit!

338.Garlic Pork And Ginger Sauce

Servings: 4
Cooking Time: 35 Minutes
Ingredients:
- 1 pound pork tenderloin, cut into strips
- 1 garlic clove, minced
- A pinch of salt and black pepper
- 1 tablespoon ginger, grated
- 3 tablespoons coconut aminos
- 2 tablespoons coconut oil, melted

Directions:
1. Heat up a pan that fits the air fryer with the oil over medium-high heat, add the meat and brown for 3 minutes. Add the rest of the ingredients, cook for 2 minutes more, put the pan in the fryer and cook at 380 degrees F for 30 minutes Divide between plates and serve with a side salad.

339.Easy Cheeseburger Meatballs

Servings: 3
Cooking Time: 15 Minutes
Ingredients:
- 1 pound ground pork
- 1 tablespoon coconut aminos
- 1 teaspoon garlic, minced
- 2 tablespoons spring onions, finely chopped
- 1/2 cup pork rinds
- 1/2 cup parmesan cheese, preferably freshly grated

Directions:
1. Combine the ground pork, coconut aminos, garlic, and spring onions in a mixing dish. Mix until everything is well incorporated.
2. Form the mixture into small meatballs.
3. In a shallow bowl, mix the pork rinds and grated parmesan cheese. Roll the meatballs over the parmesan mixture.
4. Cook at 380 degrees F for 3 minutes; shake the basket and cook an additional 4 minutes or until meatballs are browned on all sides. Bon appétit!

340.Pork Shoulder With Pineapple Sauce

Servings:3
Cooking Time: 24 Minutes
Ingredients:
- For Pork:
- 10½ ounces pork shoulder, cut into bite-sized pieces
- 2 pinches of Maggi seasoning
- 1 teaspoon light soy sauce
- Dash of sesame oil
- 1 egg
- ¼ cup plain flour
- For Sauce:
- 1 teaspoon olive oil
- 1 medium onion, sliced
- 1 tablespoon garlic, minced
- 1 large pineapple slice, cubed
- 1 medium tomato, chopped
- 2 tablespoons tomato sauce
- 2 tablespoons oyster sauce
- 1 tablespoon Worcestershire sauce
- 1 teaspoon sugar
- 1 tablespoon water
- ½ tablespoon corn flour

Directions:

1. For pork: in a large bowl, mix together the Maggi seasoning, soy sauce, and sesame oil.
2. Add the pork cubes and generously mix with the mixture.
3. Refrigerate to marinate for about 4-6 hours.
4. In a shallow dish, beat the egg.
5. In another dish, place the plain flour.
6. Dip the cubed pork in beaten egg and then, coat evenly with the flour.
7. Set the temperature of air fryer to 248 degrees F. Grease an air fryer basket.
8. Arrange pork cubes into the prepared air fryer basket in a single layer.
9. Air fry for about 20 minutes.
10. Meanwhile, for the sauce: in a skillet, heat oil over medium heat and sauté the onion and garlic for about 1 minute.
11. Add the pineapple, and tomato and cook for about 1 minute.
12. Add the tomato sauce, oyster sauce, Worcestershire sauce, and sugar and stir to combine.
13. Meanwhile, in a bowl, mix together the water and corn flour.
14. Add the corn flour mixture into the sauce, stirring continuously.
15. Cook until the sauce is thicken enough, stirring continuously.
16. Remove pork cubes from air fryer and add into the sauce.
17. Cook for about 1-2 minutes or until coated completely.
18. Remove from the heat and serve hot.

341.Chinese Style Pork Meatballs

Servings:3
Cooking Time:20 Minutes
Ingredients:
- 1 egg, beaten
- 6-ounce ground pork
- ¼ cup cornstarch
- 1 teaspoon oyster sauce
- ½ tablespoon light soy sauce
- ½ teaspoon sesame oil
- ¼ teaspoon five spice powder
- ½ tablespoon olive oil
- ¼ teaspoon brown sugar

Directions:
1. Preheat the Air fryer to 390 °F and grease an Air fryer basket.
2. Mix all the ingredients in a bowl except cornstarch and oil until well combined.
3. Shape the mixture into equal-sized balls and place the cornstarch in a shallow dish.
4. Roll the meatballs evenly into cornstarch mixture and arrange in the Air fryer basket.
5. Cook for about 10 minutes and dish out to serve warm.

342.Beef And Plums Mix

Servings: 6
Cooking Time: 40 Minutes
Ingredients:
- 1½ pounds beef stew meat, cubed
- 3 tablespoons honey
- 2 tablespoons olive oil
- 9 ounces plums, pitted and halved
- 8 ounces beef stock
- 2 yellow onions, chopped
- 2 garlic cloves, minced
- Salt and black pepper to tastes
- 1 teaspoon turmeric powder
- 1 teaspoon ginger powder
- 1 teaspoon cinnamon powder

Directions:
1. In a pan that fits your air fryer, heat up the oil over medium heat.
2. Add the beef, stir, and brown for 2 minutes.
3. Add the honey, onions, garlic, salt, pepper, turmeric, ginger, and cinnamon; toss, and cook for 2-3 minutes more.
4. Add the plums and the stock; toss again.
5. Place the pan in the fryer and cook at 380 degrees for 30 minutes.
6. Divide everything into bowls and serve.

343.Salted Corned Beef With Onions

Servings:12
Cooking Time: 50 Minutes
Ingredients:
- 1 large onion, chopped
- 2 tablespoons Dijon mustard
- 3 pounds corned beef brisket, cut into chunks
- 4 cups water
- Salt and pepper to taste

Directions:
1. Preheat the air fryer for 5 minutes
2. Place all ingredients in a baking dish that will fit in the air fryer.
3. Cook for 50 minutes at 400 °F.

344.Spicy Bacon-pork Pops

Servings: 6
Cooking Time: 30 Minutes + Marinating Time
Ingredients:
- 1 cup cream of celery soup
- 1 (13.5-ounce) can coconut milk, unsweetened
- 2 tablespoons tamari sauce
- 1 teaspoon yellow mustard
- Salt and freshly ground white pepper, to taste
- 1/2 teaspoon cayenne pepper
- 1/2 teaspoon chili powder
- 1 teaspoon curry powder
- 2 pounds pork tenderloin, cut into bite-sized cubes
- 4 ounces bacon, cut into pieces
- 12 bamboo skewers, soaked in water

Directions:
1. In a large pot, bring the cream of the celery soup, coconut milk, tamari sauce, mustard, salt, white pepper, cayenne pepper, chili powder, and curry powder to a boil.
2. Then, reduce the heat to simmer; cook until the sauce is heated through, about 13 minutes.
3. Add the pork, gently stir, and place in your refrigerator for 2 hours.
4. Thread the pork onto the skewers, alternating the cubes of meat with the pieces of bacon.
5. Preheat your Air Fryer to 370 degrees F. Cook for 15 minutes, turning over a couple of times. Bon appétit!

345.Lamb Sausages

Servings: 4
Cooking Time: 10 Minutes
Ingredients:
- 4 sausage links
- 12 oz ground lamb
- 1 teaspoon minced garlic
- ½ teaspoon onion powder
- 1 teaspoon dried parsley
- ½ teaspoon salt
- 1 teaspoon ghee
- ½ teaspoon ground ginger
- 1 tablespoon sesame oil

Directions:
1. In the mixing bowl mix up ground lamb, minced garlic, onion powder, dried parsley, salt, and ground ginger. Then fill the sausage links with the ground lamb mixture. Secure the ends of the sausages. Brush the air fryer basket with sesame oil from inside and put the sausages. Then sprinkle the sausages with ghee. Cook the lamb sausages for 10 minutes at 400F. Flip them on another side after 5 minutes of cooking.

346.Pork Rolls

Servings:4
Cooking Time:15 Minutes
Ingredients:
- 1 scallion, chopped
- ¼ cup sun-dried tomatoes, finely chopped
- 2 tablespoons fresh parsley, chopped
- 4 (6-ounces) pork cutlets, pounded slightly
- Salt and black pepper, as required
- 2 teaspoons paprika
- ½ tablespoon olive oil

Directions:

1. Preheat the Air fryer to 390 °F and grease an Air fryer basket.
2. Mix the scallion, tomatoes, parsley, salt, and black pepper in a bowl.
3. Spread the tomato mixture over each pork cutlet and roll each cutlet, securing with cocktail sticks
4. Coat the outer part of rolls with paprika, salt and black pepper and drizzle with olive oil.
5. Arrange the pork rolls in the Air fryer basket and cook for about 15 minutes.
6. Dish out onto serving plates and serve hot.

347.Grilled Steak On Tomato-olive Salad

Servings:5
Cooking Time: 50 Minutes
Ingredients:
- ¼ cup extra virgin olive oil
- ¼ teaspoon cayenne pepper
- ½ cup green olives, pitted and sliced
- 1 cup red onion, chopped
- 1 tablespoon oil
- 1 teaspoon paprika
- 2 ½ pound flank
- 2 pounds cherry tomatoes, halved
- 2 tablespoons Sherry vinegar
- Salt and pepper to taste

Directions:
1. Preheat the air fryer to 390 °F.
2. Place the grill pan accessory in the air fryer.
3. Season the steak with salt, pepper, paprika, and cayenne pepper. Brush with oil
4. Place on the grill pan and cook for 45 to 50 minutes.
5. Meanwhile, prepare the salad by mixing the remaining ingredients.
6. Serve the beef with salad.

348.Burger Patties

Servings: 6
Cooking Time: 15 Minutes
Ingredients:
- 1 lb. ground beef
- 6 cheddar cheese slices
- Pepper and salt to taste

Directions:
1. Pre-heat the Air Fryer to 350°F.
2. Sprinkle the salt and pepper on the ground beef.
3. Shape six equal portions of the ground beef into patties and put each one in the Air Fryer basket.
4. Air fry the patties for 10 minutes.
5. Top the patties with the cheese slices and air fry for one more minute.
6. Serve the patties on top of dinner rolls.

349.Ranch Ribs

Servings: 4
Cooking Time: 40 Minutes
Ingredients:
- 12 oz pork ribs, boneless
- 1 tablespoon ranch dressing
- 1 teaspoon keto tomato sauce
- 1 teaspoon apple cider vinegar
- 1 teaspoon Splenda
- 1 teaspoon avocado oil
- ½ teaspoon ground black pepper
- ½ teaspoon salt

Directions:
1. In the mixing bowl mix up ranch dressing, tomato sauce, apple cider vinegar Splenda, avocado oil, ground black pepper, and salt. Then brush the pork ribs with the ranch dressing mix well and leave for 15 minutes to marinate. Meanwhile, preheat the air fryer to 350F. Arrange the pork ribs in the air fryer basket and cook them for 40 minutes. Flip the ribs on another side during cooking to avoid burning.

350.Grilled Beef With Grated Daikon Radish

Servings:2
Cooking Time: 40 Minutes
Ingredients:
- ¼ cup grated daikon radish
- ½ cup rice wine vinegar
- ½ cup soy sauce
- 1 tablespoon olive oil
- 2 strip steaks
- Salt and pepper to taste

Directions:
1. Preheat the air fryer to 390 °F.
2. Place the grill pan accessory in the air fryer.
3. Season the steak with salt and pepper.
4. Brush with oil.
5. Grill for 20 minutes per piece and make sure to flip the beef halfway through the cooking time
6. Prepare the dipping sauce by combining the soy sauce and vinegar.
7. Serve the steak with the sauce and daikon radish.

351.Top Loin Beef Strips With Blue Cheese

Servings:4
Cooking Time: 50 Minutes
Ingredients:
- 1 tablespoon pine nuts, toasted
- 2 pounds crumbled blue cheese
- 2 tablespoons butter, softened
- 2 tablespoons cream cheese
- 4 boneless beef top loin steaks
- Salt and pepper to taste

Directions:

1. Preheat the air fryer to 390 °F.
2. Place the grill pan accessory in the air fryer.
3. Season the beef with salt and pepper. Brush all sides with butter.
4. Grill for 25 minutes per batch making sure to flip halfway through the cooking time.
5. Slice the beef and serve with blue cheese, cream cheese and pine nuts.

352.Pineapple-teriyaki Beef Skewer

Servings:6
Cooking Time: 12 Minutes
Ingredients:

- 2 tablespoons pineapple juice (optional)
- 2 tablespoons water
- 1 tablespoon vegetable oil
- 1/4 cup and 2 tablespoons light brown sugar
- 1/4 cup soy sauce
- 1-pound boneless round steak, cut into 1/4-inch slices
- 3/4 large garlic cloves, chopped

Directions:

1. In a resealable bag, mix all Ingredients thoroughly except for beef. Then add beef, remove excess air, and seal. Place in ref and marinate for at least a day.
2. Thread beef into skewers and place on skewer rack in air fryer. If needed, cook in batches.
3. For 6 minutes, cook on 390°F.
4. Serve and enjoy.

353.Vegetables & Beef Cubes

Servings: 4
Cooking Time: 20 Minutes + Marinating Time
Ingredients:

- 1 lb. top round steak, cut into cubes
- 2 tbsp. olive oil
- 1 tbsp. apple cider vinegar
- 1 tsp. fine sea salt
- ½ tsp. ground black pepper
- 1 tsp. shallot powder
- ¾ tsp. smoked cayenne pepper
- ½ tsp. garlic powder
- ¼ tsp. ground cumin
- ¼ lb. broccoli, cut into florets
- ¼ lb. mushrooms, sliced
- 1 tsp. dried basil
- 1 tsp. celery seeds

Directions:

1. Massage the olive oil, vinegar, salt, black pepper, shallot powder, cayenne pepper, garlic powder, and cumin into the cubed steak, ensuring to coat each piece evenly.
2. Allow to marinate for a minimum of 3 hours.

3. Put the beef cubes in the Air Fryer cooking basket and allow to cook at 365°F for 12 minutes.
4. When the steak is cooked through, place it in a bowl.
5. Wipe the grease from the cooking basket and pour in the vegetables. Season them with basil and celery seeds.
6. Cook at 400°F for 5 to 6 minutes. When the vegetables are hot, serve them with the steak.

354.Beefy Bell Pepper'n Egg Scramble

Servings:4
Cooking Time: 30 Minutes
Ingredients:

- 1 green bell pepper, seeded and chopped
- 1 onion, chopped
- 1-pound ground beef
- 3 cloves of garlic, minced
- 3 tablespoons olive oil
- 6 cups eggs, beaten
- Salt and pepper to taste

Directions:

1. Preheat the air fryer for 5 minutes with baking pan insert.
2. In a baking dish mix the ground beef, onion, garlic, olive oil, and bell pepper. Season with salt and pepper to taste.
3. Pour in the beaten eggs and give a good stir.
4. Place the dish with the beef and egg mixture in the air fryer.
5. Bake for 30 minutes at 330 °F.

355.Grilled Tri Tip Over Beet Salad

Servings:6
Cooking Time: 45 Minutes
Ingredients:

- 1 bunch arugula, torn
- 1 bunch scallions, chopped
- 1-pound tri-tip, sliced
- 2 tablespoons olive oil
- 3 beets, peeled and sliced thinly
- 3 tablespoons balsamic vinegar
- Salt and pepper to taste

Directions:

1. Preheat the air fryer to 390 °F.
2. Place the grill pan accessory in the air fryer.
3. Season the tri-tip with salt and pepper. Drizzle with oil.
4. Grill for 15 minutes per batch.
5. Meanwhile, prepare the salad by tossing the rest of the ingredients in a salad bowl.
6. Toss in the grilled tri-trip and drizzle with more balsamic vinegar.

356.Grilled Prosciutto Wrapped Fig

Servings:2
Cooking Time: 8 Minutes

Ingredients:
- 2 whole figs, sliced in quarters
- 8 prosciutto slices
- Pepper and salt to taste

Directions:
1. Wrap a prosciutto slice around one slice of fid and then thread into skewer. Repeat process for remaining Ingredients. Place on skewer rack in air fryer.
2. For 8 minutes, cook on 390°F. Halfway through cooking time, turnover skewers.
3. Serve and enjoy.

357. Stuffed Pork Steaks Recipe

Servings: 4
Cooking Time:30 Minutes
Ingredients:
- Zest from 2 limes; grated
- Zest from 1 orange; grated
- Juice from 1 orange
- Juice from 2 limes
- 4 tsp. garlic; minced
- 3/4 cup olive oil
- 1 cup cilantro; chopped.
- 1 cup mint; chopped
- 1 tsp. oregano; dried
- 2 tsp. cumin; ground
- 4 pork loin steaks
- 2 pickles; chopped
- 4 ham slices
- 6 Swiss cheese slices
- 2 tbsp. mustard
- Salt and black pepper to the taste

Directions:
1. In your food processor, mix lime zest and juice with orange zest and juice, garlic, oil, cilantro, mint, oregano, cumin, salt and pepper and blend well.
2. Season steaks with salt and pepper, place them into a bowl, add marinade and toss to coat.
3. Place steaks on a working surface, divide pickles, cheese, mustard and ham on them, roll and secure with toothpicks.
4. Put stuffed pork steaks in your air fryer and cook at 340 °F, for 20 minutes. Divide among plates and serve with a side salad.

358. Beef Rolls

Servings: 2
Cooking Time: 30 Minutes
Ingredients:
- 2 lb. beef flank steak
- 3 tsp. pesto
- 1 tsp. black pepper
- 6 slices of provolone cheese
- 3 oz. roasted red bell peppers
- ¾ cup baby spinach
- 1 tsp. sea salt

Directions:
1. Spoon equal amounts of the pesto onto each flank steak and spread it across evenly.
2. Place the cheese, roasted red peppers and spinach on top of the meat, about three-quarters of the way down.
3. Roll the steak up, holding it in place with toothpicks. Sprinkle on the sea salt and pepper.
4. Place inside the Air Fryer and cook for 14 minutes at 400°F, turning halfway through the cooking time.
5. Allow the beef to rest for 10 minutes before slicing up and serving.

359. Rich Meatloaf With Mustard And Peppers

Servings: 5
Cooking Time: 35 Minutes
Ingredients:
- 1 pound beef, ground
- 1/2 pound veal, ground
- 1 egg
- 4 tablespoons vegetable juice
- 1/2 cup pork rinds
- 2 bell peppers, chopped
- 1 onion, chopped
- 2 garlic cloves, minced
- 2 tablespoons tomato paste
- 2 tablespoons soy sauce
- 1 (1-ounce) package ranch dressing mix
- Sea salt, to taste
- 1/2 teaspoon ground black pepper, to taste
- 7 ounces tomato puree
- 1 tablespoon Dijon mustard

Directions:
1. Start by preheating your Air Fryer to 330 degrees F.
2. In a mixing bowl, thoroughly combine the ground beef, veal, egg, vegetable juice, pork rinds, bell peppers, onion, garlic, tomato paste, soy sauce, ranch dressing mix, salt, and ground black pepper.
3. Mix until everything is well incorporated and press into a lightly greased meatloaf pan.
4. Cook approximately 25 minutes in the preheated Air Fryer. Whisk the tomato puree with the mustard and spread the topping over the top of your meatloaf.
5. Continue to cook 2 minutes more. Let it stand on a cooling rack for 6 minutes before slicing and serving. Enjoy!

360. Italian Sausage & Tomato Egg Bake

Servings:1
Cooking Time: 16 Minutes
Ingredients:
- ½ Italian sausage, sliced into ¼-inch thick

- 1 tablespoon olive oil
- 3 eggs
- 4 cherry tomatoes (in half)
- Chopped parsley
- Grano Padano cheese (or parmesan)
- Salt/Pepper

Directions:
1. Lightly grease baking pan of air fryer with cooking spray.
2. Add Italian sausage and cook for 5 minutes at 360°F.
3. Add olive oil and cherry tomatoes. Cook for another 6 minutes.
4. Meanwhile, whisk well eggs, parsley, cheese, salt, and pepper in a bowl.
5. Remove basket and toss the mixture a bit. Pour eggs over mixture.
6. Cook for another 5 minutes.
7. Serve and enjoy.

361.Pork Roulade

Servings: 2
Cooking Time: 17 Minutes
Ingredients:
- 2 pork chops
- 1 teaspoon German mustard
- 1 teaspoon scallions, diced
- 1 pickled cucumber, diced
- 1 teaspoon almond butter
- ½ teaspoon ground black pepper
- 1 teaspoon olive oil

Directions:
1. Beat the pork chops gently with the help of the kitchen hammer and place them o the chopping board overlap. Then rub the meat with ground black pepper and German mustard. Top it with scallions, diced pickled cucumber, and almond butter. Roll the meat into the roulade and secure it with the kitchen thread. Then sprinkle the roulade with olive oil. Preheat the air fryer to 390F. Put the roulade in the air fryer and cook it for 17 minutes. Slice the cooked roulade.

362.Favorite Beef Stroganoff

Servings: 4
Cooking Time: 20 Minutes + Marinating Time
Ingredients:
- 1 ¼ pounds beef sirloin steak, cut into small-sized strips
- 1/4 cup balsamic vinegar
- 1 tablespoon brown mustard
- 1 tablespoon butter
- 1 cup beef broth
- 1 cup leek, chopped
- 2 cloves garlic, crushed
- 1 teaspoon cayenne pepper
- Sea salt flakes and crushed red pepper, to taste

- 1 cup sour cream
- 2 ½ tablespoons tomato paste

Directions:
1. Place the beef along with the balsamic vinegar and the mustard in a mixing dish; cover and marinate in your refrigerator for about 1 hour.
2. Butter the inside of a baking dish and put the beef into the dish.
3. Add the broth, leeks and garlic. Cook at 380 degrees for 8 minutes. Pause the machine and add the cayenne pepper, salt, red pepper, sour cream and tomato paste; cook for additional 7 minutes.
4. Bon appétit!

363.Hanger Steak In Mole Rub

Servings:2
Cooking Time: 60 Minutes
Ingredients:
- 1 tablespoon ground black pepper
- 2 hanger steaks
- 2 tablespoons coriander seeds
- 2 tablespoons ground coffee
- 2 tablespoons olive oil
- 2 tablespoons salt
- 4 teaspoons unsweetened cocoa powder
- 4 teaspoons brown sugar

Directions:
1. Preheat the air fryer to 390 °F.
2. Place the grill pan accessory in the air fryer.
3. In a bowl, make the spice rub by combining the coriander seeds, ground coffee, salt, brown sugar, cocoa powder, and black pepper.
4. Rub the spice mixture on the steaks and brush with oil.
5. Grill for 30 minutes and make sure to flip the meat every 10 minutes for even grilling and cook in batches.

364.Bacon Wrapped Filet Mignon

Servings:2
Cooking Time:15 Minutes
Ingredients:
- 2 bacon slices
- 2 (6-ounces) filet mignon steaks
- Salt and black pepper, to taste
- 1 teaspoon avocado oil

Directions:
1. Preheat the Air fryer to 375 °F and grease an Air fryer basket.
2. Wrap each mignon steak with 1 bacon slice and secure with a toothpick.
3. Season the steak generously with salt and black pepper and coat with avocado oil.
4. Arrange the steaks in the Air fryer basket and cook for about 15 minutes, flipping once in between.

5. Dish out the steaks and cut into desired size slices to serve.

365.Chinese-style Pork Shoulder

Servings: 3
Cooking Time: 25 Minutes + Marinating Time
Ingredients:
- 2 tablespoons coconut aminos
- 2 tablespoons Shaoxing wine
- 2 garlic cloves, minced
- 1 teaspoon fresh ginger, minced
- 1 tablespoon cilantro stems and leaves, finely chopped
- 1 pound boneless pork shoulder
- 2 tablespoons sesame oil

Directions:
1. In a large-sized ceramic dish, thoroughly combine the coconut aminos, Shaoxing wine, garlic, ginger, and cilantro; add the pork shoulder and allow it to marinate for 2 hours in the refrigerator.
2. Then, grease the cooking basket with sesame oil. Place the pork shoulder in the cooking basket; reserve the marinade.
3. Cook in the preheated Air Fryer at 395 degrees F for 14 to 17 minutes, flipping and basting with the marinade halfway through. Let it rest for 5 to 6 minutes before slicing and serving.
4. While the pork is roasting, cook the marinade in a preheated skillet over medium heat; cook until it has thickened.
5. Brush the pork shoulder with the sauce and enjoy!

366.Flavorsome Pork Chops With Peanut Sauce

Servings:4

Cooking Time:12 Minutes
Ingredients:
- 1 pound pork chops, cubed into 1-inch size
- 1 shallot, chopped finely
- ¾ cup ground peanuts
- ¾ cup coconut milk
- For Pork:
- 1 teaspoon fresh ginger, minced
- 1 garlic clove, minced
- 2 tablespoon soy sauce
- 1 tablespoon olive oil
- 1 teaspoon hot pepper sauce
- For Peanut Sauce:
- 1 tablespoon olive oil
- 1 garlic clove, minced
- 1 teaspoon ground coriander
- 1 tablespoon olive oil
- 1 teaspoon hot pepper sauce

Directions:
1. Preheat the Air fryer to 390 °F and grease an Air fryer basket.
2. For Pork:
3. Mix all the ingredients in a bowl and keep aside for about 30 minutes.
4. Arrange the chops in the Air fryer basket and cook for about 12 minutes, flipping once in between.
5. For Peanut Sauce:
6. Heat olive oil in a pan on medium heat and add shallot and garlic.
7. Sauté for about 3 minutes and stir in coriander.
8. Sauté for about 1 minute and add rest of the ingredients.
9. Cook for about 5 minutes and pour over the pork chops to serve.

FISH & SEAFOOD RECIPES

367.Italian Sardinas Fritas

Servings: 4
Cooking Time: 1 Hour 15 Minutes
Ingredients:
- 1 ½ pounds sardines, cleaned and rinsed
- Salt and ground black pepper, to savor
- 1 tablespoon Italian seasoning mix
- 1 tablespoon lemon juice
- 1 tablespoon soy sauce
- 2 tablespoons olive oil

Directions:
1. Firstly, pat the sardines dry with a kitchen towel. Add salt, black pepper, Italian seasoning mix, lemon juice, soy sauce, and olive oil; marinate them for 30 minutes.
2. Air-fry the sardines at 350 degrees F for approximately 5 minutes. Increase the temperature to 385 degrees F and air-fry them for further 7 to 8 minutes.
3. Then, place the sardines in a nice serving platter. Bon appétit!

368.Easy Lobster Tail With Salted Butetr

Servings:4
Cooking Time: 6 Minutes
Ingredients:
- 2 tablespoons melted butter
- 4 lobster tails
- Salt and pepper to taste

Directions:
1. Preheat the air fryer to 390 °F.
2. Place the grill pan accessory.
3. Cut the lobster through the tail section using a pair of kitchen scissors.
4. Brush the lobster tails with melted butter and season with salt and pepper to taste.
5. Place on the grill pan and cook for 6 minutes.

369.Chili Red Snapper

Servings: 4
Cooking Time: 15 Minutes
Ingredients:
- 4 red snapper fillets, boneless
- A pinch of salt and black pepper
- 2 garlic cloves, minced
- 2 tablespoons coconut aminos
- 2 tablespoons lime juice
- 1 tablespoon hot chili paste
- 2 tablespoons olive oil

Directions:
1. In a bowl, mix all the ingredients except the fish and whisk well. Rub the fish with this mix, place it in your air fryer's basket and cook at 380 degrees F for 15 minutes. Serve with a side salad.

370.Shrimp With Veggie

Servings: 4
Cooking Time: 20 Minutes
Ingredients:
- 50 small shrimp
- 1 tbsp Cajun seasoning
- 1 bag of frozen mix vegetables
- 1 tbsp olive oil

Directions:
1. Line air fryer basket with aluminum foil.
2. Add all ingredients into the large mixing bowl and toss well.
3. Transfer shrimp and vegetable mixture into the air fryer basket and cook at 350 F for 10 minutes.
4. Toss well and cook for 10 minutes more.
5. Serve and enjoy.

371.Cajun Spiced Lemon-shrimp Kebabs

Servings:2
Cooking Time: 10 Minutes
Ingredients:
- 1 tsp cayenne
- 1 tsp garlic powder
- 1 tsp kosher salt
- 1 tsp onion powder
- 1 tsp oregano
- 1 tsp paprika
- 12 pcs XL shrimp
- 2 lemons, sliced thinly crosswise
- 2 tbsp olive oil

Directions:
1. In a bowl, mix all Ingredients except for sliced lemons. Marinate for 10 minutes.
2. Thread 3 shrimps per steel skewer.
3. Place in skewer rack.
4. Cook for 5 minutes at 390°F.
5. Serve and enjoy with freshly squeezed lemon.

372.Fijan Coconut Fish

Servings: 2
Cooking Time: 20 Minutes + Marinating Time
Ingredients:
- 1 cup coconut milk
- 2 tablespoons lime juice
- 2 tablespoons Shoyu sauce
- Salt and white pepper, to taste
- 1 teaspoon turmeric powder
- 1/2 teaspoon ginger powder
- 1/2 Thai Bird's Eye chili, seeded and finely chopped
- 1 pound tilapia
- 2 tablespoons olive oil

Directions:

1. In a mixing bowl, thoroughly combine the coconut milk with the lime juice, Shoyu sauce, salt, pepper, turmeric, ginger, and chili pepper. Add tilapia and let it marinate for 1 hour.
2. Brush the Air Fryer basket with olive oil. Discard the marinade and place the tilapia fillets in the Air Fryer basket.
3. Cook the tilapia in the preheated Air Fryer at 400 degrees F for 6 minutes; turn them over and cook for 6 minutes more. Work in batches.
4. Serve with some extra lime wedges if desired. Enjoy!

373.Classic Coconut Shrimp

Servings: 4
Cooking Time: 25 Minutes
Ingredients:
- 1/3 teaspoon paprika
- 3 egg whites
- 1/3 cup unsweetened coconut, shredded
- 1 teaspoon salt
- 12 large shrimps, peeled and de-veined
- 1/2 cup flaxseed meal
- Lime slices, for garnish
- A pinch of ground allspice
- Grated zest of 1/2 small-sized lime

Directions:
1. Set up a dredging station with three mixing bowls. Dump the flaxseed meal into the first bowl. Beat the eggs whites in another bowl.
2. In the third bowl, combine the coconut, lime zest, allspice, salt and paprika. Set the Air Fryer to cook at 395 degrees F.
3. Dredge your shrimps in the flaxseed mixture; then, coat them with egg whites on all sides; lastly, press them into the coconut mixture. Make sure to coat well.
4. Spritz each shrimp on all sides with cooking oil. Air-fry for 7 to 8 minutes, working in two batches.
5. Turn the temperature to 335 degrees F. Air-fry an additional 3 minutes. Serve with lime slices on a nice serving platter. Bon appétit!

374.Lime, Oil 'n Leeks On Grilled Swordfish

Servings:4
Cooking Time: 20 Minutes
Ingredients:
- 2 tablespoons olive oil
- 3 tablespoons lime juice
- 4 medium leeks, cut into an inch long
- 4 swordfish steaks
- Salt and pepper to taste

Directions:
1. Preheat the air fryer to 390 °F.
2. Place the grill pan accessory in the air fryer.
3. Season the swordfish with salt, pepper and lime juice.
4. Brush the fish with olive oil
5. Place fish fillets on grill pan and top with leeks.
6. Grill for 20 minutes.

375.Parsley Shrimp

Servings: 4
Cooking Time: 12 Minutes
Ingredients:
- 1 pound shrimp, peeled and deveined
- 1 teaspoon cumin, ground
- 2 tablespoons parsley, chopped
- 2 tablespoons olive oil
- A pinch of salt and black pepper
- 4 garlic cloves, minced
- 1 tablespoon lime juice

Directions:
1. In a pan that fits your air fryer, mix all the ingredients, toss, put the pan in your air fryer and cook at 370 degrees F and cook for 12 minutes, shaking the fryer halfway. Divide into bowls and serve.

376.Crispy Prawn In Bacon Wraps

Servings:4
Cooking Time: 30 Minutes
Ingredients:
- 8 jumbo prawns, peeled and deveined
- Lemon Wedges for garnishing

Directions:
1. Wrap each prawn from head to tail with each bacon slice overlapping to keep the bacon in place. Secure the end of the bacon with a toothpick. It's ok not to cover the ends of the cheese with bacon. Refrigerate for 15 minutes.
2. Preheat air fryer to 400 F. Arrange the bacon-wrapped prawns on the fryer's basket, cook for 7 minutes or until the bacon is crispy. Transfer prawns to a paper towel to cool. Remove the toothpicks and serve the bacon-wrapped prawns with lemon wedges and a side of steamed green vegetables.

377.Air Fried Scallops

Servings: 2
Cooking Time: 10 Minutes
Ingredients:
- 8 sea scallops
- 1 tbsp tomato paste
- 3/4 cup heavy whipping cream
- 12 oz frozen spinach, thawed and drained
- 1 tsp garlic, minced
- 1 tbsp fresh basil, chopped
- 1/2 tsp pepper
- 1/2 tsp salt

Directions:

1. Spray air fryer baking pan with cooking spray.
2. Add spinach in the pan.
3. Spray scallops with cooking spray and season with pepper and salt.
4. Place scallops on top of spinach.
5. In a small bowl, mix together garlic, basil, tomato paste, whipping cream, pepper, and salt and pour over scallops and spinach.
6. Place pan into the air fryer and cook at 350 F for 10 minutes.
7. Serve and enjoy.

378.Creamy Cod Strips

Servings: 4
Cooking Time: 6 Minutes
Ingredients:

- 10 oz cod fillet
- 1 tablespoon coconut flour
- 1 tablespoon coconut flakes
- 1 egg, beaten
- 1 teaspoon ground turmeric
- ½ teaspoon salt
- 1 tablespoon heavy cream
- 1 teaspoon olive oil

Directions:

1. Cut the cod fillets on the fries strips. After this, in the mixing bowl mix up coconut flour, coconut flakes, ground turmeric, and salt. In the other bowl mix up egg and heavy cream. After this, dip the fish fries in the egg mixture. Then coat them in the coconut flour mixture. Repeat the steps again. Preheat the air fryer to 400F. Put the fish fries in the air fryer basket in one layer and sprinkle them with olive oil. Cook the meal for 3 minutes. Then flip the fish fries on another side and cook for 3 minutes more.

379.Black Cod

Servings: 2
Cooking Time: 30 Minutes
Ingredients:

- 2 [6- to 8-oz.] fillets of black cod or sablefish
- Salt
- Freshly ground black pepper
- Olive oil
- 1 cup grapes, halved
- 1 small bulb fennel, sliced ¼-inch thick
- ½ cup pecans
- 3 cups shredded kale
- 2 tsp. white balsamic vinegar or white wine vinegar
- 2 tbsp. extra-virgin olive oil

Directions:

1. 1 Pre-heat the Air Fryer to 400°F.

2. 2 Sprinkle the cod fillets with salt and pepper and drizzle some olive oil over the fish.
3. 3 Put the fish skin-side-down in the Air Fryer basket. Air fry for 10 minutes. Transfer the fillets to a side plate and loosely cover with aluminum foil.
4. 4 Coat the grapes, fennel and pecans with a drizzle of olive oil and sprinkle on some salt and pepper.
5. 5 Place the grapes, fennel and pecans in the fryer's basket and cook for 5 minutes at 400°F. Shake the basket occasionally throughout the cooking time.
6. 6 Put the grapes, fennel and pecans in a bowl and add the kale.
7. 7 Pour over the balsamic vinegar and olive oil and sprinkle with salt and pepper as desired. Serve with the fish and enjoy.

380.Creamy Salmon

Servings: 2
Cooking Time: 20 Minutes
Ingredients:

- ¾ lb. salmon, cut into 6 pieces
- ¼ cup yogurt
- 1 tbsp. olive oil
- 1 tbsp. dill, chopped
- 3 tbsp. sour cream
- Salt to taste

Directions:

1. 1 Sprinkle some salt on the salmon.
2. 2 Put the salmon slices in the Air Fryer basket and add in a drizzle of olive oil.
3. 3 Air fry the salmon at 285°F for 10 minutes.
4. 4 In the meantime, combine together the cream, dill, yogurt, and salt.
5. 5 Plate up the salmon and pour the creamy sauce over it. Serve hot.

381.Buttered Crab Shells

Servings:4
Cooking Time:10 Minutes
Ingredients:

- 4 soft crab shells, cleaned
- 1 cup buttermilk
- 3 eggs
- 2 cups panko breadcrumb
- 2 tablespoons butter, melted
- 2 teaspoons seafood seasoningo
- 1½ teaspoons lemon zest, grated

Directions:

1. Preheat the Air fryer to 375 °F and grease an Air fryer basket.
2. Place the buttermilk in a shallow bowl and whisk the eggs in a second bowl.
3. Mix the breadcrumbs, seafood seasoning, and lemon zest in a third bowl.

4. Soak the crab shells into the buttermilk for about 10 minutes, then dip in the eggs.
5. Dredge in the breadcrumb mixture and arrange the crab shells into the Air fryer basket.
6. Cook for about 10 minutes and dish out in a platter.
7. Drizzle melted butter over the crab shells and immediately serve.

382.Tuna Stuffed Avocado

Servings: 2
Cooking Time: 12 Minutes
Ingredients:
- 1 avocado, pitted, halved
- ½ pound smoked tuna, boneless and shredded
- 1 egg, beaten
- ½ teaspoon salt
- ½ teaspoon chili powder
- ½ teaspoon ground nutmeg
- 1 teaspoon dried parsley
- Cooking spray

Directions:
1. Scoop ½ part of the avocado meat from the avocado to get the avocado boats. Use the scooper for this step. After this, in the mixing bowl mix up tuna and egg. Shred the mixture with the help of the fork. Add salt, chili powder, ground nutmeg, and dried parsley. Stir the tuna mixture until homogenous. Add the scooped avocado meat and mix up the mixture well. Fill the avocado boats with tuna mixture. Preheat the air fryer to 385F. Arrange the tuna boats in the air fryer basket and cook them for 12 minutes.

383.Quick-fix Seafood Breakfast

Servings: 2
Cooking Time: 30 Minutes
Ingredients:
- 1 tablespoon olive oil
- 2 garlic cloves, minced
- 1 small yellow onion, chopped
- 1/4 pound tilapia pieces
- 1/4 pound rockfish pieces
- 1/2 teaspoon dried basil
- Salt and white pepper, to taste
- 4 eggs, lightly beaten
- 1 tablespoon dry sherry
- 4 tablespoons cheese, shredded

Directions:
1. Start by preheating your Air Fryer to 350 degrees F; add the olive oil to a baking pan. Once hot, cook the garlic and onion for 2 minutes or until fragrant.
2. Add the fish, basil, salt, and pepper. In a mixing dish, thoroughly combine the eggs

with sherry and cheese. Pour the mixture into the baking pan.
3. Cook at 360 degrees F approximately 20 minutes. Bon appétit!

384.Cod Cakes(2)

Servings:6
Cooking Time:14 Minutes
Ingredients:
- 1 pound cod fillet
- 1 egg
- 1/3 cup coconut, grated and divided
- 1 scallion, finely chopped
- 2 tablespoons fresh parsley, chopped
- 1 teaspoon fresh lime zest, finely grated
- 1 teaspoon red chili paste
- Salt, as required
- 1 tablespoon fresh lime juice

Directions:
1. Preheat the Air fryer to 375 °F and grease an Air fryer basket.
2. Put the cod fillet, lime zest, egg, chili paste, salt and lime juice in a food processor and pulse until smooth.
3. Transfer the cod mixture into a bowl and add scallion, parsley and 2 tablespoons of coconut.
4. Mix until well combined and make 12 equal-sized round cakes from the mixture.
5. Place the remaining coconut in a shallow bowl and coat the cod cakes with coconut.
6. Arrange cod cakes into the Air fryer basket in 2 batches and cook for about 7 minutes.
7. Dish out in 2 serving plates and serve warm.

385.Drunken Skewered Shrimp, Tomatoes 'n Sausages

Servings:6
Cooking Time: 20 Minutes
Ingredients:
- 1/2 teaspoon dried crushed red pepper
- 1/2 teaspoon freshly ground black pepper
- 12 1-inch-long pieces andouille or other fully cooked smoked sausage
- 12 2-layer sections of red onion wedges
- 12 cherry tomatoes
- 12 uncooked extra-large shrimp (13 to 15 per pound), peeled, deveined
- 2 tablespoons chopped fresh thyme
- 3/4 cup olive oil
- 3/4 teaspoon salt
- 4 large garlic cloves, pressed
- 4 teaspoons Sherry wine vinegar
- 5 teaspoons smoked paprika*
- Nonstick vegetable oil spray

Directions:
1. In medium bowl, mix well red pepper, black pepper, salt, wine vinegar, smoked paprika,

thyme, garlic, and oil. Transfer half to a small bowl for dipping.
2. Thread alternately sausage and shrimp in skewers. Place on skewer rack on air fryer and baste with the paprika glaze. Cook in batches.
3. For 10 minutes, cook on 360°F. Halfway through cooking time, baste and turnover skewers.
4. Serve and enjoy with the reserved dip on the side.

386.Parmesan Walnut Salmon

Servings: 4
Cooking Time: 12 Minutes
Ingredients:
- 4 salmon fillets
- 1/4 cup parmesan cheese, grated
- 1/2 cup walnuts
- 1 tsp olive oil
- 1 tbsp lemon rind

Directions:
1. Preheat the air fryer to 370 F.
2. Spray an air fryer baking dish with cooking spray.
3. Place salmon on a baking dish.
4. Add walnuts into the food processor and process until finely ground.
5. Mix ground walnuts with parmesan cheese, oil, and lemon rind. Stir well.
6. Spoon walnut mixture over the salmon and press gently.
7. Place in the air fryer and cook for 12 minutes.
8. Serve and enjoy.

387.Minty Trout And Pine Nuts

Servings: 4
Cooking Time: 16 Minutes
Ingredients:
- 4 rainbow trout
- 1 cup olive oil + 3 tablespoons
- Juice of 1 lemon
- A pinch of salt and black pepper
- 1 cup parsley, chopped
- 3 garlic cloves, minced
- ½ cup mint, chopped
- Zest of 1 lemon
- 1/3 pine nuts
- 1 avocado, peeled, pitted and roughly chopped

Directions:
1. Pat dry the trout, season with salt and pepper and rub with 3 tablespoons oil. Put the fish in your air fryer's basket and cook for 8 minutes on each side. Divide the fish between plates and drizzle half of the lemon juice all over. In a blender, combine the rest of the oil with the remaining lemon juice,

parsley, garlic, mint, lemon zest, pine nuts and the avocado and pulse well. Spread this over the trout and serve.

388.Grilled Shellfish With Vegetables

Servings:8
Cooking Time: 30 Minutes
Ingredients:
- 1 bunch broccolini
- 8 asparagus spears
- 8 small carrots, peeled and sliced
- 4 tomatoes, halved
- 1 red onion, wedged
- 2 tablespoons olive oil
- Salt and pepper to taste
- 16 small oysters, scrubbed
- 16 littleneck clams, scrubbed
- 24 large mussels, scrubbed
- 2 tablespoons lemon juice
- 4 basil sprigs

Directions:
1. Preheat the air fryer at 390 °F.
2. Place the grill pan accessory in the air fryer.
3. Place all vegetables in a bowl and drizzle with oil. Season with salt and pepper then toss to coat the vegetables with the seasoning.
4. Place on the grill pan and grill for 15 minutes or until the edges of the vegetables are charred. Set aside
5. On a large foil, place all the shellfish and season with salt, lemon juice, and basil. Fold the foil and crimp the edges.
6. Place the foil packet on the grill pan and cook for another 15 minutes or until the shellfish have opened.
7. Serve the shellfish with the charred vegetables.

389.Salmon With Shrimp & Pasta

Servings:4
Cooking Time: 18 Minutes
Ingredients:
- 14 ounces pasta (of your choice)
- 4 tablespoons pesto, divided
- 4 (4-ounces) salmon steaks
- 2 tablespoons olive oil
- ½ pound cherry tomatoes, chopped
- 8 large prawns, peeled and deveined
- 2 tablespoons fresh lemon juice
- 2 tablespoons fresh thyme, chopped

Directions:
1. In a large pan of salted boiling water, add the pasta and cook for about 8-10 minutes or until desired doneness.
2. Meanwhile, in the bottom of a baking dish, spread 1 tablespoon of pesto.

3. Place salmon steaks and tomatoes over pesto in a single layer and drizzle evenly with the oil.
4. Now, add the prawns on top in a single layer.
5. Drizzle with lemon juice and sprinkle with thyme.
6. Set the temperature of air fryer to 390 degrees F.
7. Arrange the baking dish in air fryer and air fry for about 8 minutes.
8. Once done, remove the salmon mixture from air fryer.
9. Drain the pasta and transfer into a large bowl.
10. Add the remaining pesto and toss to coat well.
11. Add the pasta evenly onto each serving plate and top with salmon mixture.
12. Serve immediately.

390.Marinated Sardines

Servings: 4
Cooking Time: 1 Hr. 15 Minutes
Ingredients:
- ¾ lb. sardines, cleaned and rinsed
- Salt and ground black pepper, to taste
- 1 tsp. smoked cayenne pepper
- 1 tbsp. lemon juice
- 1 tbsp. soy sauce
- 2 tbsp. olive oil
- For the Potatoes:
- 8 medium Russet potatoes, peeled and quartered
- ½ stick melted butter
- Salt and pepper, to taste
- 1 tsp. granulated garlic

Directions:
1. Dry the sardines with a paper towel.
2. Cover the sardines in the salt, black pepper, cayenne pepper, lemon juice, soy sauce, and olive oil, and leave to marinate for half an hour.
3. Air-fry the sardines at 350°F for roughly 5 minutes.
4. Raise the heat to 385°F and cook for an additional 7 - 8 minutes. Remove the sardines and plate up.
5. Wipe the cooking basket clean and pour in the potatoes, butter, salt, pepper, and garlic.
6. Roast at 390°F for 30 minutes. Serve the vegetables and the sardines together.

391.Peppercorn Cod

Servings: 4
Cooking Time: 15 Minutes
Ingredients:
- 4 cod fillets, boneless
- A pinch of salt and black pepper

- 1 tablespoon thyme, chopped
- ½ teaspoon black peppercorns
- 2 tablespoons olive oil
- 1 fennel, sliced
- 2 garlic cloves, minced
- 1 red bell pepper, chopped
- 2 teaspoons Italian seasoning

Directions:
1. In a bowl, mix the fennel with bell pepper and the other ingredients except the fish fillets and toss. Put this into a pan that fits the air fryer, add the fish on top, introduce the pan in your air fryer and cook at 380 degrees F for 15 minutes. Divide between plates and serve.

392.Double Cheese Fish Casserole

Servings: 4
Cooking Time: 30 Minutes
Ingredients:
- 1 tablespoon avocado oil
- 1 pound hake fillets
- 1 teaspoon garlic powder
- Sea salt and ground white pepper, to taste
- 2 tablespoons shallots, chopped
- 1 bell pepper, seeded and chopped
- 1/2 cup Cottage cheese
- 1/2 cup sour cream
- 1 egg, well whisked
- 1 teaspoon yellow mustard
- 1 tablespoon lime juice
- 1/2 cup Swiss cheese, shredded

Directions:
1. Brush the bottom and sides of a casserole dish with avocado oil. Add the hake fillets to the casserole dish and sprinkle with garlic powder, salt, and pepper.
2. Add the chopped shallots and bell peppers.
3. In a mixing bowl, thoroughly combine the Cottage cheese, sour cream, egg, mustard, and lime juice. Pour the mixture over fish and spread evenly.
4. Cook in the preheated Air Fryer at 370 degrees F for 10 minutes.
5. Top with the Swiss cheese and cook an additional 7 minutes. Let it rest for 10 minutes before slicing and serving. Bon appétit!

393.Kimchi-spiced Salmon

Servings:4
Cooking Time: 15 Minutes
Ingredients:
- 2 tbsp sesame oil
- 2 tbsp mirin
- 2 tbsp ginger puree
- 1 tsp kimchi spice
- 1 tsp sriracha sauce
- 2 pounds salmon fillets

- 1 lime, cut into wedges

Directions:
1. Preheat the Air fryer to 350 F. Grease the air fryer basket with cooking spray. In a bowl, mix together soy sauce, mirin, ginger puree, kimchi spice, and sriracha sauce. Add the salmon fillets and toss to coat. Place in the air fryer basket and drizzle with sesame oil. Cook for 10 minutes, flipping once halfway through. Garnish with lime wedges and serve.

394.Miso Sauce Over Grilled Salmon

Servings:4
Cooking Time: 16 Minutes
Ingredients:
- 1 1/4 pounds skinless salmon fillets, thinly sliced
- 1/4 cup yellow miso paste
- 2 tablespoons mirin (Japanese rice wine)
- 2 teaspoons dashi powder
- 2 teaspoons superfine sugar
- Amaranth leaves (optional), to serve
- Shichimi togarashi, to serve

Directions:
1. In a bowl mix well sugar, mirin, dashi powder, and miso.
2. Thread salmon into skewers. Baste with miso glaze. Place on skewer rack in air fryer. If needed, cook in batches.
3. For 8 minutes, cook on 360°F. Halfway through cooking time, turnover and baste.
4. Serve and enjoy.

395.Sautéed Shrimp

Servings:4
Cooking Time: 10 Minutes
Ingredients:
- 1 tbsp olive oil
- ½ a tbsp old bay seasoning
- ¼ a tbsp cayenne pepper
- ¼ a tbsp smoked paprika
- A pinch of sea salt

Directions:
1. Preheat the air fryer to 380 F, and mix all ingredients in a large bowl. Coat the shrimp with a little bit of oil and spices. Place the shrimp in the air fryer's basket and fry for 6-7 minutes. Serve with rice or salad.

396.Halibut With Thai Lemongrass Marinade

Servings: 2
Cooking Time: 45 Minutes
Ingredients:
- 2 tablespoons tamari sauce
- 2 tablespoons fresh lime juice
- 2 tablespoons olive oil
- 1 teaspoon Thai curry paste

- 1/2 inch lemongrass, finely chopped
- 1 teaspoon basil
- 2 cloves garlic, minced
- 2 tablespoons shallot, minced
- Sea salt and ground black pepper, to taste
- 2 halibut steaks

Directions:
1. Place all ingredients in a ceramic dish; let it marinate for 30 minutes.
2. Place the halibut steaks in the lightly greased cooking basket.
3. Bake in the preheated Air Fryer at 400 degrees F for 9 to 10 minutes, basting with the reserved marinade and flipping them halfway through the cooking time. Bon appétit!

397.Italian Shrimp

Servings: 4
Cooking Time: 12 Minutes
Ingredients:
- 1 pound shrimp, peeled and deveined
- A pinch of salt and black pepper
- 1 tablespoon sesame seeds, toasted
- ½ teaspoon Italian seasoning
- 1 tablespoon olive oil

Directions:
1. In a bowl, mix the shrimp with the rest of the ingredients and toss well. Put the shrimp in the air fryer's basket, cook at 370 degrees F for 12 minutes, divide into bowls and serve,

398.Tuna & Potato Cakes

Servings:4
Cooking Time: 12 Minutes
Ingredients:
- ½ tablespoon olive oil
- 1 onion, chopped
- 1 tablespoon fresh ginger, grated
- 1 green chili, seeded and finely chopped
- 2 (6-ounces) cans tuna, drained
- 1 medium boiled potato, mashed
- 2 tablespoons celery, finely chopped
- Salt, as required
- 1 cup breadcrumbs
- 1 egg

Directions:
1. Heat the olive oil in a frying pan and sauté onions, ginger, and green chili for about 30 seconds.
2. Add the tuna and stir fry for about 2-3 minutes or until all the liquid is absorbed.
3. Remove from heat and transfer the tuna mixture onto a large bowl. Set aside to cool.
4. In the bowl of tuna mixture, mix well mashed potato, celery, and salt.
5. Make 4 equal-sized patties from the mixture.
6. In a shallow bowl, place the breadcrumbs.

7. In another bowl, beat the egg.
8. Coat each patty with breadcrumbs, then dip into egg and finally, again coat with the breadcrumbs.
9. Set the temperature of air fryer to 390 degrees F. Grease an air fryer basket.
10. Arrange tuna cakes into the prepared air fryer basket in a single layer.
11. Air fry for about 2-3 minutes.
12. Flip the side and air fry for about 4-5 minutes.
13. Remove from air fryer and transfer the tuna cakes onto serving plates.
14. Serve warm.

399.Sesame Tuna Steak

Servings: 2
Cooking Time: 12 Minutes
Ingredients:
- 1 tbsp. coconut oil, melted
- 2 x 6-oz. tuna steaks
- ½ tsp. garlic powder
- 2 tsp. black sesame seeds
- 2 tsp. white sesame seeds

Directions:
1. Apply the coconut oil to the tuna steaks with a brunch, then season with garlic powder.
2. Combine the black and white sesame seeds. Embed them in the tuna steaks, covering the fish all over. Place the tuna into your air fryer.
3. Cook for eight minutes at 400°F, turning the fish halfway through.
4. The tuna steaks are ready when they have reached a temperature of 145°F. Serve straightaway.

400.Scallops With Capers Sauce

Servings:2
Cooking Time:6 Minutes
Ingredients:
- 10 (1-ounce) sea scallops, cleaned and patted very dry
- 2 tablespoons fresh parsley, finely chopped
- 2 teaspoons capers, finely chopped
- Salt and ground black pepper, as required
- ¼ cup extra-virgin olive oil
- 1 teaspoon fresh lemon zest, finely grated
- ½ teaspoon garlic, finely chopped

Directions:
1. Preheat the Air fryer to 390 °F and grease an Air fryer basket.
2. Season the scallops evenly with salt and black pepper.
3. Arrange the scallops in the Air fryer basket and cook for about 6 minutes.
4. Mix parsley, capers, olive oil, lemon zest and garlic in a bowl.

5. Dish out the scallops in a platter and top with capers sauce.

401.Lemon Butter Scallops

Servings: 1
Cooking Time: 30 Minutes
Ingredients:
- 1 lemon
- 1 lb. scallops
- ½ cup butter
- ¼ cup parsley, chopped

Directions:
1. Juice the lemon into a Ziploc bag.
2. Wash your scallops, dry them, and season to taste. Put them in the bag with the lemon juice. Refrigerate for an hour.
3. Remove the bag from the refrigerator and leave for about twenty minutes until it returns to room temperature. Transfer the scallops into a foil pan that is small enough to be placed inside the fryer.
4. Pre-heat the fryer at 400°F and put the rack inside.
5. Place the foil pan on the rack and cook for five minutes.
6. In the meantime, melt the butter in a saucepan over a medium heat. Zest the lemon over the saucepan, then add in the chopped parsley. Mix well.
7. Take care when removing the pan from the fryer. Transfer the contents to a plate and drizzle with the lemon-butter mixture. Serve hot.

402.Greek-style Monkfish With Vegetables

Servings: 2
Cooking Time: 20 Minutes
Ingredients:
- 2 teaspoons olive oil
- 1 cup celery, sliced
- 2 bell peppers, sliced
- 1 teaspoon dried thyme
- 1/2 teaspoon dried marjoram
- 1/2 teaspoon dried rosemary
- 2 monkfish fillets
- 1 tablespoon soy sauce
- 2 tablespoons lime juice
- Coarse salt and ground black pepper, to taste
- 1 teaspoon cayenne pepper
- 1/2 cup Kalamata olives, pitted and sliced

Directions:
1. In a nonstick skillet, heat the olive oil for 1 minute. Once hot, sauté the celery and peppers until tender, about 4 minutes. Sprinkle with thyme, marjoram, and rosemary and set aside.
2. Toss the fish fillets with the soy sauce, lime juice, salt, black pepper, and cayenne

pepper. Place the fish fillets in a lightly greased cooking basket and bake at 390 degrees F for 8 minutes.

3. Turn them over, add the olives, and cook an additional 4 minutes. Serve with the sautéed vegetables on the side. Bon appétit!

403. Amazing Salmon Fillets

Servings:2
Cooking Time:7 Minutes
Ingredients:
- 2 (7-ounce) (¾-inch thick) salmon fillets
- 1 tablespoon Italian seasoning
- 1 tablespoon fresh lemon juice

Directions:
1. Preheat the Air fryer to 355 °F and grease an Air fryer grill pan.
2. Rub the salmon evenly with Italian seasoning and transfer into the Air fryer grill pan, skin-side up.
3. Cook for about 7 minutes and squeeze lemon juice on it to serve.

404. Steamed Salmon With Dill Sauce

Servings:2
Cooking Time:11 Minutes
Ingredients:
- 1 cup water
- 2 (6-ounce) salmon fillets
- ½ cup Greek yogurt
- 2 tablespoons fresh dill, chopped and divided
- 2 teaspoons olive oil
- Salt, to taste
- ½ cup sour cream

Directions:
1. Preheat the Air fryer to 285 °F and grease an Air fryer basket.
2. Place water the bottom of the Air fryer pan.
3. Coat salmon with olive oil and season with a pinch of salt.
4. Arrange the salmon in the Air fryer and cook for about 11 minutes.
5. Meanwhile, mix remaining ingredients in a bowl to make dill sauce.
6. Serve the salmon with dill sauce.

405. Coconut Prawns

Servings: 4
Cooking Time: 10 Minutes
Ingredients:
- 12 prawns, cleaned and deveined
- Salt and ground black pepper, to taste
- ½ tsp. cumin powder
- 1 tsp. fresh lemon juice
- 1 medium egg, whisked
- ⅓ cup of beer
- ½ cup flour
- 1 tsp. baking powder

- 1 tbsp. curry powder
- ½ tsp. grated fresh ginger
- 1 cup flaked coconut

Directions:
1. Coat the prawns in the salt, pepper, cumin powder, and lemon juice.
2. In a bowl, combine together the whisked egg, beer, a quarter-cup of the flour, baking powder, curry, and ginger.
3. In a second bowl, put the remaining quarter-cup of flour, and in a third bowl, the flaked coconut.
4. Dredge the prawns in the flour, before coating them in the beer mixture. Finally, coat your prawns in the flaked coconut.
5. Air-fry at 360°F for 5 minutes. Flip them and allow to cook on the other side for another 2 to 3 minutes before serving.

406. Fried Branzino

Servings: 4
Cooking Time:20 Minutes
Ingredients:
- 4 medium branzino fillets; boneless
- 1/2 cup parsley; chopped
- 2 tbsp. olive oil
- A pinch of red pepper flakes; crushed
- Zest from 1 lemon; grated
- Zest from 1 orange; grated
- Juice from 1/2 lemon
- Juice from 1/2 orange
- Salt and black pepper to the taste

Directions:
1. In a large bowl; mix fish fillets with lemon zest, orange zest, lemon juice, orange juice, salt, pepper, oil and pepper flakes; toss really well, transfer fillets to your preheated air fryer at 350 °F and bake for 10 minutes; flipping fillets once. Divide fish on plates, sprinkle with parsley and serve right away.

407. Shrimp And Sausage Gumbo

Servings: 4
Cooking Time: 12 Minutes
Ingredients:
- 10 oz shrimps, peeled
- 5 oz smoked sausages, chopped
- 1 teaspoon olive oil
- 1 teaspoon ground black pepper
- 3 spring onions, diced
- 1 jalapeno pepper, chopped
- ½ cup chicken broth
- 1 teaspoon chili flakes
- ½ teaspoon dried cilantro
- ½ teaspoon salt

Directions:
1. Preheat the air fryer to 400F. In the mixing bowl mix up smoked sausages, ground black pepper, and chili flakes. Put the

smoked sausages in the air fryer and cook them for 4 minutes. Meanwhile, in the mixing bowl mix up onion, jalapeno pepper, and salt. Put the ingredients in the air fryer baking pan and sprinkle with olive oil. After this, remove the sausages from the air fryer. Put the pan with onion in the air fryer and cook it for 2 minutes. After this, add smoked sausages, dried cilantro, and shrimps. Add chicken broth. Stir the ingredients gently and cook the meal for 6 minutes at 400F.

408.Parmesan And Garlic Trout

Servings: 4
Cooking Time: 15 Minutes
Ingredients:
- 2 tablespoons olive oil
- 2 garlic cloves, minced
- ½ cup chicken stock
- Salt and black pepper to the taste
- 4 trout fillets, boneless
- ¾ cup parmesan, grated
- ¼ cup tarragon, chopped

Directions:
1. In a pan that fits your air fryer, mix all the ingredients except the fish and the parmesan and whisk. Add the fish and grease it well with this mix. Sprinkle the parmesan on top, put the pan in the air fryer and cook at 380 degrees F for 15 minutes. Divide everything between plates and serve.

409.Juicy Salmon And Asparagus Parcels

Servings:2
Cooking Time:13 Minutes
Ingredients:
- 2 salmon fillets
- 4 asparagus stalks
- ¼ cup champagne
- Salt and black pepper, to taste
- ¼ cup white sauce
- 1 teaspoon olive oil

Directions:
1. Preheat the Air fryer to 355 °F and grease an Air fryer basket.
2. Mix all the ingredients in a bowl and divide this mixture evenly over 2 foil papers.
3. Arrange the foil papers in the Air fryer basket and cook for about 13 minutes.
4. Dish out in a platter and serve hot.

410.Rockfish With Greek Avocado Cream

Servings: 4
Cooking Time: 15 Minutes + Marinating Time
Ingredients:
- For the Fish Fillets:
- 1 1/2 tablespoons balsamic vinegar
- 1/2 cup vegetable broth

- 1/3 teaspoon shallot powder
- 1 tablespoon soy sauce
- 4 Rockfish fillets
- 1 teaspoon ground black pepper
- 1 ½ tablespoons olive oil
- Fine sea salt, to taste
- 1/3 teaspoon garlic powder
- For the Avocado Cream:
- 2 tablespoons Greek-style yogurt
- 1 clove garlic, peeled and minced
- 1 teaspoon ground black pepper
- 1/2 tablespoon olive oil
- 1/3 cup vegetable broth
- 1 avocado
- 1/2 teaspoon lime juice
- 1/3 teaspoon fine sea salt

Directions:
1. In a bowl, wash and pat the fillets dry using some paper towels. Add all the seasonings. In another bowl, stir in the remaining ingredients for the fish fillets.
2. Add the seasoned fish fillets; cover and let the fillets marinate in your refrigerator at least 3 hours.
3. Then, set your Air Fryer to cook at 325 degrees F. Cook marinated rockfish fillets in the air fryer grill basket for 9 minutes.
4. In the meantime, prepare the avocado sauce by mixing all the ingredients with an immersion blender or regular blender. Serve the rockfish fillets topped with the avocado sauce. Enjoy!

411.Ale-battered Fish With Potato Mash

Servings:4
Cooking Time: 20 Minutes
Ingredients:
- 2 eggs
- 1 cup ale beer
- 1 ½ cups flour
- Salt and black pepper to taste
- 4 white fish fillets
- 2 cups mashed potatoes

Directions:
1. Preheat your Air Fryer to 390 F. Spray the air fryer basket with cooking spray.
2. Beat the eggs in a bowl with ale beer, salt, and black pepper. Pat dry the fish fillets with paper towels and dredge them in the flour; shake off the excess. Dip in the egg mixture and then in the flour again. Spray with cooking spray and add to the cooking basket. Cook for 15 minutes, flipping halfway through. Serve with potato mash and lemon wedges.

412.Cod Fillets With Garlic And Herbs

Servings: 4
Cooking Time: 15 Minutes

Ingredients:

- 4 cod fillets
- 1/4 teaspoon fine sea salt
- 1/4 teaspoon ground black pepper, or more to taste
- 1 teaspoon cayenne pepper
- 1/2 cup non-dairy milk
- 1/2 cup fresh Italian parsley, coarsely chopped
- 1 teaspoon dried basil
- 1/2 teaspoon dried oregano
- 1 Italian pepper, chopped
- 4 garlic cloves, minced

Directions:

1. Coat the inside of a baking dish with a thin layer of vegetable oil.
2. Season the cod fillets with salt, pepper, and cayenne pepper.
3. Next, puree the remaining ingredients in your food processor. Toss the fish fillets with this mixture.
4. Set the Air Fryer to cook at 380 degrees F. Cook for 10 to 12 minutes or until the cod flakes easily. Bon appétit!

413.Spiced Coco-lime Skewered Shrimp

Servings:6
Cooking Time: 12 Minutes
Ingredients:

- 1 lime, zested and juiced
- 1/3 cup chopped fresh cilantro
- 1/3 cup shredded coconut
- 1/4 cup olive oil
- 1/4 cup soy sauce
- 1-pound uncooked medium shrimp, peeled and deveined
- 2 garlic cloves
- 2 jalapeno peppers, seeded

Directions:

1. In food processor, process until smooth the soy sauce, olive oil, coconut oil, cilantro, garlic, lime juice, lime zest, and jalapeno.
2. In a shallow dish, mix well shrimp and processed marinade. Toss well to coat and marinate in the ref for 3 hours.
3. Thread shrimps in skewers. Place on skewer rack in air fryer.
4. For 6 minutes, cook on 360°F. If needed, cook in batches.
5. Serve and enjoy.

414.Coconut Calamari

Servings: 2
Cooking Time: 6 Minutes
Ingredients:

- 6 oz calamari, trimmed
- 2 tablespoons coconut flakes
- 1 egg, beaten
- 1 teaspoon Italian seasonings
- Cooking spray

Directions:

1. Slice the calamari into the rings and sprinkle them with Italian seasonings. Then transfer the calamari rings in the bowl with a beaten egg and stir them gently. After this, sprinkle the calamari rings with coconut flakes and shake well. Preheat the air fryer to 400F. Put the calamari rings in the air fryer basket and spray them with cooking spray. Cook the meal for 3 minutes. Then gently stir the calamari and cook them for 3 minutes more.

415.Fish Cakes With Horseradish Sauce

Servings: 4
Cooking Time: 20 Minutes
Ingredients:

- Halibut Cakes:
- 1 pound halibut
- 2 tablespoons olive oil
- 1/2 teaspoon cayenne pepper
- 1/4 teaspoon black pepper
- Salt, to taste
- 2 tablespoons cilantro, chopped
- 1 shallot, chopped
- 2 garlic cloves, minced
- 1 cup Romano cheese, grated
- 1 egg, whisked
- 1 tablespoon Worcestershire sauce
- Mayo Sauce:
- 1 teaspoon horseradish, grated
- 1/2 cup mayonnaise

Directions:

1. Start by preheating your Air Fryer to 380 degrees F. Spritz the Air Fryer basket with cooking oil.
2. Mix all ingredients for the halibut cakes in a bowl; knead with your hands until everything is well incorporated.
3. Shape the mixture into equally sized patties. Transfer your patties to the Air Fryer basket. Cook the fish patties for 10 minutes, turning them over halfway through.
4. Mix the horseradish and mayonnaise. Serve the halibut cakes with the horseradish mayo. Bon appétit!

416.Leamony-parsley Linguine With Grilled Tuna

Servings:2
Cooking Time: 20 Minutes
Ingredients:

- 1 tablespoon capers, chopped
- 1 tablespoon olive oil
- 12 ounces linguine, cooked according to package Directions:
- 1-pound fresh tuna fillets
- 2 cups parsley leaves, chopped

- Juice from 1 lemon
- Salt and pepper to taste

Directions:
1. Preheat the air fryer to 390 °F.
2. Place the grill pan accessory in the air fryer.
3. Season the tuna with salt and pepper. Brush with oil.
4. Grill for 20 minutes.
5. Once the tuna is cooked, shred using forks and place on top of cooked linguine. Add parsley and capers. Season with salt and pepper and add lemon juice.

417.Black Cod & Plum Sauce

Servings: 2
Cooking Time:25 Minutes
Ingredients:
- 2 medium black cod fillets; skinless and boneless
- 1 red plum; pitted and chopped
- 2 tsp. raw honey
- 1/4 tsp. black peppercorns; crushed
- 1 egg white
- 1/2 cup red quinoa; already cooked
- 2 tsp. whole wheat flour
- 4 tsp. lemon juice
- 1/2 tsp. smoked paprika
- 1 tsp. olive oil
- 2 tsp. parsley
- 1/4 cup water

Directions:
1. In a bowl; mix 1 tsp. lemon juice with egg white, flour and 1/4 tsp. paprika and whisk well.
2. Put quinoa in a bowl and mix it with ⅓ of egg white mix.
3. Put the fish into the bowl with the remaining egg white mix and toss to coat.
4. Dip fish in quinoa mix; coat well and leave aside for 10 minutes.
5. Heat up a pan with 1 tsp. oil over medium heat; add peppercorns, honey and plum; stir, bring to a simmer and cook for 1 minute.
6. Add the rest of the lemon juice, the rest of the paprika and the water; stir well and simmer for 5 minutes.
7. Add parsley; stir, take sauce off heat and leave aside for now.
8. Put fish in your air fryer and cook at 380 °F, for 10 minute. Arrange fish on plates, drizzle plum sauce on top and serve.

418.Thai Shrimp

Servings: 4
Cooking Time: 10 Minutes
Ingredients:
- 1 lb shrimp, peeled and deveined
- 1 tsp sesame seeds, toasted
- 2 garlic cloves, minced

- 2 tbsp soy sauce
- 2 tbsp Thai chili sauce
- 1 tbsp arrowroot powder
- 1 tbsp green onion, sliced
- 1/8 tsp ginger, minced

Directions:
1. Spray air fryer basket with cooking spray.
2. Toss shrimp with arrowroot powder and place into the air fryer basket.
3. Cook shrimp at 350 F for 5 minutes. Shake basket well and cook for 5 minutes more.
4. Meanwhile, in a bowl, mix together soy sauce, ginger, garlic, and chili sauce.
5. Add shrimp to the bowl and toss well.
6. Garnish with green onions and sesame seeds.
7. Serve and enjoy.

419.Seafood Fritters

Servings: 2 – 4
Cooking Time: 50 Minutes
Ingredients:
- 2 cups clam meat
- 1 cup shredded carrot
- ½ cup shredded zucchini
- 1 cup flour, combined with 3/4 cup water to make a batter
- 2 tbsp. olive oil
- ¼ tsp. pepper

Directions:
1. 1 Pre-heat your Air Fryer to 390°F.
2. 2 Combine the clam meat with the olive oil, shredded carrot, pepper and zucchini.
3. 3 Using your hands, shape equal portions of the mixture into balls and roll each ball in the chickpea mixture.
4. 4 Put the balls in the fryer and cook for 30 minutes, ensuring they turn nice and crispy before serving.

420.Crispy Lemon-parsley Fish Cakes

Servings:3
Cooking Time: 20 Minutes
Ingredients:
- ½ cup dried coconut flakes
- 1 cup almond flour
- 1 cup cooked salmon, shredded
- 1 tablespoon chopped parsley
- 1 tablespoon lemon juice
- 2 eggs, beaten
- 3 tablespoons coconut oil
- Salt and pepper to taste

Directions:
1. Mix the salmon, almond flour, eggs, salt, pepper, lemon juice and parsley in a bowl.
2. Form small balls using your hands and dredge in coconut flakes.
3. Brush the surface of the balls with coconut oil.

4. Place in the air fryer basket and cook in a preheated air fryer for 20 minutes at 325 °F.
5. Halfway through the cooking time, give the fryer basket a shake.

421.Butter Crab Muffins

Servings: 2
Cooking Time: 20 Minutes
Ingredients:
- 5 oz crab meat, chopped
- 2 eggs, beaten
- 2 tablespoons almond flour
- ¼ teaspoon baking powder
- ½ teaspoon apple cider vinegar
- ½ teaspoon ground paprika
- 1 tablespoon butter, softened
- Cooking spray

Directions:
1. Grind the chopped crab meat and put it in the bowl. Add eggs, almond flour, baking powder, apple cider vinegar, ground paprika, and butter. Stir the mixture until homogenous. Preheat the air fryer to 365F. Spray the muffin molds with cooking spray. Then pour the crab meat batter in the muffin molds and place them in the preheated air fryer. Cook the crab muffins for 20 minutes or until they are light brown. Cool the cooked muffins to the room temperature and remove from the muffin mold.

422.3-ingredients Catfish

Servings:4
Cooking Time: 23 Minutes
Ingredients:
- 4 (6-ounces) catfish fillets
- ¼ cup seasoned fish fry
- 1 tablespoon olive oil

Directions:
1. Set the temperature of air fryer to 400 degrees F. Grease an air fryer basket.
2. In a bowl, add the catfish fillets and seasoned fish fry. Toss to coat well.
3. Then, drizzle each fillet evenly with oil.
4. Arrange catfish fillets into the prepared air fryer basket in a single layer.
5. Air fry for about 10 minutes.
6. Flip the side and spray with the cooking spray.
7. Air fry for another 10 minutes.
8. Flip one last time and air fry for about 2-3 more minutes.
9. Remove from air fryer and transfer the catfish fillets onto serving plates.
10. Serve hot.

423.Crunchy Topped Fish Bake

Servings: 4

Cooking Time: 20 Minutes
Ingredients:
- 1 tablespoon butter, melted
- 1 medium-sized leek, thinly sliced
- 1 tablespoon chicken stock
- 1 tablespoon dry white wine
- 1 pound tuna
- 1/2 teaspoon red pepper flakes, crushed
- Sea salt and ground black pepper, to taste
- 1/2 teaspoon dried rosemary
- 1/2 teaspoon dried basil
- 1/2 teaspoon dried thyme
- 2 ripe tomatoes, pureed
- 1/4 cup breadcrumbs
- 1/4 cup Parmesan cheese, grated

Directions:
1. Melt 1/2 tablespoon of butter in a sauté pan over medium-high heat. Now, cook the leek and garlic until tender and aromatic. Add the stock and wine to deglaze the pan.
2. Preheat your Air Fryer to 370 degrees F.
3. Grease a casserole dish with the remaining 1/2 tablespoon of melted butter. Place the fish in the casserole dish. Add the seasonings. Top with the sautéed leek mixture.
4. Add the tomato puree. Cook for 10 minutes in the preheated Air Fryer. Top with the breadcrumbs and cheese; cook an additional 7 minutes until the crumbs are golden. Bon appétit!

424.Tilapia With Cheesy Caper Sauce

Servings: 4
Cooking Time: 15 Minutes
Ingredients:
- 4 tilapia fillets
- 1 tablespoon extra-virgin olive oil
- Celery salt, to taste
- Freshly cracked pink peppercorns, to taste
- For the Creamy Caper Sauce:
- 1/2 cup crème fraîche
- 2 tablespoons mayonnaise
- 1/4 cup Cottage cheese, at room temperature
- 1 tablespoon capers, finely chopped

Directions:
1. Toss the tilapia fillets with olive oil, celery salt, and cracked peppercorns until they are well coated.
2. Place the fillets in a single layer at the bottom of the Air Fryer cooking basket. Air-fry at 360 degrees F for about 12 minutes; turn them over once during cooking.
3. Meanwhile, prepare the sauce by mixing the remaining items.
4. Lastly, garnish air-fried tilapia fillets with the sauce and serve immediately!

425.Air Fried Catfish

Servings: 4
Cooking Time: 20 Minutes
Ingredients:
- 4 catfish fillets
- 1 tbsp olive oil
- 1/4 cup fish seasoning
- 1 tbsp fresh parsley, chopped

Directions:
1. Preheat the air fryer to 400 F.
2. Spray air fryer basket with cooking spray.
3. Seasoned fish with seasoning and place into the air fryer basket.
4. Drizzle fish fillets with oil and cook for 10 minutes.
5. Turn fish to another side and cook for 10 minutes more.
6. Garnish with parsley and serve.

426.Buttered Baked Cod With Wine

Servings:2
Cooking Time: 12 Minutes
Ingredients:
- 1 tablespoon butter
- 1 tablespoon butter
- 2 tablespoons dry white wine
- 1/2 pound thick-cut cod loin
- 1-1/2 teaspoons chopped fresh parsley
- 1-1/2 teaspoons chopped green onion
- 1/2 lemon, cut into wedges
- 1/4 sleeve buttery round crackers (such as Ritz®), crushed
- 1/4 lemon, juiced

Directions:
1. In a small bowl, melt butter in microwave. Whisk in crackers.
2. Lightly grease baking pan of air fryer with remaining butter. And melt for 2 minutes at 390°F.
3. In a small bowl whisk well lemon juice, white wine, parsley, and green onion.
4. Coat cod filets in melted butter. Pour dressing. Top with butter-cracker mixture.
5. Cook for 10 minutes at 390°F.
6. Serve and enjoy with a slice of lemon.

427.Lemon Branzino

Servings: 4
Cooking Time: 8 Minutes
Ingredients:
- 1-pound branzino, trimmed, washed
- 1 teaspoon Cajun seasoning
- 1 tablespoon sesame oil
- 1 tablespoon lemon juice
- 1 teaspoon salt

Directions:
1. Rub the branzino with salt and Cajun seasoning carefully. Then sprinkle the fish with the lemon juice and sesame oil. Preheat the air fryer to 380F. Place the fish in the air fryer and cook it for 8 minutes.

428.Cucumber And Spring Onions Salsa

Servings: 4
Cooking Time: 5 Minutes
Ingredients:

- 1 and ½ pounds cucumbers, sliced
- 2 spring onions, chopped
- 2 tomatoes cubed
- 2 red chili peppers, chopped
- 2 tablespoons ginger, grated
- 1 tablespoon balsamic vinegar
- A drizzle of olive oil

Directions:

1. In a pan that fits your air fryer, mix all the ingredients, toss, introduce in the fryer and cook at 340 degrees F for 5 minutes. Divide into bowls and serve cold as an appetizer.

429.Bow Tie Pasta Chips

Servings:6
Cooking Time:10 Minutes
Ingredients:

- 2 cups white bow tie pasta
- 1 tablespoon olive oil
- 1 tablespoon nutritional yeast
- 1½ teaspoons Italian seasoning blend
- ½ teaspoon salt

Directions:

1. Cook the pasta for 1/2 the time called for on the package. Toss the drained pasta
2. with the olive oil or aquafaba, nutritional yeast, Italian seasoning, and salt.
3. Place about half of the mixture in your air fryer basket if yours is small; larger ones may be able to do cook in one batch.
4. Cook on 390°F (200°C) for 5 minutes. Shake the basket and cook 3 to 5 minutesmore or until crunchy.

430.Veggie Cream Stuff Mushrooms

Servings: 12
Cooking Time: 8 Minutes
Ingredients:

- 24 oz mushrooms, cut stems
- 1/2 cup sour cream
- 1 cup cheddar cheese, shredded
- 1 small carrot, diced
- 1/2 bell pepper, diced
- 1/2 onion, diced
- 2 bacon slices, diced

Directions:

1. Chop mushroom stems finely.
2. Spray pan with cooking spray and heat over medium heat.
3. Add chopped mushrooms, bacon, carrot, onion, and bell pepper into the pan and cook until tender.
4. Remove pan from heat. Add cheese and sour cream into the cooked vegetables and stir well.
5. Stuff vegetable mixture into the mushroom cap and place into the air fryer basket.
6. Cook mushrooms at 350 F for 8 minutes.
7. Serve and enjoy.

431.Parmesan Turnip Slices

Servings: 8
Cooking Time: 10 Minutes
Ingredients:

- 1 lb turnip, peel and cut into slices
- 1 tbsp olive oil
- 3 oz parmesan cheese, shredded
- 1 tsp garlic powder
- 1 tsp salt

Directions:

1. Preheat the air fryer to 360 F.
2. Add all ingredients into the mixing bowl and toss to coat.
3. Transfer turnip slices into the air fryer basket and cook for 10 minutes.
4. Serve and enjoy.

432.Vegetable Mix

Servings: 4
Cooking Time: 45 Minutes
Ingredients:

- 3.5 oz. radish
- ½ tsp. parsley
- 3.5 oz. celeriac
- 1 yellow carrot
- 1 orange carrot
- 1 red onion
- 3.5 oz. pumpkin
- 3.5 oz. parsnips
- Salt to taste
- Epaulette pepper to taste
- 1 tbsp. olive oil
- 4 cloves garlic, unpeeled

Directions:

1. Peel and slice up all the vegetables into 2- to 3-cm pieces.
2. Pre-heat your Air Fryer to 390°F.
3. Pour in the oil and allow it to warm before placing the vegetables in the fryer, followed by the garlic, salt and pepper.
4. Roast for 18 – 20 minutes.
5. Top with parsley and serve hot with rice if desired.

433.Coconut Cheese Sticks

Servings:4
Cooking Time: 4 Minutes
Ingredients:

- 1 egg, beaten

- 4 tablespoons coconut flakes
- 1 teaspoon ground paprika
- 6 oz Provolone cheese
- Cooking spray

Directions:
1. Cut the cheese into sticks. Then dip every cheese stick in the beaten egg. After this, mix up coconut flakes and ground paprika. Coat the cheese sticks in the coconut mixture. Preheat the air fryer to 400F. Put the cheese sticks in the air fryer and spray them with cooking spray. Cook the meal for 2 minutes from each side. Cool them well before serving.

434.Party Greek Keftedes

Servings: 6
Cooking Time: 20 Minutes
Ingredients:
- Greek Keftedes:
- 1/2 pound mushrooms, chopped
- 1/2 pound pork sausage, chopped
- 1 teaspoon shallot powder
- 1 teaspoon granulated garlic
- 1 teaspoon dried rosemary
- 1 teaspoon dried basil
- 1 teaspoon dried oregano
- 2 eggs
- 2 tablespoons cornbread crumbs
- Tzatziki Dip:
- 1 Lebanese cucumbers, grated, juice squeezed out
- 1 cup full-fat Greek yogurt
- 1 tablespoon fresh lemon juice
- 1 garlic clove, minced
- 1 tablespoon extra-virgin olive oil
- 1/2 teaspoon salt

Directions:
1. In a mixing bowl, thoroughly combine all ingredients for the Greek keftedes.
2. Shape the meat mixture into bite-sized balls.
3. Cook in the preheated Air Fryer at 380 degrees for 10 minutes, shaking the cooking basket once or twice to ensure even cooking.
4. Meanwhile, make the tzatziki dip by mixing all ingredients. Serve the keftedes with cocktail sticks and tzatziki dip on the side. Enjoy!

435.Basic Salmon Croquettes

Servings:16
Cooking Time:14 Minutes
Ingredients:
- 1 large can red salmon, drained
- 2 eggs, lightly beaten
- 2 tablespoons fresh parsley, chopped
- 1 cup breadcrumbs
- 2 tablespoons milk
- Salt and black pepper, to taste

- 1/3 cup vegetable oil

Directions:
1. Preheat the Air fryer to 390 °F and grease an Air fryer basket.
2. Mash the salmon completely in a bowl and stir in eggs, parsley, breadcrumbs, milk, salt and black pepper.
3. Mix until well combined and make 16 equal-sized croquettes from the mixture.
4. Mix together oil and breadcrumbs in a shallow dish and coat the croquettes in this mixture.
5. Place half of the croquettes in the Air fryer basket and cook for about 7 minutes.
6. Repeat with the remaining croquettes and serve warm.

436.Hillbilly Cheese Surprise

Servings: 6
Cooking Time: 40 Minutes
Ingredients:
- 4 cups broccoli florets
- ¼ cup ranch dressing
- ½ cup sharp cheddar cheese, shredded
- ¼ cup heavy whipping cream
- Kosher salt and pepper to taste

Directions:
1. Preheat your fryer to 375°F/190°C.
2. In a bowl, combine all of the ingredients until the broccoli is well-covered.
3. In a casserole dish, spread out the broccoli mixture.
4. Bake for 30 minutes.
5. Take out of your fryer and mix.
6. If the florets are not tender, bake for another 5 minutes until tender.
7. Serve!

437.Crust-less Meaty Pizza

Servings: 1
Cooking Time: 15 Minutes
Ingredients:
- ½ cup mozzarella cheese, shredded
- 2 slices sugar-free bacon, cooked and crumbled
- ¼ cup ground sausage, cooked
- 7 slices pepperoni
- 1 tbsp. parmesan cheese, grated

Directions:
1. Spread the mozzarella across the bottom of a six-inch cake pan. Throw on the bacon, sausage, and pepperoni, then add a sprinkle of the parmesan cheese on top. Place the pan inside your air fryer.
2. Cook at 400°F for five minutes. The cheese is ready once brown in color and bubbly. Take care when removing the pan from the fryer and serve.

438.Easy And Delicious Pizza Puffs

Servings: 6
Cooking Time: 15 Minutes
Ingredients:
- 6 ounces crescent roll dough
- 1/2 cup mozzarella cheese, shredded
- 3 ounces pepperoni
- 3 ounces mushrooms, chopped
- 1 teaspoon oregano
- 1 teaspoon garlic powder
- 1/4 cup Marina sauce, for dipping

Directions:
1. Unroll the crescent dough. Roll out the dough using a rolling pin; cut into 6 pieces.
2. Place the cheese, pepperoni, and mushrooms in the center of each pizza puff. Sprinkle with oregano and garlic powder.
3. Fold each corner over the filling using wet hands. Press together to cover the filling entirely and seal the edges.
4. Now, spritz the bottom of the Air Fryer basket with cooking oil. Lay the pizza puffs in a single layer in the cooking basket. Work in batches.
5. Bake at 370 degrees F for 5 to 6 minutes or until golden brown. Serve with the marinara sauce for dipping.

439.Coconut Cookies

Servings:8
Cooking Time: 12 Minutes
Ingredients:
- 2¼ ounces caster sugar
- 3½ ounces butter
- 1 small egg
- 1 teaspoon vanilla extract
- 5 ounces self-rising flour
- 1¼ ounces white chocolate, chopped
- 3 tablespoons desiccated coconut

Directions:
1. In a large bowl, add the sugar, and butter and beat until fluffy and light.
2. Add the egg, and vanilla extract and whisk until well combined.
3. Now, add the flour, and chocolate and mix well.
4. In a shallow bowl, place the coconut.
5. With your hands, make small balls from the mixture and roll evenly into the coconut.
6. Place the balls onto an ungreased baking sheet about 1- inch apart and gently, press each ball.
7. Set the temperature of air fryer to 355 degrees F.
8. Place baking sheet into the air fryer basket.
9. Air fry for about 8 minutes and then, another 4 minutes at 320 degrees F.
10. Remove from air fryer and place the baking sheet onto a wire rack to cool for about 5 minutes.
11. Now, invert the cookies onto wire rack to cool completely before serving.
12. Serve.

440.Masala Cashew

Servings: 3
Cooking Time: 20 Minutes
Ingredients:
- ½ lb. cashew nuts
- ½ tsp. garam masala powder
- 1 tsp. coriander powder
- 1 tsp. ghee
- 1 tsp. red chili powder
- ½ tsp. black pepper
- 2 tsp. dry mango powder
- 1 tsp. sea salt

Directions:
1. 1 Put all the ingredients in a large bowl and toss together well.
2. 2 Arrange the cashew nuts in the basket of your Air Fryer.
3. 3 Cook at 250°F for 15 minutes until the nuts are brown and crispy.
4. 4 Let the nuts cool before serving or transferring to an airtight container to be stored for up to 2 weeks.

441.Crab Mushrooms

Servings: 16
Cooking Time: 8 Minutes
Ingredients:
- 16 mushrooms, clean and chop stems
- 1/4 tsp chili powder
- 1/4 tsp onion powder
- 1/4 cup mozzarella cheese, shredded
- 2 oz crab meat, chopped
- 8 oz cream cheese, softened
- 2 tsp garlic, minced
- 1/4 tsp pepper

Directions:
1. In a mixing bowl, mix together stems, chili powder, onion powder, pepper, cheese, crabmeat, cream cheese, and garlic until well combined.
2. Stuff mushrooms with bowl mixture and place into the air fryer basket.
3. Cook mushrooms at 370 F for 8 minutes.
4. Serve and enjoy.

442.Feta Triangles

Servings: 5
Cooking Time: 55 Minutes
Ingredients:
- 1 egg yolk, beaten
- 4 oz. feta cheese
- 2 tbsp. flat-leafed parsley, finely chopped

- 1 scallion, finely chopped
- 2 sheets of frozen filo pastry, defrosted
- 2 tbsp. olive oil ground black pepper to taste

Directions:
1. 1 In a bowl, combine the beaten egg yolk with the feta, parsley and scallion. Sprinkle on some pepper to taste.
2. 2 Slice each sheet of filo dough into three strips.
3. 3 Place a teaspoonful of the feta mixture on each strip of pastry.
4. 4 Pinch the tip of the pastry and fold it up to enclose the filling and create a triangle. Continue folding the strip in zig-zags until the filling is wrapped in a triangle. Repeat with all of the strips of pastry.
5. 5 Pre-heat the Air Fryer to 390°F.
6. 6 Coat the pastry with a light coating of oil and arrange in the cooking basket.
7. 7 Place the basket in the Air Fryer and cook for 3 minutes.
8. 8 Lower the heat to 360°F and cook for a further 2 minutes or until a golden brown color is achieved

443.Paprika Zucchini Bombs With Goat Cheese

Servings: 4
Cooking Time: 20 Minutes
Ingredients:
- 1 cup zucchini, grated, juice squeezed out
- 1 egg
- 1 garlic clove, minced
- 1/2 cup all-purpose flour
- 1/2 cup cornbread crumbs
- 1/2 cup parmesan cheese, grated
- 1/2 cup goat cheese, grated
- Salt and black pepper, to taste
- 1 teaspoon paprika

Directions:
1. Start by preheating your Air Fryer to 330 degrees F. Spritz the cooking basket with nonstick cooking oil.
2. Mix all ingredients until everything is well incorporated. Shape the zucchini mixture into golf sized balls and place them in the cooking basket.
3. Cook in the preheated Air Fryer for 15 to 18 minutes, shaking the basket periodically to ensure even cooking.
4. Garnish with some extra paprika if desired and serve at room temperature. Bon appétit!

444.Coconut Salmon Bites

Servings: 12
Cooking Time: 10 Minutes
Ingredients:
- 2 avocados, peeled, pitted and mashed

- 4 ounces smoked salmon, skinless, boneless and chopped
- 2 tablespoons coconut cream
- 1 teaspoon avocado oil
- 1 teaspoon dill, chopped
- A pinch of salt and black pepper

Directions:
1. In a bowl, mix all the ingredients, stir well and shape medium balls out of this mix. Place them in your air fryer's basket and cook at 350 degrees F for 10 minutes. Serve as an appetizer.

445.Mexican Cheesy Zucchini Bites

Servings: 4
Cooking Time: 25 Minutes
Ingredients:
- 1 large-sized zucchini, thinly sliced
- 1/2 cup flour
- 1/4 cup yellow cornmeal
- 1 egg, whisked
- 1/2 cup tortilla chips, crushed
- 1/2 cup Queso Añejo, grated
- Salt and cracked pepper, to taste

Directions:
1. Pat dry the zucchini slices with a kitchen towel.
2. Mix the remaining ingredients in a shallow bowl; mix until everything is well combined. Dip each zucchini slice in the prepared batter.
3. Cook in the preheated Air Fryer at 400 degrees F for 12 minutes, shaking the basket halfway through the cooking time.
4. Work in batches until the zucchini slices are crispy and golden brown. Enjoy!

446.Bacon Butter

Servings:5
Cooking Time: 2 Minutes
Ingredients:
- ½ cup butter
- 3 oz bacon, chopped

Directions:
1. Preheat the air fryer to 400F and put the bacon inside. Cook it for 8 minutes. Stir the bacon every 2 minutes. Meanwhile, soften the butter in the oven and put it in the butter mold. Add cooked bacon and churn the butter. Refrigerate the butter for 30 minutes.

447.Cocktail Sausage And Veggies On A Stick

Servings: 4
Cooking Time: 25 Minutes
Ingredients:
- 16 cocktail sausages, halved
- 16 pearl onions

- 1 red bell pepper, cut into 1 ½-inch pieces
- 1 green bell pepper, cut into 1 ½-inch pieces
- Salt and cracked black pepper, to taste
- 1/2 cup tomato chili sauce

Directions:
1. Thread the cocktail sausages, pearl onions, and peppers alternately onto skewers. Sprinkle with salt and black pepper.
2. Cook in the preheated Air Fryer at 380 degrees for 15 minutes, turning the skewers over once or twice to ensure even cooking.
3. Serve with the tomato chili sauce on the side. Enjoy!

448.Green Bean Crisps

Servings: 4
Cooking Time: 20 Minutes
Ingredients:
- 1 egg, beaten
- 1/4 cup cornmeal
- 1/4 cup parmesan, grated
- 1 teaspoon sea salt
- 1/2 teaspoon red pepper flakes, crushed
- 1 pound green beans
- 2 tablespoons grapeseed oil

Directions:
1. In a mixing bowl, combine together the egg, cornmeal, parmesan, salt, and red pepper flakes; mix to combine well.
2. Dip the green beans into the batter and transfer them to the cooking basket. Brush with the grapeseed oil.
3. Cook in the preheated Air Fryer at 390 degrees F for 4 minutes. Shake the basket and cook for a further 3 minutes. Work in batches.
4. Taste, adjust the seasonings and serve. Bon appétit!

449.Chocolate Cookie Dough Balls

Servings:6
Cooking Time: 20 Minutes
Ingredients:
- 16½ ounces store-bought chilled chocolate chip cookie dough
- ¼ cup butter, melted
- ½ cup chocolate cookie crumbs
- 2 tablespoons sugar

Directions:
1. Cut the cookie dough into 12 equal-sized pieces and then, shape each into a ball.
2. Add the melted butter in a shallow dish.
3. In another dish, mix together the cookie crumbs, and sugar.
4. Dip each cookie ball in the melted butter and then evenly coat with the cookie crumbs.

5. In the bottom of a baking sheet, place the coated cookie balls and freeze for at least 2 hours.
6. Preheat the air fryer to 350 degrees F.
7. Line the air fryer basket with a piece of foil.
8. Place the cookies balls in an Air Fryer basket in a single layer in 2 batches.
9. Air Fry for about 10 minutes.
10. Enjoy!

450.Bruschetta With Fresh Tomato And Basil

Servings: 3
Cooking Time: 15 Minutes
Ingredients:
- 1/2 Italian bread, sliced
- 2 garlic cloves, peeled
- 2 tablespoons extra-virgin olive oil
- 2 ripe tomatoes, chopped
- 1 teaspoon dried oregano
- Salt, to taste
- 8 fresh basil leaves, roughly chopped

Directions:
1. Place the bread slices on the lightly greased Air Fryer grill pan. Bake at 370 degrees F for 3 minutes.
2. Cut a clove of garlic in half and rub over one side of the toast; brush with olive oil. Add the chopped tomatoes. Sprinkle with oregano and salt.
3. Increase the temperature to 380 degrees F. Cook in the preheated Air Fryer for 3 minutes more.
4. Garnish with fresh basil and serve. Bon appétit!

451.Grilled Tomatoes

Servings: 2
Cooking Time: 25 Minutes
Ingredients:
- 2 tomatoes, medium to large
- Herbs of your choice, to taste
- Pepper to taste
- High quality cooking spray

Directions:
1. 1 Wash and dry the tomatoes, before chopping them in half.
2. 2 Lightly spritz them all over with cooking spray.
3. 3 Season each half with herbs (oregano, basil, parsley, rosemary, thyme, sage, etc.) as desired and black pepper.
4. 4 Put the halves in the tray of your Air Fryer. Cook for 20 minutes at 320°F, or longer if necessary. Larger tomatoes will take longer to cook.

452.Air Fryer Plantains

Servings:4

Cooking Time:10 Minutes
Ingredients:
- 2 ripe plantains
- 2 teaspoons avocado oil
- 1/8 teaspoon salt

Directions:
1. Preheat the Air fryer to 400 °F and grease an Air fryer basket.
2. Mix the plantains with avocado oil and salt in a bowl.
3. Arrange the coated plantains in the Air fryer basket and cook for about 10 minutes.
4. Dish out in a bowl and serve immediately.

453.Almond Coconut Granola

Servings:4
Cooking Time: 12 Minutes
Ingredients:
- 1 teaspoon monk fruit
- 1 teaspoon almond butter
- 1 teaspoon coconut oil
- 2 tablespoons almonds, chopped
- 1 teaspoon pumpkin puree
- ½ teaspoon pumpkin pie spices
- 2 tablespoons coconut flakes
- 2 tablespoons pumpkin seeds, crushed
- 1 teaspoon hemp seeds
- 1 teaspoon flax seeds
- Cooking spray

Directions:
1. In the big bowl mix up almond butter and coconut oil. Microwave the mixture until it is melted. After this, in the separated bowl mix up monk fruit, pumpkin spices, coconut flakes, pumpkin seeds, hemp seeds, and flax seeds. Add the melted coconut oil and pumpkin puree. Then stir the mixture until it is homogenous. Preheat the air fryer to 350F. Then put the pumpkin mixture on the baking paper and make the shape of the square. After this, cut the square on the serving bars and transfer in the preheated air fryer. Cook the pumpkin granola for 12 minutes.

454.Banana Peppers

Servings: 8
Cooking Time: 20 Minutes
Ingredients:
- 1 cup full-fat cream cheese
- Cooking spray
- 16 avocado slices
- 16 slices salami
- Salt and pepper to taste
- 16 banana peppers

Directions:
1. 1 Pre-heat the Air Fryer to 400°F.
2. 2 Spritz a baking tray with cooking spray.

3. 3 Remove the stems from the banana peppers with a knife.
4. 4 Cut a slit into one side of each banana pepper.
5. 5 Season the cream cheese with the salt and pepper and combine well.
6. 6 Fill each pepper with one spoonful of the cream cheese, followed by one slice of avocado.
7. 7 Wrap the banana peppers in the slices of salami and secure with a toothpick.
8. 8 Place the banana peppers in the baking tray and transfer it to the Air Fryer. Bake for roughly 8 - 10 minutes.

455.Tasty Tofu

Servings: 4
Cooking Time: 35 Minutes
Ingredients:
- 1x 12 oz. package low-fat and extra firm tofu
- 2 tbsp. low-sodium soy sauce
- 2 tbsp. fish sauce
- 1 tbsp. coriander paste
- 1 tsp. sesame oil
- 1 tsp. duck fat or coconut oil
- 1 tsp. Maggi sauce

Directions:
1. 1 Remove the liquid from the package of tofu and chop the tofu into 1-inch cubes. Line a plate with paper towels and spread the tofu out on top in one layer. Place another paper towel on top, followed by another plate, weighting it down with a heavier object if necessary. This is to dry the tofu out completely. Leave for a minimum of 30 minutes or a maximum of 24 hours, replacing the paper towels once or twice throughout the duration.
2. 2 In a medium bowl, mix together the sesame oil, Maggi sauce, coriander paste, fish sauce, and soy sauce. Stir to combine fully.
3. 3 Coat the tofu cubes with this mixture and allow to marinate for at least a half-hour, tossing the cubes a few times throughout to ensure even coating. Add another few drops of fish sauce or soy sauce to thin out the marinade if necessary.
4. 4 Melt the duck fat/coconut oil in your Air Fryer at 350°F for about 2 minutes. Place the tofu cubes in the basket and cook for about 20 minutes or longer to achieve a crispier texture. Flip the tofu over or shake the basket every 10 minutes.
5. 5 Serve hot with the dipping sauce of your choosing.

456.Shrimp Bites

Servings: 10

Cooking Time: 45 Minutes

Ingredients:
- 1 ¼ lb. shrimp, peeled and deveined
- 1 tsp. paprika
- ½ tsp. ground black pepper
- ½ tsp. red pepper flakes, crushed
- 1 tbsp. salt
- 1 tsp. chili powder
- 1 tbsp. shallot powder
- ¼ tsp. cumin powder
- 1 ¼ lb. thin bacon slices

Directions:
1. Coat the shrimps with all of the seasonings.
2. Wrap a slice of bacon around each shrimp, and hold it in place with a toothpick. Refrigerate for half an hour.
3. Transfer to the Air Fryer and fry at 360°F for 7 - 8 minutes.

457.Spicy Chickpeas

Servings:4
Cooking Time: 20 Minutes

Ingredients:
- 1 (15-ounces) can chickpeas, rinsed and drained
- 1 tablespoon olive oil
- ½ teaspoon ground cumin
- ½ teaspoon cayenne pepper
- ½ teaspoon smoked paprika
- Salt, to taste

Directions:
1. Set the temperature of Air Fryer to 390 degrees F.
2. In a bowl, add all the ingredients and toss to coat well.
3. Add the chickpeas in an Air Fryer basket in 2 batches. (you can lay a piece of grease-proof baking paper)
4. Air Fry for about 8-10 minutes.
5. Once done, transfer the hot nuts in a glass or steel bowl and serve.

458.Loaded Tater Tot Bites

Servings: 6
Cooking Time: 20 Minutes

Ingredients:
- 24 tater tots, frozen
- 1 cup Swiss cheese, grated
- 6 tablespoons Canadian bacon, cooked and chopped
- 1/4 cup Ranch dressing

Directions:
1. Spritz the silicone muffin cups with non-stick cooking spray. Now, press the tater tots down into each cup.
2. Divide the cheese, bacon, and Ranch dressing between tater tot cups.

3. Cook in the preheated Air Fryer at 395 degrees for 10 minutes. Serve in paper cake cups. Bon appétit!

459.Herb-roasted Cauliflower

Servings: 2
Cooking Time: 20 Minutes

Ingredients:
- 3 cups cauliflower florets
- 2 tablespoons sesame oil
- 1 teaspoon onion powder
- 1 teaspoon garlic powder
- 1 teaspoon thyme
- 1 teaspoon sage
- 1 teaspoon rosemary
- Sea salt and cracked black pepper, to taste
- 1 teaspoon paprika

Directions:
1. Start by preheating your Air Fryer to 400 degrees F.
2. Toss the cauliflower with the remaining ingredients; toss to coat well.
3. Cook for 12 minutes, shaking the cooking basket halfway through the cooking time. They will crisp up as they cool. Bon appétit!

460.Fried Kale Chips

Servings: 2
Cooking Time: 10 Minutes

Ingredients:
- 1 head kale, torn into 1 ½-inch pieces
- 1 tbsp. olive oil
- 1 tsp. soy sauce

Directions:
1. Wash and dry the kale pieces.
2. Transfer the kale to a bowl and coat with the soy sauce and oil.
3. Place it in the Air Fryer and cook at 400°F for 3 minutes, tossing it halfway through the cooking process.

461.Mascarpone Duck Wraps

Servings:6
Cooking Time: 6 Minutes

Ingredients:
- 1-pound duck fillet, boiled
- 1 tablespoon mascarpone
- 1 teaspoon chili flakes
- 1 teaspoon onion powder
- 6 wonton wraps
- 1 egg yolk, whisked
- Cooking spray

Directions:
1. Shred the boiled duck fillet and mix it up with mascarpone, chili flakes, and onion powder. After this, fill the wonton wraps with the duck mixture and roll them in the shape of pies. Brush the duck pies with the egg yolk. Preheat the air fryer to 385F. Put

the duck pies in the air fryer and spray them with the cooking spray. Cook the snack for 3 minutes from each side.

462.Air Fry Bacon

Servings:11
Cooking Time: 10 Minutes
Ingredients:
- 11 bacon slices

Directions:
1. Place half bacon slices in air fryer basket.
2. Cook at 400 F for 10 minutes.
3. Cook remaining half bacon slices using same steps.
4. Serve and enjoy.

463.Yummy Chicken Dip

Servings: 6
Cooking Time: 20 Minutes
Ingredients:
- 2 cups chicken, cooked and shredded
- 3/4 cup sour cream
- 1/4 tsp onion powder
- 8 oz cream cheese, softened
- 3 tbsp hot sauce
- 1/4 tsp garlic powder

Directions:
1. Preheat the air fryer to 325 F.
2. Add all ingredients in a large bowl and mix until well combined.
3. Transfer mixture in air fryer baking dish and place in the air fryer.
4. Cook chicken dip for 20 minutes.
5. Serve and enjoy.

464.Parsnip Chips With Spicy Citrus Aioli

Servings: 4
Cooking Time: 20 Minutes
Ingredients:
- 1 pound parsnips, peel long strips
- 2 tablespoons sesame oil
- Sea salt and ground black pepper, to taste
- 1 teaspoon red pepper flakes, crushed
- 1/2 teaspoon curry powder
- 1/2 teaspoon mustard seeds
- Spicy Citrus Aioli:
- 1/4 cup mayonnaise
- 1 tablespoon fresh lime juice
- 1 clove garlic, smashed
- Salt and black pepper, to taste

Directions:
1. Start by preheating the Air Fryer to 380 degrees F.
2. Toss the parsnip chips with the sesame oil, salt, black pepper, red pepper, curry powder, and mustard seeds.
3. Cook for 15 minutes, shaking the Air Fryer basket periodically.

4. Meanwhile, make the sauce by whisking the mayonnaise, lime juice, garlic, salt, and pepper. Place in the refrigerator until ready to use. Bon appétit!

465.Mexican Muffins

Servings:4
Cooking Time: 15 Minutes
Ingredients:
- 1 cup ground beef
- 1 teaspoon taco seasonings
- 2 oz Mexican blend cheese, shredded
- 1 teaspoon keto tomato sauce
- Cooking spray

Directions:
1. Preheat the air fryer to 375F. Meanwhile, in the mixing bowl mix up ground beef and taco seasonings. Spray the muffin molds with cooking spray. Then transfer the ground beef mixture in the muffin molds and top them with cheese and tomato sauce. Transfer the muffin molds in the preheated air fryer and cook them for 15 minutes.

466.Dill Pickle Fries

Servings:12
Cooking Time:28 Minutes
Ingredients:
- 1½ (16-ounces) jars spicy dill pickle spears, drained and pat dried
- 1 cup all-purpose flour
- 1 egg, beaten
- ¼ cup milk
- 1 cup panko breadcrumbs
- ½ teaspoon paprika

Directions:
1. Preheat the Air fryer to 440 °F and grease an Air fryer basket.
2. Place flour and paprika in a shallow dish and whisk the egg with milk in a second dish.
3. Place the breadcrumbs in a third shallow dish.
4. Coat the pickle spears evenly in flour and dip in the egg mixture.
5. Roll into the breadcrumbs evenly and arrange half of the pickle spears in an Air fryer basket.
6. Cook for about 14 minutes, flipping once in between.
7. Repeat with the remaining pickle spears and dish out to serve warm.

467.Bacon-wrapped Jalapeno Popper

Servings: 4
Cooking Time: 20 Minutes
Ingredients:
- 6 jalapenos
- 1/3 cup medium cheddar cheese, shredded

- ¼ tsp. garlic powder
- 3 oz. full-fat cream cheese
- 12 slices sugar-free bacon

Directions:
1. Prepare the jalapenos by slicing off the tops and halving each one lengthwise. Take care when removing the seeds and membranes, wearing gloves if necessary.
2. In a microwavable bowl, combine the cheddar cheese, garlic powder, and cream cheese. Microwave for half a minute and mix again, before spoon equal parts of this mixture into each of the jalapeno halves.
3. Take a slice of bacon and wrap it around one of the jalapeno halves, covering it entirely. Place it in the basket of your fryer. Repeat with the rest of the bacon and jalapenos.
4. Cook at 400°F for twelve minutes, flipping the peppers halfway through in order to ensure the bacon gets crispy. Make sure not to let any of the contents spill out of the jalapeno halves when turning them.
5. Eat the peppers hot or at room temperature.

468.Baby Corn

Servings: 4
Cooking Time: 20 Minutes
Ingredients:
- 8 oz. baby corns, boiled
- 1 cup flour
- 1 tsp. garlic powder
- ½ tsp. carom seeds
- ¼ tsp. chili powder
- Pinch of baking soda
- Salt to taste

Directions:
1. In a bowl, combine the flour, chili powder, garlic powder, cooking soda, salt and carom seed. Add in a little water to create a batter-like consistency.
2. Coat each baby corn in the batter.
3. Pre-heat the Air Fryer at 350°F.
4. Cover the Air Fryer basket with aluminum foil before laying the coated baby corns on top of the foil.
5. Cook for 10 minutes.

469.Thyme-roasted Sweet Potatoes

Servings: 3
Cooking Time: 35 Minutes
Ingredients:
- 1 pound sweet potatoes, peeled, cut into bite-sized pieces
- 2 tablespoons olive oil
- 1 teaspoon sea salt
- 1/4 teaspoon freshly ground black pepper
- 1/2 teaspoon cayenne pepper
- 2 fresh thyme sprigs

Directions:
1. Arrange the potato slices in a single layer in the lightly greased cooking basket. Add the olive oil, salt, black pepper, and cayenne pepper; toss to coat.
2. Bake at 380 degrees F for 30 minutes, shaking the cooking basket occasionally.
3. Bake until tender and slightly browned, working in batches. Serve warm, garnished with thyme sprigs. Bon appétit!

470.Vegetable Pastries

Servings:8
Cooking Time:10 Minutes
Ingredients:
- 2 large potatoes, boiled and mashed
- ½ cup carrot, peeled and chopped
- ½ cup onion, chopped
- ½ cup green peas, shelled
- 3 puff pastry sheets, each cut into 4 round pieces
- 1 tablespoon olive oil
- Salt and black pepper, to taste
- 2 garlic cloves, minced
- 1 tablespoon curry powder
- 2 tablespoons fresh ginger, minced

Directions:
1. Preheat the Air fryer to 390 °F and grease an Air fryer basket.
2. Heat olive oil on medium heat in a skillet and add carrot, onion, ginger and garlic.
3. Sauté for about 5 minutes and stir in the mashed potatoes, peas, curry powder, salt and black pepper.
4. Cook for about 2 minutes and dish out in a bowl.
5. Put about 2 tablespoons of vegetable filling mixture over each pastry round.
6. Fold each pastry round into half-circle and press the edges firmly with a fork.
7. Place half of the pastries in the Air fryer basket and cook for about 5 minutes.
8. Dish out in a platter and serve warm.

471.Famous Blooming Onion With Mayo Dip

Servings: 3
Cooking Time: 25 Minutes
Ingredients:
- 1 large Vidalia onion
- 1/2 cup all-purpose flour
- 1 teaspoon salt
- 1/2 teaspoon ground black pepper
- 1 teaspoon cayenne pepper
- 1/2 teaspoon dried thyme
- 1/2 teaspoon dried oregano
- 1/2 teaspoon ground cumin
- 2 eggs
- 1/4 cup milk

- Mayo Dip:
- 3 tablespoons mayonnaise
- 3 tablespoons sour cream
- 1 tablespoon horseradish, drained
- Kosher salt and freshly ground black pepper, to taste

Directions:
1. Cut off the top 1/2 inch of the Vidalia onion; peel your onion and place it cut-side down. Starting 1/2 inch from the root, cut the onion in half. Make a second cut that splits each half in two. You will have 4 quarters held together by the root.
2. Repeat these cuts, splitting the 4 quarters to yield eighths; then, you should split them again until you have 16 evenly spaced cuts. Turn the onion over and gently separate the outer pieces using your fingers.
3. In a mixing bowl, thoroughly combine the flour and spices. In a separate bowl, whisk the eggs and milk. Dip the onion into the egg mixture, followed by the flour mixture.
4. Spritz the onion with cooking spray and transfer to the lightly greased cooking basket. Cook for 370 degrees F for 12 to 15 minutes.
5. Meanwhile, make the mayo dip by whisking the remaining ingredients. Serve and enjoy!

472.Cheese Cookies

Servings:10
Cooking Time: 12 Minutes
Ingredients:
- For Dough:
- 3.38 fluid ounces cream
- 5.30 ounces margarine
- 6.35 ounces Gruyere cheese, grated
- 1 teaspoon paprika
- Salt, as required
- 5.30 ounces flour, sifted
- ½ teaspoon baking powder
- For Topping:
- 1 tablespoon milk
- 2 egg yolks, beaten
- 2 tablespoons poppy seeds

Directions:
1. For cookies: in a bowl, mix together the cream, margarine, cheese, paprika, and salt.
2. Place the flour, and baking powder onto a smooth surface. Mix them well.
3. Using your hands, create a well in the center of flour.
4. Add the cheese mixture and knead until a soft dough forms.
5. Roll the dough into 1-1½-inch thickness.
6. Cut the cookies using a cookie cutter.
7. In another bowl, mix together the milk, and egg yolks.

8. Coat the cookies with milk mixture and then, sprinkle with poppy seeds.
9. Set the temperature of Air Fryer to 340 degrees F.
10. Place cookies onto the grill pan of an Air Fryer in a single layer.
11. Air Fry for about 12 minutes.
12. Serve.

473.Old-fashioned Onion Rings

Servings:4
Cooking Time:10 Minutes
Ingredients:
- 1 large onion, cut into rings
- 1¼ cups all-purpose flour
- 1 cup milk
- 1 egg
- ¾ cup dry bread crumbs
- Salt, to taste

Directions:
1. Preheat the Air fryer to 360 °F and grease the Air fryer basket.
2. Mix together flour and salt in a dish.
3. Whisk egg with milk in a second dish until well mixed.
4. Place the breadcrumbs in a third dish.
5. Coat the onion rings with the flour mixture and dip into the egg mixture.
6. Lastly dredge in the breadcrumbs and transfer the onion rings in the Air fryer basket.
7. Cook for about 10 minutes and dish out to serve warm.

474.Cabbage Chips

Servings: 6
Cooking Time: 30 Minutes
Ingredients:
- 1 large cabbage head, tear cabbage leaves into pieces
- 2 tbsp olive oil
- 1/4 cup parmesan cheese, grated
- Pepper
- Salt

Directions:
1. Preheat the air fryer to 250 F.
2. Add all ingredients into the large mixing bowl and toss well.
3. Spray air fryer basket with cooking spray.
4. Divide cabbage in batches.
5. Add one cabbage chips batch in air fryer basket and cook for 25-30 minutes at 250 F or until chips are crispy and lightly golden brown.
6. Serve and enjoy.

475.Leeks Dip

Servings: 6
Cooking Time: 12 Minutes

Ingredients:
- 2 spring onions, minced
- 2 tablespoons butter, melted
- 3 tablespoons coconut milk
- 4 leeks, sliced
- ¼ cup coconut cream
- Salt and white pepper to the taste

Directions:
1. In a pan that fits your air fryer, mix all the ingredients and whisk them well. Introduce the pan in the fryer and cook at 390 degrees F for 12 minutes. Divide into bowls and serve.

476.Sage & Onion Stuffing

Servings: 6
Cooking Time: 35 Minutes
Ingredients:
- 2 lb. sausage meat
- ½ onion
- ½ tsp. garlic puree
- 1 tsp. sage
- 3 tbsp. friendly bread crumbs
- Pinch of salt
- Black pepper

Directions:
1. 1 Combine all of the ingredients in a large bowl.
2. 2 Take equal portions of the mixture, mold them into medium sized balls and put them in the Air Fryer.
3. 3 Cook at 355°F for 15 minutes.

477.Healthy Vegetable Kabobs

Servings: 4
Cooking Time: 10 Minutes
Ingredients:
- 1/2 onion
- 1 zucchini
- 1 eggplant
- 2 bell peppers
- Pepper
- Salt

Directions:
1. Cut all vegetables into 1-inch pieces.
2. Thread vegetables onto the soaked wooden skewers and season with pepper and salt.
3. Place skewers into the air fryer basket and cook for 10 minutes at 390 F. Turn halfway through.
4. Serve and enjoy.

478.Chives Meatballs

Servings: 6
Cooking Time: 20 Minutes
Ingredients:
- 1 pound beef meat, ground
- 1 teaspoon onion powder
- 1 teaspoon garlic powder

- A pinch of salt and black pepper
- 2 tablespoons chives, chopped
- Cooking spray

Directions:
1. In a bowl, mix all the ingredients except the cooking spray, stir well and shape medium meatballs out of this mix. Pace them in your lined air fryer's basket, grease with cooking spray and cook at 360 degrees F for 20 minutes. Serve as an appetizer.

479.Crispy Zucchini Fries

Servings: 4
Cooking Time: 10 Minutes
Ingredients:
- 2 medium zucchinis, cut into fries shape
- 1/2 tsp garlic powder
- 1 tsp Italian seasoning
- 1/2 cup parmesan cheese, grated
- 1/2 cup almond flour
- 1 egg, lightly beaten
- Pepper
- Salt

Directions:
1. Add egg in a bowl and whisk well.
2. In a shallow bowl, mix together almond flour, spices, parmesan cheese, pepper, and salt.
3. Spray air fryer basket with cooking spray.
4. Dip zucchini fries in egg then coat with almond flour mixture and place in the air fryer basket.
5. Cook zucchini fries for 10 minutes at 400 F.
6. Serve and enjoy.

480.Flax Cheese Chips

Servings: 2
Cooking Time: 20 Minutes
Ingredients:
- 1 ½ cup cheddar cheese
- 4 tbsp ground flaxseed meal
- Seasonings of your choice

Directions:
1. Preheat your fryer to 425°F/220°C.
2. Spoon 2 tablespoons of cheddar cheese into a mound, onto a non-stick pad.
3. Spread out a pinch of flax seed on each chip.
4. Season and bake for 10-15 minutes.

481.Parmesan Zucchini Chips

Servings: 1
Cooking Time: 10 Minutes
Ingredients:
- 2 medium zucchini
- 1 oz. pork rinds, finely ground
- ½ cup parmesan cheese, grated
- 1 egg

Directions:

1. Cut the zucchini into slices about a quarter-inch thick. Lay on a paper towel to dry.
2. In a bowl, combine the ground pork rinds and the grated parmesan.
3. In a separate bowl, beat the egg with a fork.
4. Take a zucchini slice and dip it into the egg, then into the pork rind-parmesan mixture, making sure to coat it evenly. Repeat with the rest of the slices. Lay them in the basket of your fryer, taking care not to overlap. This step may need to be completed in more than one batch.
5. Cook at 320°F for five minutes. Turn the chips over and allow to cook for another five minutes.
6. Allow to cool to achieve a crispier texture or serve warm. Enjoy!

482.Seasoned Crab Sticks

Servings:4
Cooking Time:12 Minutes
Ingredients:
- 1 packet crab sticks, shred into small pieces
- 2 teaspoon sesame oil
- Cajun seasoning, to taste

Directions:
1. Preheat the Air fryer to 320 °F and grease an Air fryer basket.
2. Drizzle crab stick pieces with sesame oil and arrange in the Air fryer basket.
3. Cook for about 12 minutes and serve, sprinkled with Cajun seasoning.

483.Vegetable Nuggets

Servings:4
Cooking Time:10 Minutes
Ingredients:
- 1 zucchini, chopped roughly
- ½ of carrot, chopped roughly
- 1 cup all-purpose flour
- 1 egg
- 1 cup panko breadcrumbs
- 1 tablespoon garlic powder
- ½ tablespoon mustard powder
- 1 tablespoon onion powder
- Salt and black pepper, to taste

Directions:
1. Preheat the Air fryer to 380 °F and grease an Air fryer basket.
2. Put zucchini, carrot, mustard powder, garlic powder, onion powder, salt and black pepper in a food processor and pulse until combined.
3. Place flour in a shallow dish and whisk the eggs with milk in a second dish.
4. Place breadcrumbs in a third shallow dish.
5. Coat the vegetable nuggets evenly in flour and dip in the egg mixture.

6. Roll into the breadcrumbs evenly and arrange the nuggets in an Air fryer basket.
7. Cook for about 10 minutes and dish out to serve warm.

484.Lemon Tofu Cubes

Servings:2
Cooking Time: 7 Minutes
Ingredients:
- ½ teaspoon ground coriander
- 1 tablespoon avocado oil
- 1 teaspoon lemon juice
- ½ teaspoon chili flakes
- 6 oz tofu

Directions:
1. In the shallow bowl mix up ground coriander, avocado oil, lemon juice, and chili flakes. Chop the tofu into cubes and sprinkle with coriander mixture. Shake the tofu. After this, preheat the air fryer to 400F and put the tofu cubes in it. Cook the tofu for 4 minutes. Then flip the tofu on another side and cook for 3 minutes more.

485.Wonton Sausage Appetizers

Servings: 5
Cooking Time: 20 Minutes
Ingredients:
- 1/2 pound ground sausage
- 2 tablespoons scallions, chopped
- 1 garlic clove, minced
- 1/2 tablespoon fish sauce
- 1 teaspoon Sriracha sauce
- 20 wonton wrappers
- 1 egg, whisked with 1 tablespoon water

Directions:
1. In a mixing bowl, thoroughly combine the ground sausage, scallions, garlic, fish sauce, and Sriracha.
2. Divide the mixture between the wonton wrappers. Dip your fingers in the egg wash
3. Fold the wonton in half. Bring up the 2 ends of the wonton and use the egg wash to stick them together. Pinch the edges and coat each wonton with the egg wash.
4. Place the folded wontons in the lightly greased cooking basket. Cook at 360 degrees F for 10 minutes. Work in batches and serve warm. Bon appétit!

486.Amazing Blooming Onion

Servings: 4
Cooking Time: 40 Minutes
Ingredients:
- 4 medium/small onions
- 1 tbsp. olive oil
- 4 dollops of butter

Directions:
1. 1 Peel the onion. Cut off the top and bottom.

2. 2 To make it bloom, cut as deeply as possible without slicing through it completely. 4 cuts [i.e. 8 segments] should do it.
3. 3 Place the onions in a bowl of salted water and allow to absorb for 4 hours to help eliminate the sharp taste and induce the blooming process.
4. 4 Pre-heat your Air Fryer to 355°F.
5. 5 Transfer the onions to the Air Fryer. Pour over a light drizzle of olive oil and place a dollop of butter on top of each onion.
6. 6 Cook or roast for 30 minutes. Remove the outer layer before serving if it is too brown.

487.Potato Totes

Servings: 2
Cooking Time: 20 Minutes
Ingredients:
- 1 large potato, diced
- 1 tsp. onion, minced
- 1 tsp. olive oil
- Pepper to taste
- Salt to taste

Directions:
1. Boil the potatoes in a saucepan of water over a medium-high heat.
2. Strain the potatoes, transfer them to bowl, and mash them thoroughly.
3. Combine with the olive oil, onion, pepper and salt in mashed potato.
4. Shape equal amounts of the mixture into small tots and place each one in the Air Fryer basket. Cook at 380°F for 8 minutes.
5. Give the basket a good shake and cook for an additional 5 minutes before serving.

488.Bacon-wrapped Shrimp

Servings:6
Cooking Time:7 Minutes
Ingredients:
- 1 pound bacon, sliced thinly
- 1 pound shrimp, peeled and deveined
- Salt, to taste

Directions:
1. Preheat the Air fryer to 390 °F and grease an Air fryer basket.
2. Wrap 1 shrimp with a bacon slices, covering completely.
3. Repeat with the remaining shrimp and bacon slices.
4. Arrange the bacon wrapped shrimps in a baking dish and freeze for about 15 minutes.
5. Place the shrimps in an Air fryer basket and cook for about 7 minutes.
6. Dish out and serve warm.

DESERTS RECIPES

489.Lemon Butter Pound Cake

Servings: 8
Cooking Time: 2 Hours 20 Minutes
Ingredients:
- 1 stick softened butter
- 1 cup sugar
- 1 medium egg
- 1 ¼ cups flour
- 1 tsp. butter flavoring
- 1 tsp. vanilla essence
- Pinch of salt
- ¾ cup milk
- Grated zest of 1 medium-sized lemon
- For the Glaze:
- 2 tbsp. freshly squeezed lemon juice

Directions:
1. In a large bowl, use a creamer to mix together the butter and sugar. Fold in the egg and continue to stir.
2. Add in the flour, butter flavoring, vanilla essence, and salt, combining everything well.
3. Pour in the milk, followed by the lemon zest, and continue to mix.
4. Lightly brush the inside of a cake pan with the melted butter.
5. Pour the cake batter into the cake pan.
6. Place the pan in the Air Fryer and bake at 350°F for 15 minutes.
7. After removing it from the fryer, run a knife around the edges of the cake to loosen it from the pan and transfer it to a serving plate.
8. Leave it to cool completely.
9. In the meantime, make the glaze by combining with the lemon juice.
10. Pour the glaze over the cake and let it sit for a further 2 hours before serving.

490.Apple Dumplings

Servings: 2
Cooking Time: 40 Minutes
Ingredients:
- 2 tbsp. sultanas
- 2 sheets puff pastry
- 2 tbsp. butter, melted
- 2 small apples
- 1 tbsp. sugar

Directions:
1. Pre-heat your Air Fryer to 350°F
2. Peel the apples and remove the cores.
3. In a bowl, stir together the sugar and the sultanas.
4. Lay one apple on top of each pastry sheet and stuff the sugar and sultanas into the holes where the cores used to be.
5. Wrap the pastry around the apples, covering them completely.
6. Put them on a sheet of aluminum foil and coat each dumpling with a light brushing of melted butter
7. Transfer to the Air Fryer and bake for 25 minutes until a golden brown color is achieved and the apples have softened inside.

491.Coconut And Berries Cream

Servings: 6
Cooking Time: 30 Minutes
Ingredients:
- 12 ounces blackberries
- 6 ounces raspberries
- 12 ounces blueberries
- ¾ cup swerve
- 2 ounces coconut cream

Directions:
1. In a bowl, mix all the ingredients and whisk well. Divide this into 6 ramekins, put them in your air fryer and cook at 320 degrees F for 30 minutes. Cool down and serve it.

492.Chocolate Custard

Servings: 4
Cooking Time: 32 Minutes
Ingredients:
- 2 eggs
- 1 tsp vanilla
- 1 cup heavy whipping cream
- 1 cup unsweetened almond milk
- 2 tbsp unsweetened cocoa powder
- 1/4 cup Swerve
- Pinch of salt

Directions:
1. Preheat the air fryer to 305 F.
2. Add all ingredients into the blender and blend until well combined.
3. Pour mixture into the ramekins and place into the air fryer.
4. Cook for 32 minutes.
5. Serve and enjoy.

493.Creamy Raspberry Cake

Servings: 4
Cooking Time: 30 Minutes
Ingredients:
- 3 eggs, beaten
- ½ cup coconut flour
- ½ teaspoon baking powder
- 2 teaspoons Erythritol
- 1 teaspoon vanilla extract
- 1 tablespoon Truvia
- ½ cup heavy cream
- 1 oz raspberries, sliced

- Cooking spray

Directions:
1. Make the cake batter: in the mixing bowl mix up beaten egg, coconut flour, baking powder, and Erythritol. Add vanilla extract and stir the mixture until smooth. Then preheat the air fryer to 330F. Spray the air fryer baking pan with cooking spray and pour the cake batter inside. Put the pan with batter in the preheated air fryer and cook it for 30 minutes. Meanwhile, make the cake frosting: whip the heavy cream. Then add Truvia and stir it well. When the cake is cooked, cool it well and remove it from the air fryer pan. Slice the cake into 2 cakes. Then spread one piece of cake with ½ part of whipped cream and top with sliced raspberries. After this, cover it with the second piece of cakes. Top the cake with the remaining whipped cream.

494.Chocolate And Blueberry Cupcakes

Servings: 6
Cooking Time: 20 Minutes
Ingredients:
- 3 teaspoons cocoa powder, unsweetened
- 1/2 cup blueberries
- 1 ¼ cups almond flour
- 1/2 cup milk
- 1 stick butter, room temperature
- 3 eggs
- 3/4 cup granulated erythritol
- 1 teaspoon pure rum extract
- 1/2 teaspoon baking soda
- 1 teaspoon baking powder
- 1/4 teaspoon grated nutmeg
- 1/2 teaspoon ground cinnamon
- 1/8 teaspoon salt

Directions:
1. Grab two mixing bowls. In the first bowl, thoroughly combine the erythritol, almond flour, baking soda, baking powder, salt, nutmeg, cinnamon and cocoa powder.
2. Take the second bowl and cream the butter, egg, rum extract, and milk; whisk to combine well. Now, add the wet mixture to the dry mixture. Fold in blueberries.
3. Press the prepared batter mixture into a lightly greased muffin tin. Bake at 345 degrees for 15 minutes. Use a toothpick to check if your cupcakes are baked. Bon appétit!

495.Cardamom Squares

Servings: 4
Cooking Time: 20 Minutes
Ingredients:
- 4 tablespoons peanut butter
- 1 tablespoon peanut, chopped

- 1 teaspoon vanilla extract
- ½ cup coconut flour
- 1 tablespoon Erythritol
- ½ teaspoon ground cardamom

Directions:
1. Put the peanut butter and peanut in the bowl. Add vanilla extract, coconut flour, and ground cardamom. Then add Erythritol and stir the mixture until homogenous. Preheat the air fryer to 330F. Line the air fryer basket with baking paper and pour the peanut butter mixture over it. Flatten it gently and cook for 20 minutes. Then remove the cooked mixture from the air fryer and cool it completely. Cut the dessert into the squares.

496.Blueberry & Lemon Cake

Servings:4
Cooking Time: 17 Minutes
Ingredients:
- 2 eggs
- 1 cup blueberries
- zest from 1 lemon
- juice from 1 lemon
- 1 tsp. vanilla
- brown sugar for topping (a little sprinkling on top of each muffin-less than a teaspoon)
- 2 1/2 cups self-rising flour
- 1/2 cup Monk Fruit (or use your preferred sugar)
- 1/2 cup cream
- 1/4 cup avocado oil (any light cooking oil)

Directions:
1. In mixing bowl, beat well wet Ingredients. Stir in dry ingredients and mix thoroughly.
2. Lightly grease baking pan of air fryer with cooking spray. Pour in batter.
3. For 12 minutes, cook on 330°F.
4. Let it stand in air fryer for 5 minutes.
5. Serve and enjoy.

497.Classic Lava Cake

Servings: 4
Cooking Time: 20 Minutes
Ingredients:
- 4 ounces butter, melted
- 4 ounces dark chocolate
- 2 eggs, lightly whisked
- 2 tablespoons monk fruit sweetener
- 2 tablespoons almond meal
- 1 teaspoon baking powder
- 1/2 teaspoon ground cinnamon
- 1/4 teaspoon ground star anise

Directions:
1. Begin by preheating your Air Fryer to 370 degrees F. Spritz the sides and bottom of a baking pan with nonstick cooking spray.

2. Melt the butter and dark chocolate in a microwave-safe bowl. Mix the eggs and monk fruit until frothy.
3. Pour the butter/chocolate mixture into the egg mixture. Stir in the almond meal, baking powder, cinnamon, and star anise. Mix until everything is well incorporated.
4. Scrape the batter into the prepared pan. Bake in the preheated Air Fryer for 9 to 11 minutes.
5. Let stand for 2 minutes. Invert on a plate while warm and serve. Bon appétit!

498.Baked Pears With Chocolate

Servings:4
Cooking Time:45 Minutes
Ingredients:

- 4 firm ripe pears, peeled, cored and sliced
- 1/3 cup turbinado sugar
- 1/2 teaspoon ground anise star
- 1 teaspoon pure vanilla extract
- 1 teaspoon pure orange extract
- 1/2 stick butter, cold
- 1/2 cup chocolate chips, for garnish

Directions:
1. Grease the baking dish with a pan spray; lay the pear slices on the bottom of the prepared dish.
2. In a mixing dish, combine the sugar, anise star, vanilla, and orange extract. Then, sprinkle this mixture over the fruit layer.
3. Cut in butter and scatter evenly over the top of the pear layer. Air-fryer at 380 degrees F for 35 minutes. Serve sprinkled with chocolate chips. Enjoy!

499.Autumn Walnut Crisp

Servings: 8
Cooking Time: 40 Minutes
Ingredients:

- 1 cup walnuts
- 1/2 cup swerve
- Topping:
- 1 ½ cups almond flour
- 1/2 cup coconut flour
- 1/2 cup swerve
- 1 teaspoon crystallized ginger
- 1/2 teaspoon ground cardamom
- A pinch of salt
- 1 stick butter, cut into pieces

Directions:
1. Place walnuts and 1/2 cup of swerve in a baking pan lightly greased with nonstick cooking spray.
2. In a mixing dish, thoroughly combine all the topping ingredients. Sprinkle the topping ingredients over the walnut layer.
3. Bake in the preheated Air Fryer at 330 degrees F for 35 minutes. Bon appétit!

500.Swirled German Cake

Servings: 8
Cooking Time: 25 Minutes
Ingredients:

- 1 cup flour
- 1 tsp. baking powder
- 1 cup sugar
- 1/8 tsp. kosher salt
- ¼ tsp. ground cinnamon
- ¼ tsp. grated nutmeg
- 1 tsp. orange zest
- 1 stick butter, melted
- 2 eggs
- 1 tsp. pure vanilla extract
- ¼ cup milk
- 2 tbsp. unsweetened cocoa powder

Directions:
1. Take a round pan that is small enough to fit inside your Air Fryer and lightly grease the inside with oil.
2. In a bowl, use an electric mixer to combine the flour, baking powder, sugar, salt, cinnamon, nutmeg, and orange zest.
3. Fold in the butter, eggs, vanilla, and milk, incorporating everything well.
4. Spoon a quarter-cup of the batter to the baking pan.
5. Stir the cocoa powder into the rest of the batter.
6. Use a spoon to drop small amounts of the brown batter into the white batter. Swirl them together with a knife.
7. Place the pan in the Air Fryer and cook at 360°F for about 15 minutes.
8. Remove the pan from the fryer and leave to cool for roughly 10 minutes.

501.Chocolaty Squares

Servings:4
Cooking Time:20 Minutes
Ingredients:

- 2-ounce cold butter
- 3-ounce self-rising flour
- ½ tablespoon milk
- 2-ounce chocolate, chopped
- 1¼-ounce brown sugar
- 1/8 cup honey

Directions:
1. Preheat the Air fryer to 320 °F and grease a tin lightly.
2. Mix butter, brown sugar, flour and honey and beat till smooth.
3. Stir in the chocolate and milk and pour the mixture into a tin.
4. Transfer into the Air fryer basket and cook for about 20 minutes.
5. Dish out and cut into desired squares to serve.

502.Walnut Bars

Servings: 4
Cooking Time: 16 Minutes
Ingredients:
- 1 egg
- 1/3 cup cocoa powder
- 3 tablespoons swerve
- 7 tablespoons ghee, melted
- 1 teaspoon vanilla extract
- ¼ cup almond flour
- ¼ cup walnuts, chopped
- ½ teaspoon baking soda

Directions:
1. In a bowl, mix all the ingredients and stir well. Spread this on a baking sheet that fits your air fryer lined with parchment paper, put it in the fryer and cook at 330 degrees F and bake for 16 minutes. Leave the bars to cool down, cut and serve.

503.Baked Apples

Servings:2
Cooking Time: 35 Minutes
Ingredients:
- 2 tbsp butter, cold
- 3 tbsp sugar
- 3 tbsp crushed walnuts
- 2 tbsp raisins
- 1 tsp cinnamon

Directions:
1. Preheat the Air fryer to 400 F.
2. In a bowl, add butter, sugar, walnuts, raisins and cinnamon; mix with fingers until you obtain a crumble. Arrange the apples in the air fryer. Stuff the apples with the filling mixture. Cook for 30 minutes.

504.Vanilla Souffle

Servings: 6
Cooking Time: 50 Minutes
Ingredients:
- ¼ cup flour
- ¼ cup butter, softened
- 1 cup whole milk
- ¼ cup sugar
- 2 tsp. vanilla extract
- 1 vanilla bean
- 5 egg whites
- 4 egg yolks
- 1 oz. sugar
- 1 tsp. cream of tartar

Directions:
1. Mix together the flour and butter to create a smooth paste.
2. In a saucepan, heat up the milk. Add the ¼ cup sugar and allow it to dissolve.
3. Put the vanilla bean in the mixture and bring it to a boil.
4. Pour in the flour-butter mixture. Beat the contents of the saucepan thoroughly with a wire whisk, removing all the lumps.
5. Reduce the heat and allow the mixture to simmer and thicken for a number of minutes.
6. Take the saucepan off the heat. Remove the vanilla bean and let the mixture cool for 10 minutes in an ice bath.
7. In the meantime, grease six 3-oz. ramekins or soufflé dishes with butter and add a sprinkling of sugar to each one.
8. In a separate bowl quickly, rigorously stir the egg yolks and vanilla extract together. Combine with the milk mixture.
9. In another bowl, beat the egg whites, 1 oz. sugar and cream of tartar to form medium stiff peaks.
10. Fold the egg whites into the soufflé base. Transfer everything to the ramekins, smoothing the surfaces with a knife or the back of a spoon.
11. Pre-heat the Air Fryer to 330°F.
12. Put the ramekins in the cooking basket and cook for 14 – 16 minutes. You may need to complete this step in multiple batches.
13. Serve the soufflés topped with powdered sugar and with a side of chocolate sauce.

505.Oriental Coconut Cake

Servings:8
Cooking Time: 40 Minutes
Ingredients:
- 1 cup gluten-free flour
- 2 eggs
- 1/2 cup flaked coconut
- 1-1/2 teaspoons baking powder
- 1/2 teaspoon baking soda
- 1/2 teaspoon xanthan gum
- 1/2 teaspoon salt
- 1/2 cup coconut milk
- 1/2 cup vegetable oil
- 1/2 teaspoon vanilla extract
- 1/4 cup chopped walnuts
- 3/4 cup white sugar

Directions:
1. In blender blend all wet Ingredients. Add dry ingredients and blend thoroughly.
2. Lightly grease baking pan of air fryer with cooking spray.
3. Pour in batter. Cover pan with foil.
4. For 30 minutes, cook on 330°F.
5. Let it rest for 10 minutes
6. Serve and enjoy.

506.Zucchini-choco Bread

Servings:12
Cooking Time: 20 Minutes
Ingredients:

- ¼ teaspoon salt
- ½ cup almond milk
- ½ cup maple syrup
- ½ cup sunflower oil
- ½ cup unsweetened cocoa powder
- 1 cup oat flour
- 1 cup zucchini, shredded and squeezed
- 1 tablespoon flax egg (1 tablespoon flax meal + 3 tablespoons water)
- 1 teaspoon apple cider vinegar
- 1 teaspoon baking soda
- 1 teaspoon vanilla extract
- 1/3 cup chocolate chips

Directions:
1. Preheat the air fryer to 350 °F.
2. Line a baking dish that will fit the air fryer with parchment paper.
3. In a bowl, combine the flax meal, zucchini, sunflower oil, maple, vanilla, apple cider vinegar and milk.
4. Stir in the oat flour, baking soda, cocoa powder, and salt. Mix until well combined.
5. Add the chocolate chips.
6. Pour over the baking dish and cook for 15 minutes or until a toothpick inserted in the middle comes out clean.

507.15-minute Orange Galettes

Servings: 6
Cooking Time: 15 Minutes
Ingredients:
- 1 cup almond meal
- 1/2 cup coconut flour
- 3 eggs
- 1/3 cup milk
- 2 tablespoons monk fruit
- 2 teaspoons grated lemon peel
- 1/3 teaspoon ground nutmeg, preferably freshly ground
- 1 ½ teaspoons baking powder
- 3 tablespoons orange juice
- A pinch of turmeric

Directions:
1. Grab two mixing bowls. Combine dry ingredients in the first bowl.
2. In the second bowl, combine all wet ingredients. Add wet mixture to the dry mixture and mix until smooth and uniform.
3. Air-fry for 4 to 5 minutes at 345 degrees F. Work in batches. Dust with confectioners' swerve if desired. Bon appétit!

508.Banana Cake

Servings:6
Cooking Time: 40 Minutes
Ingredients:
- 1½ cups cake flour
- 1 teaspoon baking soda
- ½ teaspoon ground cinnamon

- Salt, to taste
- ½ cup vegetable oil
- 2 eggs
- ½ cup sugar
- ½ teaspoon vanilla extract
- 3 medium bananas, peeled and mashed
- ¼ cup walnuts, chopped
- ¼ cup raisins, chopped

Directions:
1. In a large bowl, mix well flour, baking soda, cinnamon, and salt.
2. In another bowl, beat well eggs and oil.
3. Add the sugar, vanilla extract, and bananas. Whisk until well combined.
4. Add the flour mixture and stir until just combined.
5. Set the temperature of air fryer to 320 degrees F. Grease a cake pan.
6. Place mixture evenly into the prepared cake pan and top with walnuts and raisins.
7. With a piece of foil, cover the pan.
8. Arrange the cake pan into an air fryer basket.
9. Now, set the temperature of air fryer to 300 degrees F.
10. Air fry for about 30 minutes.
11. Remove the piece of foil and set the temperature to 285 degrees F.
12. Air fry for another 5-10 minutes or until a toothpick inserted in the center comes out clean.
13. Remove the cake pan from air fryer and place onto a wire rack to cool for about 10 minutes.
14. Now, invert the cake onto wire rack to completely cool before slicing.
15. Cut the cake into desired size slices and serve.

509.Cinamon Banana Bread

Servings:68
Cooking Time: 30 Minutes
Ingredients:
- 1 cup flour
- 1 tsp ground cinnamon
- ½ tsp salt
- ¼ tsp baking powder
- 2 eggs
- ½ cup sugar
- ¼ cup milk
- 2 tbsp butter, melted
- ½ tsp vanilla extract
- 2 tbsp sultanas, soaked
- 1 tbsp honey

Directions:
1. Preheat the Air fryer to 300 F. Grease a baking dish with cooking spray.
2. In a bowl, beat the eggs. Add in pumpkin, sugar, milk, canola oil, sultanas, and vanilla.

In a separate bowl, sift the flour and mix in cinnamon, salt, and baking powder.

3. Combine the 2 mixtures and stir until a thick cake mixture forms. Spoon the batter into the prepared baking dish and place it in your air fryer. Cook for 25 minutes until a toothpick inserted in the center comes out clean and dry. Remove to a wire rack to cool completely. Drizzle with honey to serve.

510.Mocha Chocolate Espresso Cake

Servings: 8
Cooking Time: 40 Minutes
Ingredients:
- 1 ½ cups flour
- 2/3 cup sugar
- 1 teaspoon baking powder
- 1/4 teaspoon salt
- 1 stick butter, melted
- 1/2 cup hot strongly brewed coffee
- 1/2 teaspoon vanilla
- 1 egg
- Topping:
- 1/4 cup flour
- 1/2 cup sugar
- 1/2 teaspoon ground cardamom
- 1 teaspoon ground cinnamon
- 3 tablespoons coconut oil

Directions:
1. Mix all dry ingredients for your cake; then, mix in the wet ingredients. Mix until everything is well incorporated.
2. Spritz a baking pan with cooking spray. Scrape the batter into the baking pan.
3. Then make the topping by mixing all ingredients. Place on top of the cake. Smooth the top with a spatula.
4. Bake at 330 degrees F for 30 minutes or until the top of the cake springs back when gently pressed with your fingers. Serve with your favorite hot beverage. Bon appétit!

511.Chocolate Peanut Butter Cups

Servings: 2
Cooking Time: 70 Minutes
Ingredients:
- 1 stick unsalted butter
- 1 oz / 1 cube unsweetened chocolate
- 5 packets Sugar in the Raw
- 1 tbsp heavy cream
- 4 tbsp peanut butter

Directions:
1. In a microwave, melt the butter and chocolate.
2. Add the Sugar.
3. Stir in the cream and peanut butter.
4. Line the muffin tins. Fill the muffin cups.
5. Freeze for 60 minutes.
6. Serve!

512.Vanilla Yogurt Cake

Servings: 12
Cooking Time: 30 Minutes
Ingredients:
- 6 eggs, whisked
- 1 teaspoon vanilla extract
- 1 teaspoon baking powder
- 9 ounces coconut flour
- 4 tablespoons stevia
- 8 ounces Greek yogurt

Directions:
1. In a bowl, mix all the ingredients and whisk well. Pour this into a cake pan that fits the air fryer lined with parchment paper, put the pan in the air fryer and cook at 330 degrees F for 30 minutes.

513.Mango Honey Cake

Servings:4
Cooking Time: 50 Minutes
Ingredients:
- 8 oz self-rising flour
- 4 oz butter, softened
- 1 mango, cubed
- ½ cup orange juice
- 1 egg
- 2 tbsp milk
- ½ cup honey

Directions:
1. Preheat air fryer to 390 F. In a bowl, mix butter and flour. Crumble the mixture with your fingers. Stir in mango, honey, chocolate, and juice. Whisk egg and milk in another bowl, and then add to the batter. Transfer the batter to a greased cake pan, put in the air fryer, and cook for 40 minutes. Let cool before serving.

514.Cocktail Party Fruit Kabobs

Servings: 6
Cooking Time: 10 Minutes
Ingredients:
- 2 pears, diced into bite-sized chunks
- 2 apples, diced into bite-sized chunks
- 2 mangos, diced into bite-sized chunks
- 1 tablespoon fresh lemon juice
- 1 teaspoon vanilla essence
- 2 tablespoons maple syrup
- 1 teaspoon ground cinnamon
- 1/2 teaspoon ground cloves

Directions:
1. Toss all ingredients in a mixing dish.
2. Tread the fruit pieces on skewers.
3. Cook at 350 degrees F for 5 minutes. Bon appétit!

515.Fruity Oreo Muffins

Servings:6

Cooking Time:10 Minutes
Ingredients:
- 1 cup milk
- 1 pack Oreo biscuits, crushed
- ¾ teaspoon baking powder
- 1 banana, peeled and chopped
- 1 apple, peeled, cored and chopped
- 1 teaspoon cocoa powder
- 1 teaspoon honey
- 1 teaspoon fresh lemon juice
- A pinch of ground cinnamon

Directions:
1. Preheat the Air fryer to 320 °F and grease 6 muffin cups lightly.
2. Mix milk, biscuits, cocoa powder, baking soda, and baking powder in a bowl until well combined.
3. Transfer the mixture into the muffin cups and cook for about 10 minutes.
4. Remove from the Air fryer and invert the muffin cups onto a wire rack to cool.
5. Meanwhile, mix the banana, apple, honey, lemon juice, and cinnamon in another bowl.
6. Scoop some portion of muffins from the center and fill with fruit mixture to serve.

516.Cinnamon And Sugar Sweet Potato Fries

Servings: 2
Cooking Time: 30 Minutes
Ingredients:
- 1 large sweet potato, peeled and sliced into sticks
- 1 teaspoon ghee
- 1 tablespoon cornstarch
- 1/4 teaspoon ground cardamom
- 1/4 cup sugar
- 1 tablespoon ground cinnamon

Directions:
1. Toss the sweet potato sticks with the melted ghee and cornstarch.
2. Cook in the preheated Air Fryer at 380 degrees F for 20 minutes, shaking the basket halfway through the cooking time.
3. Sprinkle the cardamom, sugar, and cinnamon all over the sweet potato fries and serve. Bon appétit!

517.Homemade Coconut Banana Treat

Servings: 6
Cooking Time: 20 Minutes
Ingredients:
- 2 tbsp. coconut oil
- ¾ cup friendly bread crumbs
- 2 tbsp. sugar
- ½ tsp. cinnamon powder
- ¼ tsp. ground cloves
- 6 ripe bananas, peeled and halved
- ⅓ cup flour

- 1 large egg, beaten

Directions:
1. Heat a skillet over a medium heat. Add in the coconut oil and the bread crumbs, and mix together for approximately 4 minutes.
2. Take the skillet off of the heat.
3. Add in the sugar, cinnamon, and cloves.
4. Cover all sides of the banana halves with the rice flour.
5. Dip each one in the beaten egg before coating them in the bread crumb mix.
6. Place the banana halves in the Air Fryer basket, taking care not to overlap them. Cook at 290°F for 10 minutes. You may need to complete this step in multiple batches.
7. Serve hot or at room temperature, topped with a sprinkling of flaked coconut if desired.

518.Crème Brulee

Servings:3
Cooking Time: 60 Minutes
Ingredients:
- 1 cup milk
- 2 vanilla pods
- 10 egg yolks
- 4 tbsp sugar + extra for topping

Directions:
1. In a pan, add the milk and cream. Cut the vanilla pods open and scrape the seeds into the pan with the vanilla pods also. Place the pan over medium heat on a stovetop until almost boiled while stirring regularly. Turn off the heat. Add the egg yolks to a bowl and beat it. Add the sugar and mix well but not too bubbly.
2. Remove the vanilla pods from the milk mixture; pour the mixture onto the eggs mixture while stirring constantly. Let it sit for 25 minutes. Fill 2 to 3 ramekins with the mixture. Place the ramekins in the fryer basket and cook them at 190 F for 50 minutes. Once ready, remove the ramekins and let sit to cool. Sprinkle the remaining sugar over and use a torch to melt the sugar, so it browns at the top.

519.Chocolate And Peanut Butter Brownies

Servings: 10
Cooking Time: 30 Minutes
Ingredients:
- 1 cup peanut butter
- 1 ¼ cups sugar
- 3 eggs
- 1 cup all-purpose flour
- 1 teaspoon baking powder
- 1/4 teaspoon kosher salt

- 1 cup dark chocolate, broken into chunks

Directions:
1. Start by preheating your Air Fryer to 350 degrees F. Now, spritz the sides and bottom of a baking pan with cooking spray.
2. In a mixing dish, thoroughly combine the peanut butter with the sugar until creamy. Next, fold in the egg and beat until fluffy.
3. After that, stir in the flour, baking powder, salt, and chocolate. Mix until everything is well combined.
4. Bake in the preheated Air Fryer for 20 to 22 minutes. Transfer to a wire rack to cool before slicing and serving. Bon appétit!

520.Banana And Rice Pudding

Servings: 6
Cooking Time: 20 Minutes
Ingredients:
- 1 cup brown rice
- 3 cups milk
- 2 bananas, peeled and mashed
- ½ cup maple syrup
- 1 teaspoon vanilla extract

Directions:
1. Place all the ingredients in a pan that fits your air fryer; stir well.
2. Put the pan in the fryer and cook at 360 degrees F for 20 minutes.
3. Stir the pudding, divide into cups, refrigerate, and serve cold.

521.Dessert French Toast With Blackberries

Servings: 2
Cooking Time: 20 Minutes
Ingredients:
- 2 tablespoons butter, at room temperature
- 1 egg
- 2 tablespoons granulated sugar
- 1/4 teaspoon ground cinnamon
- 1/4 teaspoon vanilla extract
- 6 slices French baguette
- 1 cup fresh blackberries
- 2 tablespoons powdered sugar

Directions:
1. Start by preheating your Air Fryer to 375 degrees F.
2. In a mixing dish, whisk the butter, egg, granulated sugar, cinnamon and vanilla.
3. Dip all the slices of the French baguette in this mixture. Transfer the French toast to the baking pan.
4. Bake in the preheated Air Fryer for 8 minutes, turning them over halfway through the cooking time to ensure even cooking.
5. To serve, divide the French toast between two warm plates. Arrange the blackberries

on top of each slice. Dust with powdered sugar and serve immediately. Enjoy!

522.Cheat Apple Pie

Servings:8
Cooking Time: 30 Minutes
Ingredients:
- 2 oz butter, melted
- 2 oz sugar
- 1 oz brown sugar
- 2 tsp cinnamon
- 1 egg, beaten
- 3 large puff pastry sheets
- ¼ tsp salt

Directions:
1. Whisk white sugar, brown sugar, cinnamon, salt, and butter. Place the apples in a baking dish and coat them with the mixture. Place the baking dish in the air fryer, and cook for 10 minutes at 350 F.
2. Meanwhile, roll out the pastry on a floured flat surface, and cut each sheet into 6 equal pieces. Divide the apple filling between the pieces. Brush the edges of the pastry squares with the egg.
3. Fold them and seal the edges with a fork. Place on a lined baking sheet and cook in the fryer at 350 F for 8 minutes. Flip over, increase the temperature to 390 F, and cook for 2 more minutes.

523.Fudge Cake With Pecans

Servings: 6
Cooking Time: 30 Minutes
Ingredients:
- 1/2 cup butter, melted
- 1/2 cup swerve
- 1 teaspoon vanilla essence
- 1 egg
- 1/2 cup almond flour
- 1/2 teaspoon baking powder
- 1/4 cup cocoa powder
- 1/2 teaspoon ground cinnamon
- 1/4 teaspoon fine sea salt
- 1 ounce bakers' chocolate, unsweetened
- 1/4 cup pecans, finely chopped

Directions:
1. Start by preheating your Air Fryer to 350 degrees F. Now, lightly grease six silicone molds.
2. In a mixing dish, beat the melted butter with the swerve until fluffy. Next, stir in the vanilla and egg and beat again.
3. After that, add the almond flour, baking powder, cocoa powder, cinnamon, and salt. Mix until everything is well combined.
4. Fold in the chocolate and pecans; mix to combine. Bake in the preheated Air Fryer for 20 to 22 minutes. Enjoy!

524.Raisin Bread Pudding

Servings:3
Cooking Time: 12 Minutes
Ingredients:
- 1 cup milk
- 1 egg
- 1 tablespoon brown sugar
- ½ teaspoon ground cinnamon
- ¼ teaspoon vanilla extract
- 2 tablespoons raisins, soaked in hot water for about 15 minutes
- 2 bread slices, cut into small cubes
- 1 tablespoon chocolate chips
- 1 tablespoon sugar

Directions:
1. In a bowl, mix well milk, egg, brown sugar, cinnamon, and vanilla extract.
2. Stir in the raisins.
3. In a baking dish, spread the bread cubes and top evenly with the milk mixture.
4. Refrigerate for about 15-20 minutes.
5. Set the temperature of air fryer to 375 degrees F.
6. Remove from refrigerator and sprinkle with chocolate chips and sugar on top.
7. Arrange the baking dish into an air fryer basket.
8. Air fry for about 12 minutes.
9. Remove from the air fryer and serve warm.

525.Air Fryer Chocolate Cake

Servings:6
Cooking Time:25 Minutes
Ingredients:
- 3 eggs
- 1 cup almond flour
- 1 stick butter, room temperature
- 1/3 cup cocoa powder
- 1½ teaspoons baking powder
- ½ cup sour cream
- 2/3 cup swerve
- 2 teaspoons vanilla

Directions:
1. Preheat the Air fryer to 360 °F and grease a cake pan lightly.
2. Mix all the ingredients in a bowl and beat well.
3. Pour the batter in the cake pan and transfer into the Air fryer basket.
4. Cook for about 25 minutes and cut into slices to serve.

526.Banana & Vanilla Pastry Puffs

Servings: 8
Cooking Time: 15 Minutes
Ingredients:
- 1 package [8-oz.] crescent dinner rolls, refrigerated
- 1 cup milk
- 4 oz. instant vanilla pudding
- 4 oz. cream cheese, softened
- 2 bananas, peeled and sliced
- 1 egg, lightly beaten

Directions:
1. Roll out the crescent dinner rolls and slice each one into 8 squares.
2. Mix together the milk, pudding, and cream cheese using a whisk.
3. Scoop equal amounts of the mixture into the pastry squares. Add the banana slices on top.
4. Fold the squares around the filling, pressing down on the edges to seal them.
5. Apply a light brushing of the egg to each pastry puff before placing them in the Air Fryer.
6. Air bake at 355°F for 10 minutes.

527.Cocoa Bombs

Servings: 12
Cooking Time: 8 Minutes
Ingredients:
- 2 cups macadamia nuts, chopped
- 4 tablespoons coconut oil, melted
- 1 teaspoon vanilla extract
- ¼ cup cocoa powder
- 1/3 cup swerve

Directions:
1. In a bowl, mix all the ingredients and whisk well. Shape medium balls out of this mix, place them in your air fryer and cook at 300 degrees F for 8 minutes. Serve cold.

528.Chocolate Brownie

Servings: 4
Cooking Time: 16 Minutes
Ingredients:
- 1 cup bananas, overripe
- 1 scoop protein powder
- 2 tbsp unsweetened cocoa powder
- 1/2 cup almond butter, melted

Directions:
1. Preheat the air fryer to 325 F.
2. Spray air fryer baking pan with cooking spray.
3. Add all ingredients into the blender and blend until smooth.
4. Pour batter into the prepared pan and place in the air fryer basket.
5. Cook brownie for 16 minutes.
6. Serve and enjoy.

529.Strawberry Frozen Dessert

Servings: 1
Cooking Time: 45 Minutes
Ingredients:
- ½ cup sugar-free strawberry preserves
- ½ cup Sugar in the Raw or Splenda

- 2 cups Fage Total 0% Greek Yogurt
- Ice cream maker

Directions:
1. In a food processor, purée the strawberries. Add the strawberry preserves.
2. Add the Greek yogurt and fully mix.
3. Put into the ice cream maker for 25-30 minute.
4. Serve!

530.Easy Cheesecake

Servings: 6
Cooking Time: 10 Minutes
Ingredients:
- 2 eggs
- 16 oz cream cheese, softened
- 2 tbsp sour cream
- 1/2 tsp fresh lemon juice
- 1 tsp vanilla
- 3/4 cup erythritol

Directions:
1. Preheat the air fryer to 350 F.
2. Add eggs, lemon juice, vanilla, and sweetener in a large bowl and beat using a hand mixer until smooth.
3. Add cream cheese and sour cream and beat until fluffy.
4. Pour batter into the 2 four-inch spring-form pan and place in air fryer basket and cook for 8-10minutes at 350 F.
5. Remove from air fryer and let it cool completely.
6. Place in refrigerator for overnight.
7. Serve and enjoy.

531.Apple Doughnuts

Servings:6
Cooking Time:5 Minutes
Ingredients:
- 2½ cups plus 2 tablespoons all-purpose flour
- 1½ teaspoons baking powder
- 2 tablespoons unsalted butter, softened
- 1 egg
- ½ pink lady apple, peeled, cored and grated
- 1 cup apple cider
- ½ teaspoon ground cinnamon
- ½ teaspoon salt
- ½ cup brown sugar

Directions:
1. Preheat the Air fryer to 360 °F and grease an Air fryer basket lightly.
2. Boil apple cider in a medium pan over medium-high heat and reduce the heat.
3. Let it simmer for about 15 minutes and dish out in a bowl.
4. Sift together flour, baking powder, baking soda, cinnamon, and salt in a large bowl.

5. Mix the brown sugar, egg, cooled apple cider and butter in another bowl.
6. Stir in the flour mixture and grated apple and mix to form a dough.
7. Wrap the dough with a plastic wrap and refrigerate for about 30 minutes.
8. Roll the dough into 1-inch thickness and cut the doughnuts with a doughnut cutter.
9. Arrange the doughnuts into the Air fryer basket and cook for about 5 minutes, flipping once in between.
10. Dish out and serve warm.

532.Old-fashioned Plum Dumplings

Servings: 4
Cooking Time: 40 Minutes
Ingredients:
- 1 (14-ounce) box pie crusts
- 2 cups plums, pitted
- 2 tablespoons granulated sugar
- 2 tablespoons coconut oil
- 1/4 teaspoon ground cardamom
- 1/2 teaspoon ground cinnamon
- 1 egg white, slightly beaten

Directions:
1. Place the pie crust on a work surface. Roll into a circle and cut into quarters.
2. Place 1 plum on each crust piece. Add the sugar, coconut oil, cardamom, and cinnamon. Roll up the sides into a circular shape around the plums.
3. Repeat with the remaining ingredients. Brush the edges with the egg white. Place in the lightly greased Air Fryer basket.
4. Bake in the preheated Air Fryer at 360 degrees F for 20 minutes, flipping them halfway through the cooking time. Work in two batches, decorate and serve at room temperature. Bon appétit!

533.Cashew Bars Recipe

Servings: 6
Cooking Time:25 Minutes
Ingredients:
- 1/4 cup almond meal
- 1 tbsp. almond butter
- 1 ½ cups cashews; chopped
- 4 dates; chopped
- 3/4 cup coconut; shredded
- 1/3 cup honey
- 1 tbsp. chia seeds

Directions:
1. In a bowl; mix honey with almond meal and almond butter and stir well.
2. Add cashews, coconut, dates and chia seeds and stir well again.
3. Spread this on a lined baking sheet that fits your air fryer and press well.

4. Introduce in the fryer and cook at 300 °F, for 15 minutes. Leave mix to cool down, cut into medium bars and serve

534.Cinnamon Doughnuts

Servings:6
Cooking Time:12 Minutes
Ingredients:
- 1 cup white almond flour
- 1 teaspoon baking powder
- 2 tablespoons water
- ¼ cup almond milk
- ¼ cup swerve
- ½ teaspoon salt
- 1 tablespoon coconut oil, melted
- 2 teaspoons cinnamon

Directions:
1. Preheat the Air fryer to 360 °F and grease an Air fryer basket.
2. Mix flour, swerve, salt, cinnamon and baking powder in a bowl.
3. Stir in the coconut oil, water, and soy milk until a smooth dough is formed.
4. Cover this dough and refrigerate for about 1 hour.
5. Mix ground cinnamon with 2 tablespoons swerve in another bowl and keep aside.
6. Divide the dough into 12 equal balls and roll each ball in the cinnamon swerve mixture.
7. Transfer 6 balls in the Air fryer basket and cook for about 6 minutes.
8. Repeat with the remaining balls and dish out to serve.

535.Cream Doughnuts

Servings:8
Cooking Time:16 Minutes
Ingredients:
- 4 tablespoons butter, softened and divided
- 2 egg yolks
- 2¼ cups plain flour
- 1½ teaspoons baking powder
- ½ cup sugar
- 1 teaspoon salt
- ½ cup sour cream
- ½ cup heavy cream

Directions:
1. Preheat the Air fryer to 355 °F and grease an Air fryer basket lightly.
2. Sift together flour, baking powder and salt in a large bowl.
3. Add sugar and cold butter and mix until a coarse crumb is formed.
4. Stir in the egg yolks, ½ of the sour cream and 1/3 of the flour mixture and mix until a dough is formed.
5. Add remaining sour cream and 1/3 of the flour mixture and mix until well combined.

6. Stir in the remaining flour mixture and combine well.
7. Roll the dough into ½ inch thickness onto a floured surface and cut into donuts with a donut cutter.
8. Coat butter on both sides of the donuts and arrange in the Air fryer basket.
9. Cook for about 8 minutes until golden and top with heavy cream to serve.

536.Blackberry Cream

Servings: 6
Cooking Time: 20 Minutes
Ingredients:
- 2 cups blackberries
- Juice of ½ lemon
- 2 tablespoons water
- 1 teaspoon vanilla extract
- 2 tablespoons swerve

Directions:
1. In a bowl, mix all the ingredients and whisk well. Divide this into 6 ramekins, put them in the air fryer and cook at 340 degrees F for 20 minutes Cool down and serve.

537.Snickerdoodle Cinnamon Cookies

Servings: 10
Cooking Time: 1 Hour
Ingredients:
- 4 tablespoons liquid monk fruit
- 1/2 cup hazelnuts, ground
- 1 stick butter, room temperature
- 2 cups almond flour
- 1 cup coconut flour
- 2 ounces granulated swerve
- 2 teaspoons ground cinnamon

Directions:
1. Firstly, cream liquid monk fruit with butter until the mixture becomes fluffy. Sift in both types of flour.
2. Now, stir in the hazelnuts. Now, knead the mixture to form a dough; place in the refrigerator for about 35 minutes.
3. To finish, shape the prepared dough into the bite-sized balls; arrange them on a baking dish; flatten the balls using the back of a spoon.
4. Mix granulated swerve with ground cinnamon. Press your cookies in the cinnamon mixture until they are completely covered.
5. Bake the cookies for 20 minutes at 310 degrees F.
6. Leave them to cool for about 10 minutes before transferring them to a wire rack. Bon appétit!

538.Brownies Muffins

Servings:12

Cooking Time:10 Minutes
Ingredients:
- 1 package Betty Crocker fudge brownie mix
- ¼ cup walnuts, chopped
- 1 egg
- 2 teaspoons water
- 1/3 cup vegetable oil

Directions:
1. Preheat the Air fryer to 300 °F and grease 12 muffin molds lightly.
2. Mix all the ingredients in a bowl and divide evenly into the muffin molds.
3. Arrange the molds in the Air Fryer basket and cook for about 10 minutes.
4. Dish out and invert the muffins onto wire rack to completely cool before serving.

539.No Flour Lime Muffins

Servings:6
Cooking Time: 30 Minutes
Ingredients:
- Juice and zest of 2 limes
- 1 cup yogurt
- ¼ cup superfine sugar
- 8 oz cream cheese
- 1 tsp vanilla extract

Directions:
1. Preheat the air fryer to 330 F, and with a spatula, gently combine the yogurt and cheese. In another bowl, beat together the rest of the ingredients. Gently fold the lime with the cheese mixture. Divide the batter between 6 lined muffin tins. Cook in the air fryer for 10 minutes.

540.Chocolate Chip Cookies

Servings: 9
Cooking Time: 25 Minutes
Ingredients:
- 1 ¼ cup flour
- 2/3 cup chocolate chips, or any kind of baker's chocolate
- ⅓ cup sugar
- ½ cup butter
- 4 tbsp. honey
- 1 tbsp. milk
- High quality cooking spray

Directions:
1. Set your Air Fryer to 320°F and allow to warm up for about 10 minutes.
2. In the meantime, in a large bowl, cream the butter to soften it.
3. Add in the sugar and combine to form a light and fluffy consistency.
4. Stir in the honey.
5. Gradually fold in the flour, incorporating it well.

6. If you are using baker's chocolate, use a rolling pin or a mallet to break it up and create chocolate chips.
7. Throw the chocolate into the bowl and mix well to ensure the chips are evenly distributed throughout the dough.
8. Finally, add in the milk and combine well.
9. Lightly spritz your Air Fryer basket with the cooking spray.
10. Transfer the cookie dough into the fryer and cook for 20 minutes.
11. Slice into 9 cookies. Serve immediately. Alternatively, the cookies can be stored in an airtight container for up to 3 days.

541.Leche Flan Filipino Style

Servings:4
Cooking Time: 30 Minutes
Ingredients:
- 1 cup heavy cream
- 1 teaspoon vanilla extract
- 1/2 (14 ounce) can sweetened condensed milk
- 1/2 cup milk
- 2-1/2 eggs
- 1/3 cup white sugar

Directions:
1. In blender, blend well vanilla, eggs, milk, cream, and condensed milk.
2. Lightly grease baking pan of air fryer with cooking spray. Add sugar and heat for 10 minutes at 370°F until melted and caramelized. Lower heat to 300°F and continue melting and swirling.
3. Pour milk mixture into caramelized sugar. Cover pan with foil.
4. Cook for 20 minutes at 330°F.
5. Let it cool completely in the fridge.
6. Place a plate on top of pan and invert pan to easily remove flan.
7. Serve and enjoy.

542.Chocolate Soufflé

Servings:2
Cooking Time: 25 Minutes
Ingredients:
- ¼ cup butter, melted
- 2 tbsp flour
- 3 tbsp sugar
- 3 oz chocolate, melted
- ½ tsp vanilla extract

Directions:
1. Preheat the air fryer to 330 F.
2. Beat the yolks along with the sugar and vanilla extract; stir in butter, chocolate, and flour. and whisk the whites until a stiff peak forms.
3. Working in batches, gently combine the egg whites with the chocolate mixture. Divide

the batter between two greased ramekins. Cook for 14 minutes.

543.Chocolate Rum Lava Cake

Servings: 4
Cooking Time: 20 Minutes
Ingredients:
- 2 ½ ounces butter, at room temperature
- 3 ounces chocolate, unsweetened
- 2 eggs, beaten
- 1/2 cup confectioners' swerve
- 1/2 cup almond flour
- 1 teaspoon rum extract
- 1 teaspoon vanilla extract

Directions:
1. Begin by preheating your Air Fryer to 370 degrees F. Spritz the sides and bottom of four ramekins with cooking spray.
2. Melt the butter and chocolate in a microwave-safe bowl. Mix the eggs and confectioners' swerve until frothy.
3. Pour the butter/chocolate mixture into the egg mixture. Stir in the almond flour, rum extract, and vanilla extract. Mix until everything is well incorporated.
4. Scrape the batter into the prepared ramekins. Bake in the preheated Air Fryer for 9 to 11 minutes.
5. Let stand for 2 to 3 minutes. Invert on a plate while warm and serve. Bon appétit!

544.Berry Cookies

Servings: 4
Cooking Time: 9 Minutes
Ingredients:
- 2 teaspoons butter, softened
- 1 tablespoon Splenda
- 1 egg yolk
- ½ cup almond flour
- 1 oz strawberry, chopped, mashed

Directions:
1. In the mixing bowl mix up butter, Splenda, egg yolk, and almond flour. Knead the non-sticky dough. Then make the small balls from the dough. Use your finger to make small holes in every ball. Then fill the balls with mashed strawberries. Preheat the air fryer to 360F. Line the air fryer basket with baking paper and put the cookies inside. Cook them for 9 minutes.

545.Ginger Lemon Pie

Servings: 6
Cooking Time: 30 Minutes
Ingredients:
- 2 eggs
- 6 tablespoons coconut flour
- ½ teaspoon vanilla extract
- 6 tablespoons ricotta cheese
- ½ teaspoon baking powder
- 1 teaspoon lemon juice
- ½ teaspoon ground ginger
- 3 tablespoons Erythritol
- 1 tablespoon butter, melted

Directions:
1. Crack the eggs and separate them on the egg whites and egg yolks. Then whisk the egg yolks with Erythritol until you get the lemon color mixture. Then whisk the egg whites to the soft peaks. Add egg whites in the egg yolk mixture. Then add ricotta cheese, baking powder, lemon juice, ground ginger, vanilla extract, Erythritol. Then add butter and coconut flour and stir the pie butter until smooth. Line the air fryer baking pan with the baking paper. Pour the pie batter inside. Preheat the air fryer to 330F. Put the baking pan with pie in the air fryer and cook it for 30 minutes.

546.Coconut Cheese Cookies

Servings: 30
Cooking Time: 12 Minutes
Ingredients:
- 8 oz cream cheese
- 1 tsp vanilla
- 1 tbsp baking powder
- ¾ cup coconut flakes
- 1 cup swerve
- ¾ cup butter, softened
- 1 ¼ cup coconut flour
- Pinch of salt

Directions:
1. Preheat the air fryer to 325 F.
2. Beat cream cheese, butter, and sweetener in a bowl using a hand mixer until fluffy.
3. Add vanilla and stir well.
4. Add coconut flour, baking powder, and salt and mix until well combined.
5. Add coconut flakes and mix to combine.
6. Make cookies from mixture and place on a plate.
7. Place cookies in batches in the air fryer and cook for 12 minutes.
8. Serve and enjoy.

547.Sunday Banana Chocolate Cookies

Servings: 8
Cooking Time: 20 Minutes
Ingredients:
- 1 stick butter, at room temperature
- 1 ¼ cups caster sugar
- 2 ripe bananas, mashed
- 1 teaspoon vanilla paste
- 1 2/3 cups all-purpose flour
- 1/3 cup cocoa powder
- 1 ½ teaspoons baking powder
- 1/4 teaspoon ground cinnamon

- 1/4 teaspoon crystallized ginger
- 1 ½ cups chocolate chips

Directions:
1. In a mixing dish, beat the butter and sugar until creamy and uniform. Stir in the mashed bananas and vanilla.
2. In another mixing dish, thoroughly combine the flour, cocoa powder, baking powder, cinnamon, and crystallized ginger.
3. Add the flour mixture to the banana mixture; mix to combine well. Afterwards, fold in the chocolate chips.
4. Drop by large spoonfuls onto a parchment-lined Air Fryer basket. Bake at 365 degrees F for 11 minutes or until golden brown on the top. Bon appétit!

548.Vanilla Coconut Cheese Cookies

Servings: 15
Cooking Time: 12 Minutes
Ingredients:
- 1 egg
- 1/2 tsp baking powder
- 1 tsp vanilla
- 1/2 cup swerve
- 1/2 cup butter, softened
- 3 tbsp cream cheese, softened
- 1/2 cup coconut flour
- Pinch of salt

Directions:
1. In a bowl, beat together butter, sweetener, and cream cheese.
2. Add egg and vanilla and beat until smooth and creamy.

3. Add coconut flour, salt, and baking powder and beat until combined. Cover and place in the fridge for 1 hour.
4. Preheat the air fryer to 325 F.
5. Make cookies from dough and place into the air fryer and cook for 12 minutes.
6. Serve and enjoy.

549.Easy Chocolate And Coconut Cake

Servings: 10
Cooking Time: 20 Minutes
Ingredients:
- 1 stick butter
- 1 ¼ cups dark chocolate, broken into chunks
- 1/4 cup tablespoon agave syrup
- 1/4 cup sugar
- 2 tablespoons milk
- 2 eggs, beaten
- 1/3 cup coconut, shredded

Directions:
1. Begin by preheating your Air Fryer to 330 degrees F.
2. In a microwave-safe bowl, melt the butter, chocolate, and agave syrup. Allow it to cool to room temperature.
3. Add the remaining ingredients to the chocolate mixture; stir to combine well. Scrape the batter into a lightly greased baking pan.
4. Bake in the preheated Air Fryer for 15 minutes or until a toothpick comes out dry and clean. Enjoy!

OTHER AIR FRYER RECIPES

550.Oatmeal Pizza Cups

Servings: 4
Cooking Time: 30 Minutes
Ingredients:
- 1 cup rolled oats
- 1 teaspoon baking powder
- 1/4 teaspoon ground black pepper
- Salt, to taste
- 2 tablespoons butter, melted
- 1 cup milk
- 4 slices smoked ham, chopped
- 4 ounces mozzarella cheese, shredded
- 4 tablespoons ketchup

Directions:
1. Start by preheating your Air Fryer to 350 degrees F. Now, lightly grease a muffin tin with nonstick spray.
2. Pulse the rolled oats, baking powder, pepper, and salt in your food processor until the mixture looks like coarse meal.
3. Add the remaining ingredients and stir to combine well. Spoon the mixture into the prepared muffin tin.
4. Bake in the preheated Air Fryer for 20 minutes until a toothpick inserted comes out clean. Bon appétit!

551.Onion Rings With Mayo Dip

Servings: 3
Cooking Time: 25 Minutes
Ingredients:
- 1 large onion
- 1/2 cup almond flour
- 1 teaspoon salt
- 1/2 teaspoon ground black pepper
- 1 teaspoon cayenne pepper
- 1/2 teaspoon dried thyme
- 1/2 teaspoon dried oregano
- 1/2 teaspoon ground cumin
- 2 eggs
- 4 tablespoons milk
- Mayo Dip:
- 3 tablespoons mayonnaise
- 3 tablespoons sour cream
- 1 tablespoon horseradish, drained
- Kosher salt and freshly ground black pepper, to taste

Directions:
1. Cut off the top 1/2 inch of the Vidalia onion; peel your onion and place it cut-side down. Starting 1/2 inch from the root, cut the onion in half. Make a second cut that splits each half in two. You will have 4 quarters held together by the root.
2. Repeat these cuts, splitting the 4 quarters to yield eighths; then, you should split them again until you have 16 evenly spaced cuts. Turn the onion over and gently separate the outer pieces using your fingers.
3. In a mixing bowl, thoroughly combine the almond flour and spices. In a separate bowl, whisk the eggs and milk. Dip the onion into the egg mixture, followed by the almond flour mixture.
4. Spritz the onion with cooking spray and transfer to the lightly greased cooking basket. Cook for 370 degrees F for 12 to 15 minutes.
5. Meanwhile, make the mayo dip by whisking the remaining ingredients. Serve and enjoy!

552.Baked Eggs With Cheese And Cauli Rice

Servings: 4
Cooking Time: 30 Minutes
Ingredients:
- 1 pound cauliflower rice
- 1 onion, diced
- 6 slices bacon, precooked
- 1 tablespoon butter, melted
- Sea salt and ground black pepper, to taste
- 6 eggs
- 1 cup cheddar cheese, shredded

Directions:
1. Place the cauliflower rice and onion in a lightly greased casserole dish. Add the bacon and the reserved quinoa. Drizzle the melted butter over cauliflower rice and sprinkle with salt and pepper.
2. Bake in the preheated Air Fryer at 390 degrees F for 10 minutes.
3. Turn the temperature down to 350 degrees F.
4. Make six indents for the eggs; crack one egg into each indent. Bake for 10 minutes, rotating the pan once or twice to ensure even cooking.
5. Top with cheese and bake for a further 5 minutes. Enjoy!

553.Easy Fried Button Mushrooms

Servings: 4
Cooking Time: 15 Minutes
Ingredients:
- 1 pound button mushrooms
- 1 cup cornstarch
- 1 cup all-purpose flour
- 1/2 teaspoon baking powder
- 2 eggs, whisked
- 2 cups seasoned breadcrumbs
- 1/2 teaspoon salt
- 2 tablespoons fresh parsley leaves, roughly chopped

Directions:
1. Pat the mushrooms dry with a paper towel.
2. To begin, set up your breading station. Mix the cornstarch, flour, and baking powder in a shallow dish. In a separate dish, whisk the eggs.
3. Finally, place your breadcrumbs and salt in a third dish.
4. Start by dredging the mushrooms in the flour mixture; then, dip them into the eggs. Press your mushrooms into the breadcrumbs, coating evenly.
5. Spritz the Air Fryer basket with cooking oil. Add the mushrooms and cook at 400 degrees F for 6 minutes, flipping them halfway through the cooking time.
6. Serve garnished with fresh parsley leaves. Bon appétit!

554. Turkey With Cheese And Pasilla Peppers

Servings: 2
Cooking Time: 30 Minutes
Ingredients:
- 1/2 cup Parmesan cheese, shredded
- 1/2 pound turkey breasts, cut into four pieces
- 1/3 cup mayonnaise
- 1 ½ tablespoons sour cream
- 1 dried Pasilla peppers
- 1 teaspoon onion salt
- 1/3 teaspoon mixed peppercorns, freshly cracked

Directions:
1. In a shallow bowl, mix Parmesan cheese, onion salt, and the cracked mixed peppercorns together.
2. In a food processor, blitz the mayonnaise, along with the cream and dried Pasilla peppers until there are no lumps.
3. Coat the turkey breasts with this mixture, ensuring that all sides are covered.
4. Then, coat each piece of turkey in the Parmesan mixture. Now, preheat the Air Fryer to 365 degrees F; cook for 28 minutes until thoroughly cooked.

555. Western Eggs With Ham And Cheese

Servings: 4
Cooking Time: 20 Minutes
Ingredients:
- 6 eggs
- 1/2 cup milk
- 2 ounces cream cheese, softened
- Sea salt, to your liking
- 1/4 teaspoon ground black pepper
- 1/4 teaspoon paprika
- 6 ounces cooked ham, diced
- 1 onion, chopped
- 1/2 cup cheddar cheese, shredded

Directions:
1. Begin by preheating the Air Fryer to 360 degrees F. Spritz the sides and bottom of a baking pan with cooking oil.
2. In a mixing dish, whisk the eggs, milk, and cream cheese until pale. Add the spices, ham, and onion; stir until everything is well incorporated.
3. Pour the mixture into the baking pan; top with the cheddar cheese.
4. Bake in the preheated Air Fryer for 12 minutes. Serve warm and enjoy!

556. Classic Egg Salad

Servings: 3
Cooking Time: 20 Minutes + Chilling Time
Ingredients:
- 6 eggs
- 1 teaspoon mustard
- 1/2 cup mayonnaise
- 1 tablespoons white vinegar
- 2 carrots, trimmed and sliced
- 1 red bell pepper, seeded and sliced
- 1 green bell pepper, seeded and sliced
- 1 shallot, sliced
- Sea salt and ground black pepper, to taste

Directions:
1. Place the wire rack in the Air Fryer basket; lower the eggs onto the wire rack.
2. Cook at 270 degrees F for 15 minutes.
3. Transfer them to an ice-cold water bath to stop the cooking. Peel the eggs under cold running water; coarsely chop the hard-boiled eggs and set aside.
4. Toss with the remaining ingredients and serve well chilled. Bon appétit!

557. Cheesy Zucchini With Queso Añejo

Servings: 4
Cooking Time: 25 Minutes
Ingredients:
- 1 large-sized zucchini, thinly sliced
- 1/4 cup almond flour
- 1 cup parmesan cheese
- 1 egg, whisked
- 1/2 cup Queso Añejo, grated
- Salt and cracked pepper, to taste

Directions:
1. Pat dry the zucchini slices with a kitchen towel.
2. Mix the remaining ingredients in a shallow bowl; mix until everything is well combined. Dip each zucchini slice in the prepared batter.
3. Cook in the preheated Air Fryer at 400 degrees F for 12 minutes, shaking the basket halfway through the cooking time.

4. Work in batches until the zucchini slices are crispy and golden brown. Enjoy!

558.Baked Apples With Crisp Topping

Servings: 3
Cooking Time: 25 Minutes
Ingredients:
- 3 Granny Smith apples, cored
- 2/3 cup rolled oats
- 3 tablespoons honey
- 1 tablespoon fresh orange juice
- 1/2 teaspoon ground cardamom
- 1/2 teaspoon ground cinnamon
- 1/4 teaspoon ground cloves
- 1/4 teaspoon ground star anise
- 2 tablespoons butter, cut in pieces
- 3 tablespoons cranberries

Directions:
1. Use a paring knife to remove the stem and seeds from the apples, making deep holes.
2. In a mixing bowl, combine together the rolled oats, honey, orange juice, cardamom, cinnamon, cloves, anise, butter, and cranberries.
3. Pour enough water into an Air Fryer safe dish. Place the apples in the dish.
4. Bake at 340 degrees F for 16 to 18 minutes. Serve at room temperature. Bon appétit!

559.Potato And Kale Croquettes

Servings: 6
Cooking Time: 9 Minutes
Ingredients:
- 4 eggs, slightly beaten
- 1/3 cup flour
- 1/3 cup goat cheese, crumbled
- 1 ½ teaspoons fine sea salt
- 4 garlic cloves, minced
- 1 cup kale, steamed
- 1/3 cup breadcrumbs
- 1/3teaspoon red pepper flakes
- 3 potatoes, peeled and quartered
- 1/3 teaspoon dried dill weed

Directions:
1. Firstly, boil the potatoes in salted water. Once the potatoes are cooked, mash them; add the kale, goat cheese, minced garlic, sea salt, red pepper flakes, dill and one egg; stir to combine well.
2. Now, roll the mixture to form small croquettes.
3. Grab three shallow bowls. Place the flour in the first shallow bowl.
4. Beat the remaining 3 eggs in the second bowl. After that, throw the breadcrumbs into the third shallow bowl.
5. Dip each croquette in the flour; then, dip them in the eggs bowl; lastly, roll each croquette in the breadcrumbs.

6. Air fry at 335 degrees F for 7 minutes or until golden. Tate, adjust for seasonings and serve warm.

560.Easy Roasted Hot Dogs

Servings: 6
Cooking Time: 25 Minutes
Ingredients:
- 6 hot dogs
- 6 hot dog buns
- 1 tablespoon mustard
- 6 tablespoons ketchup
- 6 lettuce leaves

Directions:
1. Place the hot dogs in the lightly greased Air Fryer basket.
2. Bake at 380 degrees F for 15 minutes, turning them over halfway through the cooking time to promote even cooking.
3. Place on the bun and add the mustard, ketchup, and lettuce leaves. Enjoy!

561.Eggs Florentine With Spinach

Servings: 2
Cooking Time: 20 Minutes
Ingredients:
- 2 tablespoons ghee, melted
- 2 cups baby spinach, torn into small pieces
- 2 tablespoons shallots, chopped
- 1/4 teaspoon red pepper flakes
- Salt, to taste
- 1 tablespoon fresh thyme leaves, roughly chopped
- 4 eggs

Directions:
1. Start by preheating your Air Fryer to 350 degrees F. Brush the sides and bottom of a gratin dish with the melted ghee.
2. Put the spinach and shallots into the bottom of the gratin dish. Season with red pepper, salt, and fresh thyme.
3. Make four indents for the eggs; crack one egg into each indent. Bake for 12 minutes, rotating the pan once or twice to ensure even cooking. Enjoy!

562.Grilled Lemony Pork Chops

Servings: 5
Cooking Time: 34 Minutes
Ingredients:
- 5 pork chops
- 1/3 cup vermouth
- 1/2 teaspoon paprika
- 2 sprigs thyme, only leaves, crushed
- 1/2 teaspoon dried oregano
- Fresh parsley, to serve
- 1 teaspoon garlic salt½ lemon, cut into wedges
- 1 teaspoon freshly cracked black pepper

- 3 tablespoons lemon juice
- 3 cloves garlic, minced
- 2 tablespoons canola oil

Directions:
1. Firstly, heat the canola oil in a sauté pan over a moderate heat. Now, sweat the garlic until just fragrant.
2. Remove the pan from the heat and pour in the lemon juice and vermouth. Now, throw in the seasonings. Dump the sauce into a baking dish, along with the pork chops.
3. Tuck the lemon wedges among the pork chops and air-fry for 27 minutes at 345 degrees F. Bon appétit!

563.Italian Creamy Frittata With Kale

Servings: 3
Cooking Time: 20 Minutes
Ingredients:
- 1 yellow onion, finely chopped
- 6 ounces wild mushrooms, sliced
- 6 eggs
- 1/4 cup double cream
- 1/2 teaspoon cayenne pepper
- Sea salt and ground black pepper, to taste
- 1 tablespoon butter, melted
- 2 tablespoons fresh Italian parsley, chopped
- 2 cups kale, chopped
- 1/2 cup mozzarella, shredded

Directions:
1. Begin by preheating the Air Fryer to 360 degrees F. Spritz the sides and bottom of a baking pan with cooking oil.
2. Add the onions and wild mushrooms, and cook in the preheated Air Fryer at 360 degrees F for 4 to 5 minutes.
3. In a mixing dish, whisk the eggs and double cream until pale. Add the spices, butter, parsley, and kale; stir until everything is well incorporated.
4. Pour the mixture into the baking pan with the mushrooms.
5. Top with the cheese. Cook in the preheated Air Fryer for 10 minutes. Serve immediately and enjoy!

564.Celery And Bacon Cakes

Servings: 4
Cooking Time: 25 Minutes
Ingredients:
- 2 eggs, lightly beaten
- 1/3 teaspoon freshly cracked black pepper
- 1 cup Colby cheese, grated
- 1/2 tablespoon fresh dill, finely chopped
- 1/2 tablespoon garlic paste
- 1/3 cup onion, finely chopped
- 1/3 cup bacon, chopped
- 2 teaspoons fine sea salt

- 2 medium-sized celery stalks, trimmed and grated
- 1/3 teaspoon baking powder

Directions:
1. Place the celery on a paper towel and squeeze them to remove the excess liquid.
2. Combine the vegetables with the other ingredients in the order listed above. Shape the balls using 1 tablespoon of the vegetable mixture.
3. Then, gently flatten each ball with your palm or a wide spatula. Spritz the croquettes with a nonstick cooking oil.
4. Bake the vegetable cakes in a single layer for 17 minutes at 318 degrees F. Serve warm with sour cream.

565.Spring Chocolate Doughnuts

Servings: 6
Cooking Time: 20 Minutes
Ingredients:
- 1 can (16-ounce can buttermilk biscuits
- Chocolate Glaze:
- 1 cup powdered sugar
- 4 tablespoons unsweetened baking cocoa
- 2 tablespoon butter, melted
- 2 tablespoons milk

Directions:
1. Bake your biscuits in the preheated Air Fryer at 350 degrees F for 8 minutes, flipping them halfway through the cooking time.
2. While the biscuits are baking, make the glaze.
3. Beat the ingredients with whisk until smooth, adding enough milk for the desired consistency; set aside.
4. Dip your doughnuts into the chocolate glaze and transfer to a cooling rack to set. Bon appétit!

566.Breakfast Eggs With Swiss Chard And Ham

Servings: 2
Cooking Time: 20 Minutes
Ingredients:
- 2 eggs
- 1/4 teaspoon dried or fresh marjoram
- 2 teaspoons chili powder
- 1/3 teaspoon kosher salt
- 1/2 cup steamed Swiss Chard
- 1/4 teaspoon dried or fresh rosemary
- 4 pork ham slices
- 1/3 teaspoon ground black pepper, or more to taste

Directions:
1. Divide the Swiss Chard and ham among 2 ramekins; crack an egg into each ramekin. Sprinkle with seasonings.

2. Cook for 15 minutes at 335 degrees F or until your eggs reach desired texture.
3. Serve warm with spicy tomato ketchup and pickles. Bon appétit!

567.Beer-braised Short Loin

Servings: 4
Cooking Time: 15 Minutes
Ingredients:
- 1 ½ pounds short loin
- 2 tablespoons olive oil
- 1 bottle beer
- 2-3 cloves garlic, finely minced
- 2 Turkish bay leaves

Directions:
1. Pat the beef dry; then, tenderize the beef with a meat mallet to soften the fibers. Place it in a large-sized mixing dish.
2. Add the remaining ingredients; toss to coat well and let it marinate for at least 1 hour.
3. Cook about 7 minutes at 395 degrees F; after that, pause the Air Fryer. Flip the meat over and cook for another 8 minutes, or until it's done.

568.Delicious Hot Fruit Bake

Servings: 4
Cooking Time: 40 Minutes
Ingredients:
- 2 cups blueberries
- 2 cups raspberries
- 1 tablespoon cornstarch
- 3 tablespoons maple syrup
- 2 tablespoons coconut oil, melted
- A pinch of freshly grated nutmeg
- A pinch of salt
- 1 cinnamon stick
- 1 vanilla bean

Directions:
1. Place your berries in a lightly greased baking dish. Sprinkle the cornstarch onto the fruit.
2. Whisk the maple syrup, coconut oil, nutmeg, and salt in a mixing dish; add this mixture to the berries and gently stir to combine.
3. Add the cinnamon and vanilla. Bake in the preheated Air Fryer at 370 degrees F for 35 minutes. Serve warm or at room temperature. Enjoy!

569.Cottage Cheese Stuffed Chicken Rolls

Servings: 2
Cooking Time: 20 Minutes
Ingredients:
- 1/2 cup Cottage cheese
- 2 eggs, beaten
- 2 medium-sized chicken breasts, halved
- 2 tablespoons fresh coriander, chopped
- 1 teaspoon fine sea salt
- 1/2 cup parmesan cheese, grated
- 1/3 teaspoon freshly ground black pepper, to savor
- 3 cloves garlic, finely minced

Directions:
1. Firstly, flatten out the chicken breast using a meat tenderizer.
2. In a medium-sized mixing dish, combine the Cottage cheese with the garlic, coriander, salt, and black pepper.
3. Spread 1/3 of the mixture over the first chicken breast. Repeat with the remaining ingredients. Roll the chicken around the filling; make sure to secure with toothpicks.
4. Now, whisk the egg in a shallow bowl. In another shallow bowl, combine the salt, ground black pepper, and parmesan cheese.
5. Coat the chicken breasts with the whisked egg; now, roll them in the parmesan cheese.
6. Cook in the air fryer cooking basket at 365 degrees F for 22 minutes. Serve immediately.

570.Easiest Pork Chops Ever

Servings: 6
Cooking Time: 22 Minutes
Ingredients:
- 1/3 cup Italian breadcrumbs
- Roughly chopped fresh cilantro, to taste
- 2 teaspoons Cajun seasonings
- Nonstick cooking spray
- 2 eggs, beaten
- 3 tablespoons white flour
- 1 teaspoon seasoned salt
- Garlic & onion spice blend, to taste
- 6 pork chops
- 1/3 teaspoon freshly cracked black pepper

Directions:
1. Coat the pork chops with Cajun seasonings, salt, pepper, and the spice blend on all sides.
2. Then, add the flour to a plate. In a shallow dish, whisk the egg until pale and smooth. Place the Italian breadcrumbs in the third bowl.
3. Dredge each pork piece in the flour; then, coat them with the egg; finally, coat them with the breadcrumbs. Spritz them with cooking spray on both sides.
4. Now, air-fry pork chops for about 18 minutes at 345 degrees F; make sure to taste for doneness after first 12 minutes of cooking. Lastly, garnish with fresh cilantro. Bon appétit!

571.Double Cheese Crêpes

Servings: 3
Cooking Time: 35 Minutes
Ingredients:
- 1/4 cup coconut flour

- 1 tablespoon psyllium husk
- 2 eggs, beaten
- 3 egg whites, beaten
- 1/4 teaspoon allspice
- 1/2 teaspoon salt
- 1 teaspoon cream of tartar
- 3/4 cup milk
- 1/2 cup ricotta cheese
- 1/2 cup Parmigiano-Reggiano cheese, preferably freshly grated
- 1 cup marinara sauce

Directions:
1. Mix the coconut flour, psyllium husk, eggs, allspice, salt, and cream of tartar in a large bowl. Gradually add the milk and ricotta cheese, whisking continuously, until well combined.
2. Let it stand for 20 minutes.
3. Spritz the Air Fryer baking pan with cooking spray. Pour the batter into the prepared pan.
4. Cook at 230 degrees F for 3 minutes. Flip and cook until browned in spots, 2 to 3 minutes longer.
5. Repeat with the remaining batter. Serve with Parmigiano-Reggiano cheese and marinara sauce. Bon appétit!

572.Baked Denver Omelet With Sausage

Servings: 5
Cooking Time: 14 Minutes
Ingredients:
- 3 pork sausages, chopped
- 8 well-beaten eggs
- 1 ½ bell peppers, seeded and chopped
- 1 teaspoon smoked cayenne pepper
- 2 tablespoons Fontina cheese
- 1/2 teaspoon tarragon
- 1/2 teaspoon ground black pepper
- 1 teaspoon salt

Directions:
1. In a cast-iron skillet, sweat the bell peppers together with the chopped pork sausages until the peppers are fragrant and the sausage begins to release liquid.
2. Lightly grease the inside of a baking dish with pan spray.
3. Throw all of the above ingredients into the prepared baking dish, including the sautéed mixture; stir to combine.
4. Bake at 345 degrees F approximately 9 minutes. Serve right away with the salad of choice.

573.Frittata With Turkey Breasts And Cottage Cheese

Servings: 4
Cooking Time: 50 Minutes
Ingredients:

- 1 tablespoon olive oil
- 1 pound turkey breasts, slices
- 6 large-sized eggs
- 3 tablespoons Greek yogurt
- 3 tablespoons Cottage cheese, crumbled
- 1/4 teaspoon ground black pepper
- 1/4 teaspoon red pepper flakes, crushed
- Himalayan salt, to taste
- 1 red bell pepper, seeded and sliced
- 1 green bell pepper, seeded and sliced

Directions:
1. Grease the cooking basket with olive oil. Add the turkey and cook in the preheated Air Fryer at 350 degrees F for 30 minutes, flipping them over halfway through. Cut into bite-sized strips and reserve.
2. Now, beat the eggs with Greek yogurt, cheese, black pepper, red pepper, and salt. Add the bell peppers to a baking pan that is previously lightly greased with a cooking spray.
3. Add the turkey strips; pour the egg mixture over all ingredients.
4. Bake in the preheated Air Fryer at 360 degrees F for 15 minutes. Serve right away!

574.Scrambled Eggs With Sausage

Servings: 6
Cooking Time: 25 Minutes
Ingredients:
- 1 teaspoon lard
- 1/2 pound turkey sausage
- 6 eggs
- 1 scallion, chopped
- 1 garlic clove, minced
- 1 sweet pepper, seeded and chopped
- 1 chili pepper, seeded and chopped
- Sea salt and ground black pepper, to taste
- 1/2 cup Swiss cheese, shredded

Directions:
1. Start by preheating your Air Fryer to 330 degrees F. Now, spritz 6 silicone molds with cooking spray.
2. Melt the lard in a saucepan over medium-high heat. Now, cook the sausage for 5 minutes or until no longer pink.
3. Coarsely chop the sausage; add the eggs, scallions, garlic, peppers, salt, and black pepper. Divide the egg mixture between the silicone molds. Top with the shredded cheese.
4. Bake in the preheated Air Fryer at 340 degrees F for 15 minutes, checking halfway through the cooking time to ensure even cooking. Enjoy!

575.Cheese And Chive Stuffed Chicken Rolls

Servings: 6

Cooking Time: 20 Minutes
Ingredients:
- 2 eggs, well-whisked
- Tortilla chips, crushed
- 1 1/2 tablespoons extra-virgin olive oil
- 1 ½ tablespoons fresh chives, chopped
- 3 chicken breasts, halved lengthwise
- 1 ½ cup soft cheese
- 2 teaspoons sweet paprika
- 1/2 teaspoon whole grain mustard
- 1/2 teaspoon cumin powder
- 1/3 teaspoon fine sea salt
- 1/3 cup fresh cilantro, chopped
- 1/3 teaspoon freshly ground black pepper, or more to taste

Directions:
1. Flatten out each piece of the chicken breast using a rolling pin. Then, grab three mixing dishes.
2. In the first one, combine the soft cheese with the cilantro, fresh chives, cumin, and mustard.
3. In another mixing dish, whisk the eggs together with the sweet paprika. In the third dish, combine the salt, black pepper, and crushed tortilla chips.
4. Spread the cheese mixture over each piece of chicken. Repeat with the remaining pieces of the chicken breasts; now, roll them up.
5. Coat each chicken roll with the whisked egg; dredge each chicken roll into the tortilla chips mixture. Lower the rolls onto the air fryer cooking basket. Drizzle extra-virgin olive oil over all rolls.
6. Air fry at 345 degrees F for 28 minutes, working in batches. Serve warm, garnished with sour cream if desired.

576.Baked Eggs With Kale And Ham

Servings: 2
Cooking Time: 15 Minutes
Ingredients:
- 2 eggs
- 1/4 teaspoon dried or fresh marjoram
- 2 teaspoons chili powder
- 1/3 teaspoon kosher salt
- ½ cup steamed kale
- 1/4 teaspoon dried or fresh rosemary
- 4 pork ham slices
- 1/3 teaspoon ground black pepper, or more to taste

Directions:
1. Divide the kale and ham among 2 ramekins; crack an egg into each ramekin. Sprinkle with seasonings.
2. Cook for 15 minutes at 335 degrees F or until your eggs reach desired texture.

3. Serve warm with spicy tomato ketchup and pickles. Bon appétit!

577.Decadent Frittata With Roasted Garlic And Sausage

Servings: 6
Cooking Time: 20 Minutes
Ingredients:
- 6 large-sized eggs
- 2 tablespoons butter, melted
- 3 tablespoons cream
- 1 cup chicken sausage, chopped
- 2 tablespoons roasted garlic, pressed
- 1/3 cup goat cheese such as Caprino, crumbled
- 1 teaspoon smoked cayenne pepper
- 1 teaspoon freshly ground black pepper
- 1/2 red onion, peeled and chopped
- 1 teaspoon fine sea salt

Directions:
1. First of all, grease six oven safe ramekins with melted butter. Then, divide roasted garlic and red onion among your ramekins. Add chicken sausage and toss to combine.
2. Beat the eggs with cream until well combined and pale; sprinkle with cayenne pepper, salt, and black pepper; beat again.
3. Scrape the mixture into your ramekins and air-fry for about 13 minutes at 355 degrees F.
4. Top with crumbled cheese and serve immediately.

578.Omelet With Mushrooms And Peppers

Servings: 2
Cooking Time: 20 Minutes
Ingredients:
- 1 tablespoon olive oil
- 1/2 cup scallions, chopped
- 1 bell pepper, seeded and thinly sliced
- 6 ounces button mushrooms, thinly sliced
- 4 eggs
- 2 tablespoons milk
- Sea salt and freshly ground black pepper, to taste
- 1 tablespoon fresh chives, for serving

Directions:
1. Heat the olive oil in a skillet over medium-high heat. Now, sauté the scallions and peppers until aromatic.
2. Add the mushrooms and continue to cook an additional 3 minutes or until tender. Reserve.
3. Generously grease a baking pan with nonstick cooking spray.
4. Then, whisk the eggs, milk, salt, and black pepper. Spoon into the prepared baking pan.

5. Cook in the preheated Air Fryer at 360 F for 4 minutes. Flip and cook for a further 3 minutes.
6. Place the reserved mushroom filling on one side of the omelet. Fold your omelet in half and slide onto a serving plate. Serve immediately garnished with fresh chives. Bon appétit!

579.Spicy Eggs With Sausage And Swiss Cheese

Servings: 6
Cooking Time: 25 Minutes
Ingredients:
- 1 teaspoon lard
- 1/2 pound turkey sausage
- 6 eggs
- 1 scallion, chopped
- 1 garlic clove, minced
- 1 bell pepper, seeded and chopped
- 1 chili pepper, seeded and chopped
- Sea salt and ground black pepper, to taste
- 1/2 cup Swiss cheese, shredded

Directions:
1. Start by preheating your Air Fryer to 330 degrees F. Now, spritz 4 silicone molds with cooking spray.
2. Melt the lard in a saucepan over medium-high heat. Now, cook the sausage for 5 minutes or until no longer pink.
3. Coarsely chop the sausage; add the eggs, scallions, garlic, peppers, salt, and black pepper. Divide the egg mixture between the silicone molds. Top with the shredded cheese.
4. Bake in the preheated Air Fryer at 340 degrees F for 15 minutes, checking halfway through the cooking time to ensure even cooking. Enjoy!

580.Green Pea Fritters With Parsley Yogurt Dip

Servings: 4
Cooking Time: 20 Minutes
Ingredients:
- Pea Fritters:
- 1 ½ cups frozen green peas
- 1 tablespoon sesame oil
- 1/2 cup scallions, chopped
- 2 garlic cloves, minced
- 1 cup chickpea flour
- 1 teaspoon baking powder
- 1/2 teaspoon sea salt
- 1/2 teaspoon ground black pepper
- 1/4 teaspoon dried dill
- 1/2 teaspoon dried basil
- Parsley Yogurt Dip:
- 1/2 cup Greek-Style yoghurt

- 2 tablespoons mayonnaise
- 2 tablespoons fresh parsley, chopped
- 1 tablespoon fresh lemon juice
- 1/2 teaspoon garlic, smashed

Directions:
1. Place the thawed green peas in a mixing dish; pour in hot water. Drain and rinse well.
2. Mash the green peas; add the remaining ingredients for the pea fritters and mix to combine well. Shape the mixture into patties and transfer them to the lightly greased cooking basket.
3. Bake at 330 degrees F for 14 minutes or until thoroughly heated.
4. Meanwhile, make your dipping sauce by whisking the remaining ingredients. Place in your refrigerator until ready to serve.
5. Serve the green pea fritters with the chilled dip on the side. Enjoy!

581.Farmer's Breakfast Deviled Eggs

Servings: 3
Cooking Time: 25 Minutes
Ingredients:
- 6 eggs
- 6 slices bacon
- 2 tablespoons mayonnaise
- 1 teaspoon hot sauce
- 1/2 teaspoon Worcestershire sauce
- 2 tablespoons green onions, chopped
- 1 tablespoon pickle relish
- Salt and ground black pepper, to taste
- 1 teaspoon smoked paprika

Directions:
1. Place the wire rack in the Air Fryer basket; lower the eggs onto the wire rack.
2. Cook at 270 degrees F for 15 minutes.
3. Transfer them to an ice-cold water bath to stop the cooking. Peel the eggs under cold running water; slice them into halves.
4. Cook the bacon at 400 degrees F for 3 minutes; flip the bacon over and cook an additional 3 minutes; chop the bacon and reserve.
5. Mash the egg yolks with the mayo, hot sauce, Worcestershire sauce, green onions, pickle relish, salt, and black pepper; add the reserved bacon and spoon the yolk mixture into the egg whites.
6. Garnish with smoked paprika. Bon appétit!

582.Turkey Wontons With Garlic-parmesan Sauce

Servings: 8
Cooking Time: 15 Minutes
Ingredients:
- 8 ounces cooked turkey breasts, shredded
- 16 wonton wrappers
- 1 ½ tablespoons butter, melted

- 1/3 cup cream cheese, room temperature
- 8 ounces Asiago cheese, shredded
- 3 tablespoons Parmesan cheese, grated
- 1 teaspoon garlic powder
- Fine sea salt and freshly ground black pepper, to taste

Directions:
1. In a small-sized bowl, mix the butter, Parmesan, garlic powder, salt, and black pepper; give it a good stir.
2. Lightly grease a mini muffin pan; lay 1 wonton wrapper in each mini muffin cup. Fill each cup with the cream cheese and turkey mixture.
3. Air-fry for 8 minutes at 335 degrees F. Immediately top with Asiago cheese and serve warm. Bon appétit!

583. Two Cheese And Shrimp Dip

Servings: 8
Cooking Time: 25 Minutes
Ingredients:
- 2 teaspoons butter, melted
- 8 ounces shrimp, peeled and deveined
- 2 garlic cloves, minced
- 1/4 cup chicken stock
- 2 tablespoons fresh lemon juice
- Salt and ground black pepper, to taste
- 1/2 teaspoon red pepper flakes
- 4 ounces cream cheese, at room temperature
- 1/2 cup sour cream
- 4 tablespoons mayonnaise
- 1/4 cup mozzarella cheese, shredded

Directions:
1. Start by preheating the Air Fryer to 395 degrees F. Grease the sides and bottom of a baking dish with the melted butter.
2. Place the shrimp, garlic, chicken stock, lemon juice, salt, black pepper, and red pepper flakes in the baking dish.
3. Transfer the baking dish to the cooking basket and bake for 10 minutes. Add the mixture to your food processor; pulse until the coarsely is chopped.
4. Add the cream cheese, sour cream, and mayonnaise. Top with the mozzarella cheese and bake in the preheated Air Fryer at 360 degrees F for 6 to 7 minutes or until the cheese is bubbling.
5. Serve immediately with breadsticks if desired. Bon appétit!

584. Easy Frittata With Chicken Sausage

Servings: 2
Cooking Time: 15 Minutes
Ingredients:
- 1 tablespoon olive oil
- 2 chicken sausages, sliced
- 4 eggs
- 1 garlic clove, minced
- 1/2 yellow onion, chopped
- Sea salt and ground black pepper, to taste
- 4 tablespoons Monterey-Jack cheese
- 1 tablespoon fresh parsley leaves, chopped

Directions:
1. Grease the sides and bottom of a baking pan with olive oil.
2. Add the sausages and cook in the preheated Air Fryer at 360 degrees F for 4 to 5 minutes.
3. In a mixing dish, whisk the eggs with garlic and onion. Season with salt and black pepper.
4. Pour the mixture over sausages. Top with cheese. Cook in the preheated Air Fryer at 360 degrees F for another 6 minutes.
5. Serve immediately with fresh parsley leaves. Bon appétit!

585. Cauliflower And Manchego Croquettes

Servings: 4
Cooking Time: 15 Minutes
Ingredients:
- 1 cup Manchego cheese, shredded
- 1 teaspoon paprika
- 1 teaspoon freshly ground black pepper
- 1/2 tablespoon fine sea salt
- 1/2 cup scallions, finely chopped
- 1 pound cauliflower florets
- 2 tablespoons canola oil
- 2 teaspoons dried basil

Directions:
1. Blitz the cauliflower florets in a food processor until finely crumbed. Then, combine the broccoli with the rest of the above ingredients.
2. Then, shape the balls using your hands. Now, flatten the balls to make the patties.
3. Next, cook your patties at 360 degrees F approximately 10 minutes. Bon appétit!

586. Deviled Eggs With Pickle Relish

Servings: 3
Cooking Time: 20 Minutes
Ingredients:
- 5 eggs
- 2 tablespoons mayonnaise
- 2 tablespoons pickle relish
- Sea salt, to taste
- 1/2 teaspoon mixed peppercorns, crushed

Directions:
1. Place the wire rack in the Air Fryer basket; lower the eggs onto the wire rack.
2. Cook at 270 degrees F for 15 minutes.

3. Transfer them to an ice-cold water bath to stop the cooking. Peel the eggs under cold running water; slice them into halves.
4. Mash the egg yolks with the mayo, sweet pickle relish, and salt; spoon yolk mixture into egg whites. Arrange on a nice serving platter and garnish with the mixed peppercorns. Bon appétit!

587.Keto Brioche With Caciocavallo

Servings: 6
Cooking Time: 15 Minutes
Ingredients:
- 1/2 cup ricotta cheese, crumbled
- 1 cup part skim mozzarella cheese, shredded
- 1 egg
- 1/2 cup coconut flour
- 1/2 cup almond flour
- 1 teaspoon baking soda
- 2 tablespoons plain whey protein isolate
- 3 tablespoons sesame oil
- 2 teaspoons dried thyme
- 1 ½ cups Caciocavallo, grated
- 1 cup leftover chicken, shredded
- 3 eggs
- 1 teaspoon kosher salt
- 1 teaspoon freshly cracked black pepper, or more to taste
- 1/3 teaspoon gremolata

Directions:
1. To make the keto brioche, microwave the cheese for 1 minute 30 seconds, stirring twice. Add the cheese to the bowl of a food processor and blend well. Fold in the egg and mix again.
2. Add in the flour, baking soda, and plain whey protein isolate; blend again. Scrape the batter onto the center of a lightly greased cling film.
3. Form the dough into a disk and transfer to your freezer to cool; cut into 6 pieces and transfer to a parchment-lined baking pan (make sure to grease your hands).
4. Firstly, slice off the top of each brioche; then, scoop out the insides.
5. Brush each brioche with sesame oil. Add the remaining ingredients in the order listed above.
6. Place the prepared brioche onto the bottom of the cooking basket. Bake for 7 minutes at 345 degrees F. Bon appétit!

588.Spicy Omelet With Ground Chicken

Servings: 2
Cooking Time: 15 Minutes
Ingredients:
- 4 eggs, whisked
- 4 ounces ground chicken
- 1/2 cup scallions, finely chopped
- 2 cloves garlic, finely minced
- 1/2 teaspoon salt
- 1/2 teaspoon ground black pepper
- 1/2 teaspoon paprika
- 1 teaspoon dried thyme
- A dash of hot sauce

Directions:
1. Thoroughly combine all the ingredients in a mixing dish. Now, scrape the egg mixture into two oven safe ramekins that are previously greased with a thin layer of the vegetable oil.
2. Set your machine to cook at 350 degrees F; air-fry for 13 minutes or until thoroughly cooked. Serve immediately.

589.Snapper With Gruyere Cheese

Servings: 4
Cooking Time: 25 Minutes
Ingredients:
- 2 tablespoons olive oil
- 1 shallot, thinly sliced
- 2 garlic cloves, minced
- 1 ½ pounds snapper fillets
- Sea salt and ground black pepper, to taste
- 1 teaspoon cayenne pepper
- 1/2 teaspoon dried basil
- 1/2 cup tomato puree
- 1/2 cup white wine
- 1 cup Gruyere cheese, shredded

Directions:
1. Heat 1 tablespoon of olive oil in a saucepan over medium-high heat. Now, cook the shallot and garlic until tender and aromatic.
2. Preheat your Air Fryer to 370 degrees F.
3. Grease a casserole dish with 1 tablespoon of olive oil. Place the snapper fillet in the casserole dish. Season with salt, black pepper, and cayenne pepper. Add the sautéed shallot mixture.
4. Add the basil, tomato puree and wine to the casserole dish. Cook for 10 minutes in the preheated Air Fryer.
5. Top with the shredded cheese and cook an additional 7 minutes. Serve immediately.

590.Cheese Sticks With Ketchup

Servings: 4
Cooking Time: 15 Minutes
Ingredients:
- 1/4 cup coconut flour
- 1/4 cup almond flour
- 2 eggs
- 1/2 cup parmesan cheese, grated
- 1 tablespoon Cajun seasonings
- 8 cheese sticks, kid-friendly
- 1/4 cup ketchup, low-carb

Directions:

1. To begin, set up your breading station. Place the flour in a shallow dish. In a separate dish, whisk the eggs.
2. Finally, mix the parmesan cheese and Cajun seasoning in a third dish.
3. Start by dredging the cheese sticks in the flour; then, dip them into the egg. Press the cheese sticks into the parmesan mixture, coating evenly.
4. Place the breaded cheese sticks in the lightly greased Air Fryer basket. Cook at 380 degrees F for 6 minutes.
5. Serve with ketchup and enjoy!

591.Greek-style Roasted Figs

Servings: 4
Cooking Time: 20 Minutes
Ingredients:
- 2 teaspoons butter, melted
- 8 figs, halved
- 2 tablespoons brown sugar
- 1/2 teaspoon cinnamon
- 1 teaspoon lemon zest
- 1 cup Greek yogurt
- 4 tablespoons honey

Directions:
1. Drizzle the melted butter all over the fig halves.
2. Sprinkle brown sugar, cinnamon, and lemon zest on the fig slices. Meanwhile, mix the Greek yogurt with the honey.
3. Roast in the preheated Air Fryer at 330 degrees F for 16 minutes.
4. To serve, divide the figs among 4 bowls and serve with a dollop of the yogurt sauce. Enjoy!

592.Broccoli Bites With Cheese Sauce

Servings: 6
Cooking Time: 20 Minutes
Ingredients:
- For the Broccoli Bites:
- 1 medium-sized head broccoli, broken into florets
- 1/2 teaspoon lemon zest, freshly grated
- 1/3 teaspoon fine sea salt
- 1/2 teaspoon hot paprika
- 1 teaspoon shallot powder
- 1 teaspoon porcini powder
- 1/2 teaspoon granulated garlic
- 1/3 teaspoon celery seeds
- 1 ½ tablespoons olive oil
- For the Cheese Sauce:
- 2 tablespoons butter
- 1 tablespoon golden flaxseed meal
- 1 cup milk
- 1/2 cup blue cheese

Directions:

1. Toss all the ingredients for the broccoli bites in a mixing bowl, covering the broccoli florets on all sides.
2. Cook them in the preheated Air Fryer at 360 degrees for 13 to 15 minutes.
3. In the meantime, melt the butter over a medium heat; stir in the golden flaxseed meal and let cook for 1 min or so.
4. Gradually pour in the milk, stirring constantly, until the mixture is smooth. Bring it to a simmer and stir in the cheese. Cook until the sauce has thickened slightly.
5. Pause your Air Fryer, mix the broccoli with the prepared sauce and cook for further 3 minutes. Bon appétit!

593.Roasted Turkey Sausage With Potatoes

Servings: 6
Cooking Time: 40 Minutes
Ingredients:
- 1/2 pound red potatoes, peeled and diced
- 1/2 teaspoon onion salt
- 1/2 teaspoon dried sage
- 1/2pound ground turkey
- 1/3 teaspoon ginger, ground
- 1 sprig rosemary, chopped
- 1 ½ tablespoons olive oil
- 1/2 teaspoon paprika
- 2 sprigs thyme, chopped
- 1 teaspoon ground black pepper

Directions:
1. In a bowl, mix the first six ingredients; give it a good stir. Heat a thin layer of vegetable oil in a nonstick skillet that is placed over a moderate flame.
2. Form the mixture into patties; fry until they're browned on all sides, or about 12 minutes.
3. Arrange the potatoes at the bottom of a baking dish. Sprinkle with the rosemary and thyme; add a drizzle of olive oil. Top with the turkey.
4. Roast for 32 minutes at 365 degrees F, turning once halfway through. Eat warm.

594.Filipino Ground Meat Omelet(tortang Giniling)

Servings: 3
Cooking Time: 20 Minutes
Ingredients:
- 1 teaspoon lard
- 2/3 pound ground beef
- 1/4 teaspoon chili powder
- 1/2 teaspoon ground bay leaf
- 1/2 teaspoon ground pepper
- Sea salt, to taste
- 1 green bell pepper, seeded and chopped
- 1 red bell pepper, seeded and chopped

- 6 eggs
- 1/3 cup double cream
- 1/2 cup Colby cheese, shredded
- 1 tomato, sliced

Directions:
1. Melt the lard in a cast-iron skillet over medium-high heat. Add the ground beef and cook for 4 minutes until no longer pink, crumbling with a spatula.
2. Add the ground beef mixture, along with the spices to the baking pan. Now, add the bell peppers.
3. In a mixing bowl, whisk the eggs with double cream. Spoon the mixture over the meat and peppers in the pan.
4. Cook in the preheated Air Fryer at 355 degrees F for 10 minutes.
5. Top with the cheese and tomato slices. Continue to cook for 5 minutes more or until the eggs are golden and the cheese has melted.

595.Country-style Apple Fries

Servings: 4
Cooking Time: 20 Minutes
Ingredients:
- 1/2 cup milk
- 1 egg
- 1/2 all-purpose flour
- 1 teaspoon baking powder
- 4 tablespoons brown sugar
- 1 teaspoon vanilla extract
- 1/2 teaspoon ground cloves
- A pinch of kosher salt
- A pinch of grated nutmeg
- 1 tablespoon coconut oil, melted
- 2 Pink Lady apples, cored, peeled, slice into pieces (shape and size of French fries
- 1/3 cup granulated sugar
- 1 teaspoon ground cinnamon

Directions:
1. In a mixing bowl, whisk the milk and eggs; gradually stir in the flour; add the baking powder, brown sugar, vanilla, cloves, salt, nutmeg, and melted coconut oil. Mix to combine well.
2. Dip each apple slice into the batter, coating on all sides. Spritz the bottom of the cooking basket with cooking oil.
3. Cook the apple fries in the preheated Air Fryer at 395 degrees F approximately 8 minutes, turning them over halfway through the cooking time.
4. Cook in small batches to ensure even cooking.
5. In the meantime, mix the granulated sugar with the ground cinnamon; sprinkle the cinnamon sugar over the apple fries. Serve warm.

596.Greek Omelet With Halloumi Cheese

Servings: 2
Cooking Time: 17 Minutes
Ingredients:
- 1/2 cup Halloumi cheese, sliced
- 2 teaspoons garlic paste
- 2 teaspoons fresh chopped rosemary
- 4well-whisked eggs
- 2 bell peppers, seeded and chopped
- 1 ½ tablespoons fresh basil, chopped
- 3 tablespoons onions, chopped
- Fine sea salt and ground black pepper, to taste

Directions:
1. Spritz your baking dish with a canola cooking spray.
2. Throw in all ingredients and stir until everything is well incorporated.
3. Bake for about 15 minutes at 325 degrees F. Eat warm.

597.Cheese And Garlic Stuffed Chicken Breasts

Servings: 2
Cooking Time: 20 Minutes
Ingredients:
- 1/2 cup Cottage cheese
- 2 eggs, beaten
- 2 medium-sized chicken breasts, halved
- 2 tablespoons fresh coriander, chopped
- 1teaspoon fine sea salt
- Seasoned breadcrumbs
- 1/3teaspoon freshly ground black pepper, to savor
- 3 cloves garlic, finely minced

Directions:
1. Firstly, flatten out the chicken breast using a meat tenderizer.
2. In a medium-sized mixing dish, combine the Cottage cheese with the garlic, coriander, salt, and black pepper.
3. Spread 1/3 of the mixture over the first chicken breast. Repeat with the remaining ingredients. Roll the chicken around the filling; make sure to secure with toothpicks.
4. Now, whisk the egg in a shallow bowl. In another shallow bowl, combine the salt, ground black pepper, and seasoned breadcrumbs.
5. Coat the chicken breasts with the whisked egg; now, roll them in the breadcrumbs.
6. Cook in the air fryer cooking basket at 365 degrees F for 22 minutes. Serve immediately.

598.Celery Fries With Harissa Mayo

Servings: 3
Cooking Time: 30 Minutes
Ingredients:

- 1/2 pound celery root
- 2 tablespoons olive oil
- Sea salt and ground black pepper, to taste
- Harissa Mayo
- 1/4 cup mayonnaise
- 2 tablespoons sour cream
- 1/2 tablespoon harissa paste
- 1/4 teaspoon ground cumin
- Salt, to taste

Directions:
1. Cut the celery root into desired size and shape.
2. Then, preheat your Air Fryer to 400 degrees F. Now, spritz the Air Fryer basket with cooking spray.
3. Toss the celery fries with the olive oil, salt, and black pepper. Bake in the preheated Air Fryer for 25 to 30 minutes, turning them over every 10 minutes to promote even cooking.
4. Meanwhile, mix all ingredients for the harissa mayo. Place in your refrigerator until ready to serve. Bon appétit!

599.Fluffy Omelet With Leftover Beef

Servings: 4
Cooking Time: 20 Minutes
Ingredients:
- Non-stick cooking spray
- 1/2 pound leftover beef, coarsely chopped
- 2 garlic cloves, pressed
- 1 cup kale, torn into pieces and wilted
- 1 bell pepper, chopped
- 6 eggs, beaten
- 6 tablespoons sour cream
- 1/2 teaspoon turmeric powder

- 1 teaspoon red pepper flakes
- Salt and ground black pepper, to your liking

Directions:
1. Spritz the inside of four ramekins with a cooking spray.
2. Divide all of the above ingredients among the prepared ramekins. Stir until everything is well combined.
3. Air-fry at 360 degrees F for 16 minutes; check with a wooden stick and return the eggs to the Air Fryer for a few more minutes as needed. Serve immediately.

600.Super Easy Sage And Lime Wings

Servings: 4
Cooking Time: 30 Minutes + Marinating Time
Ingredients:
- 1 teaspoon onion powder
- 1/3 cup fresh lime juice
- 1/2 tablespoon corn flour
- 1/2 heaping tablespoon fresh chopped parsley
- 1/3 teaspoon mustard powder
- 1/2 pound turkey wings, cut into smaller pieces
- 2 heaping tablespoons fresh chopped sage
- 1/2 teaspoon garlic powder
- 1/2 teaspoon seasoned salt
- 1 teaspoon freshly cracked black or white peppercorns

Directions:
1. Simply dump all of the above ingredients into a mixing dish; cover and let it marinate for about 1 hours in your refrigerator.
2. Air-fry turkey wings for 28 minutes at 355 degrees F. Bon appétit!

CPSIA information can be obtained
at www.ICGtesting.com
Printed in the USA
BVHW061039071021
618411BV00003B/129